KAMBUYA'S CATTLE

Three men discussing matters with "Teso," the appointive chief Seperia at the right.

WALTER GOLDSCHMIDT

KAMBUYA'S CATTLE
The Legacy of an African Herdsman

Berkeley and Los Angeles
UNIVERSITY OF CALIFORNIA PRESS
1969

University of California Press
Berkeley and Los Angeles, California
University of California Press, Ltd.
London, England

Printed in the United States of America

To the
KOTA OF KAMBUYA

Acknowledgments

To Salimu arap Kambuya, now head of the kota of Kambuya, to his family, his neighbors, the elders, and all who engaged in the kokwet here recorded, I acknowledge my great indebtedness and express my appreciation for their kindness and patience. Yovan Chemtai, who interpreted the events and subsequent discussions with diligence and helped me understand them, has played a crucial role in making this work possible. It is a pleasure to acknowledge my debt to him.

Once again, my gratitude to Gale, whose help and support in the field and subsequently have been of greatest importance in this enterprise. Mary Schaeffer's assistance in preparing the manuscript went far beyond the requirements of her job, and I again express my thanks.

My colleagues on the Culture and Ecology in East Africa research project have made critical evaluations of early drafts which were most helpful, and their collaboration has deepened my understanding in many ways. I want to thank Robert B. Edgerton, Francis P. Conant, Symmes C. Oliver, Philip W. Porter, and Edgar V. Winans. They should not, however, bear responsibility for any of the shortcomings in the work.

The Culture and Ecology project, under the auspices of which the research for this book was conducted, was sponsored by the University of California, Los Angeles, and supported by a grant, G-11713, from the National Science Foundation and by a United States Public Health Service grant, MH-04097, from the National Institute of Mental Health. I appreciate the action of these agencies and the scholars who staff them in supporting this research, and hope that this unanticipated product of the program helps repay their confidence.

The quotation from Arnold Toynbee's *Acquaintances* is reproduced with the kind permission of its publisher, Oxford University Press.

W. G.

Contents

Chronology of Events at Kapsirika, 1962

August 15 (est.)	Kambuya dies
August 18 (est.)	Animal slaughtered for Kambuya
August 22	Goldschmidts return to Kapsirika
September 7	Salimu returns to Kapsirika and goes to Mbale
September 8	Discourse at Salimu's kraal (chap. iii)
September 9	First abortive hearings at Andyema's (chap. iv)
September 12	Second abortive hearings (chap. iv)
September 13	Anointing ceremony (chap. v)
September 14	Dividing the tokapsoy (chap. vi)
September 17	Final discussions (chap. vii)
October 16	Hearings regarding witchcraft (chap. viii)

KAMBUYA'S CATTLE

In human affairs the source of every action is some individual person. Every human action is a product of a previous act of choice, and the power to make choices is the monopoly of human personalities. So, when we say, "Harold Wilson did this or that," we are using language that is one hundred per cent realistic. If we say, "The Prime Minister did it," our feet are no longer planted quite so firmly on the ground, for the term "Prime Minister" is an abstraction; the title is worn like a secondhand suit of clothes by one human being after another, and the wearers, not their official vestments, are the realities. If we say, "Her Majesty's Government did it," we have floated off the ground into the atmosphere of mythology. . . . "Her Majesty's Government" is a mythical character; and so are its congeners the United Kingdom, the Electorate, the Crown, the Church, the Bench, the Bar, the Trade, the Turf. These abstractions, to which we attribute humanlike acts, are of the same order of unreality as the nereids, dryads, oreads, and other anthropomorphic divine presences in human form in whose imaginary actions the ancient Greeks had mythologized the seas, woods, mountains, and other features of inanimate Nature before Thales reduced all these mythical beings to water.

Everyone will agree that history ought to be written, on Thales' lines, in terms of the realities, not in terms of myth. . . . Try, then, to write a passage of historical narrative in terms of nothing but human individuals and their relations with each other. You will find the experiment frustrating. You will discover that you will not be able to write a line without ascribing to mythical abstractions the authorship of actions that, in reality, were performed, as you know very well, not by these nonexistent wraiths evoked from fairyland, but by human beings.

Arnold J. Toynbee

Prologue

A man has died. By the standards of his community, he is rich. He has a number of sons—two by his first wife, and one by his second—who are adult members of the community he has just departed. A young wife (also dead) had two small boys whose interests must be protected. The network of kinship extends further: there are sisters and their families, brothers and their children, daughters and their husbands, grandchildren. All these have interests and obligations.

The dead man is the center of another network, fully as important as the first and more intricate to deal with: a network of economic exchanges, of debts and credits. Cattle, goats, sheep, and—nowadays—money enter into this calculus. The reckoning is intricate, for the rationalizing influence of cost accounting does not exist. Each obligation is an individual obligation; only rarely can a debt be canceled by a credit. All these obligations must be retained in the heads of the men who are to liquidate the estate in accordance with local canons of justice and propriety.

The third network, hardly independent of the other two, we may call social. Men have come to help settle the estate because they have social obligations to the deceased, because they are interested in fair play, and because the drama of the events breaks the natural monotony of a rather humdrum existence. Perhaps, too, they hope to have some small benefice from the legacy.

These ramifications are overlaid by two systems. One is the system of law. There are rules which everybody knows and which are to be followed. Certain rights inhere in certain persons by reason of kinship or economic obligation. A debt is recognized and enforceable. Nowadays the native system of community pressure is supplemented by Europeanized courts, but this alters the situation only slightly; it allows a recourse and appeal in cases where the older social pressures do not enforce a claim, but the criteria and circumstances are essentially uniform. Here, as elsewhere, the law is recognized because in the absence of rules there can be no orderly interaction; obligations cannot be incurred if performance cannot be enforced. Within the framework of these laws, persons manipulate events to their own benefit and, when they feel it to be to their advantage to do so, may disregard the law entirely.

The second system is that of sentiments. The actors in the drama are persons who have grown up together and who have lived together. They are therefore not merely counters in a game but personalities. Some are wise, and some foolish; some well informed about the matter at hand, some ignorant. The scene is dominated by one brother, who, in addition to being favored as the eldest, is well informed and perhaps wise—he is the protagonist. To his brothers he is not a locus on a kinship chart but a personality. His full brother resents the fact that the eldest was the father's favorite, and the long history of being made the butt of his brother's ridicule still rankles in his heart. Their half brother—older, cleverer, and, because of local custom, more independent than the second—is in a position of closer rivalry to the eldest though not so favorably situated. There are also the favorite grandson, the favored young sister of the deceased, as well as the old fellow-initiate, to mention only a few of the special relations that exist.

Death, a breaching of the ongoing patterns of human activities, creates a point in time when the patterns of interaction of the past must be altered. The role of the dead man is taken by another, and the relationship of each actor to every other takes on new meaning.

As a geologic fault uncovers the underlying structure of the land, as revolutionary events uncover the patterns of power in a society, so too the breach caused by a death discloses the structure of a community, demonstrating the pattern of life activities, the networks of kinship and economic obligations, the systems of rules and of sentiments. I hope that this record of the action that took place in response to Kambuya's death may reveal the reality of Sebei life and perhaps also provoke reflection on human behavior.

CHAPTER I *Introduction*

This book records the drama of events that occurred in a small and remote village of Sebei tribesmen over a period of two weeks in the late summer of 1962. It is a document of human interactions among the heirs, the relatives, and the neighbors of Kambuya. Most of the text is a translation of the actual discussion, recorded at the time.

The events were neither unusual nor typical. They were not unusual in that they were an instance of a standard set of public actions in response to a death; through such hearings, rights and obligations were usually redefined and reaffirmed. The major purpose was to establish debts owed by the estate of the deceased and owing to it, and to determine the allocation of his property. In this instance, the property was chiefly cattle; sheep and goats were not discussed. Such hearings also allocated wives, but Kambuya's only surviving wife was too old to be inherited.

Although not unusual, neither was the case typical. I do not present this record as an example of what the Sebei usually do. Whereas the program was institutionalized, the action itself was the working out of the personal needs and capabilities of the actors as they came together under the peculiar circumstances surrounding Kambuya's death. I do not mean merely that there were special circumstances here that would not apply elsewhere, though some could be cited. Kambuya was unusually rich in cattle, so that the hearings were both more important and more protracted than the average. Kambuya's having been blind gave the situation a certain poignancy and altered circumstances to a degree. His son's unexplained disappearance lent a measure of mystery to the affair. I do mean to say that *no* instance is typical; each is unique, for neither the circumstances nor the actors are ever quite the same.

Paradoxically, I feel that the unique quality of the events may lead us to a better understanding of Sebei culture as it is lived today. The usual form of ethnographic reporting sets forth the generalizations about the culturally expected behavior and the regularized social relationships in the community under study. However much these are substantiated by specific observations or direct quotation from informants, they remain constructs and generalities. This is the normal anthropological task; the science of ethnology is built on the comparative study of such orderly, regularized analyses of communities as *systems* of behavior.

By treating of the typical, of the construct, we lose sight of the reality. We transform human behavior into patterned generalities by the very act of analysis, much as the museum collector transforms a musical instrument or a sacred fetish into a museum specimen by the very act of collection. This is a problem that many anthropologists have sensed and have endeavored to overcome; they would bring back the culture alive, rather than as a specimen. Some, like Malinowski,[1] have tried to do so by lengthy and intimate accounts of daily life and special events. Some, like Elizabeth Marshall Thomas,[2] have sought to re-create the culture by the merit of sheer literary skill. Several follow the lead of Paul Radin[3] by presenting detailed life histories—native autobiographies—of members of the distant culture. Many[4] have written novels or, like Elenore Smith Bowen,[5] quasi novels involving the ethnographic experience. Some frankly autobiographical accounts of the ethnographer, like those of Claude Lévi-Strauss and Kenneth E. Read,[6] seek to

---

[1] In works too well known and too numerous to cite.

[2] *The Harmless People* (New York: Knopf, 1959).

[3] *The Autobiography of a Winnebago*, University of California Publications in American Archaeology and Ethnology, vol. 16, no. 7 (1920); reprinted by Dover Publications, New York (n.d.). A whole genre follows this lead.

[4] E.g., Hilda Kuper, *Bite of Hunger: A Novel of Africa* (New York: Harcourt, Brace and World, 1965).

[5] *Return to Laughter* (New York: Harper, 1954).

[6] Claude Lévi-Strauss, *Tristes Tropiques* (New York: Atheneum, 1964); Kenneth E. Read, *The High Valley* (New York: Charles Scribner's Sons, 1965). See also David Maybury-Lewis, *The Savage and the Innocent* (Cleve-

convey the human quality through personal experience. Oscar Lewis[7] brings his material back in the form of extensive tape-recorded interviews. All these share the conviction, it seems to me, that standard ethnographic reporting, however valuable and necessary to the scientific understanding of human behavior, deadens reality.

The present book seeks another way. It records the acting out of a real set of events in the words of the actors themselves with a minimum of intrusion upon them. The events reported were a moment of quiet drama in the lives of the people, a point of heightened self-awareness because of the redefinition of the situation that a death necessarily calls forth. So far as I am aware, this form of ethnographic reporting is unique. M. N. Srinivas[8] presents in great detail some legal disputes among Indian villagers, and Robert G. Armstrong[9] briefly records the discourse of an African legal procedure; but nowhere do we get the extended account of ongoing interaction that characterizes the presentation here.

My first purpose, then, is to reach into the life of Sebei and to offer a part of it intact, so that the reader may savor the intimate and meaningful qualities of ordinary life. This end is the more urgent because of the general character of the cultures in East Africa which the Sebei share. These cultures are peculiarly difficult to penetrate; as we go from one standard ethnography of the so-called Nilo-Hamitic peoples to another, we find these works sparse and arid, even when the analyses are thorough and detailed and have been written by the most qualified scholars. The Masai (to whom the Sebei are distantly related), whose external manifestations render them the very

land and New York: World Publishing Co., 1965). But only rarely do anthropologists write of such personal experiences.

[7] Lewis' most recent work is *La Vida* (New York: Random House, 1966); using recorded interviews, Lewis lets his characters speak for themselves. The popularity of his work emphasizes the public hunger for such internal understanding.

[8] "A Study of Disputes" (mimeo.), Department of Sociology, Delhi School of Economics, University of Delhi (n.d.).

[9] "A West African Inquest," *American Anthropologist*, 56 (1954), 1051–1075.

quintessence of the noble savage, with their hauteur, their elegance, and their commitment to their native mode of life, have
often been depicted but never portrayed. Popular accounts fare
little better. Alan Moorehead spoke of the Karamojong (neighbors to the Sebei) "squatting silently on their stools . . . quite
clearly thinking about absolutely nothing."[10] Even Elizabeth
Marshall Thomas[11] did not penetrate the character of the Dodoth
(a nearby tribe of similar cultural background) as she had
previously done for the Bushmen.

The reason for this lack must lie in the quality of these cultures themselves. And the quality that seems to me most relevant
is the scarcity of verbal and symbolic elaboration. The Sebei
and their neighbors are laconic. Their world is peopled by
spirits, but they speak very little of them. They have tales, but,
among the Sebei at least, these are told only by the young and
by the very old; ordinary adults almost literally do not even
know them. Nor do they elaborate their world with artistic
products. We cannot observe a Masai or the more closely related Pokot, with their copper arm and neck rings, their elaborate hairdress, and their very bearing (which once the Sebei must
have shared), without recognizing a strong aesthetic sense; but
the Sebei make no artifacts for beauty's sake, and embellish
utilitarian objects in only the most meager way. The portals by
which we usually enter an alien culture are thus narrow to the
point of being closed.

It is a truism that an outsider enters an alien culture through
what is of most interest to its participants, not what the visitor
finds most fascinating. It is safe to say that those Karamojong
whose conversation was described as being empty were discussing their cattle and the maneuvers men take against nature
and their fellowmen to increase their herds. As auto buffs can
talk endlessly of racing cams and dual-injection carburetors, or
baseball fans can give you the RBI and strike-out records of all
major league players, so too can the cattle-keeping Sebei and

<hr>

[10] "Reporter at Large: A Drop into the Stone Age," *The New Yorker*,
Sept. 6, 1958.
[11] *Warrior Herdsmen* (New York: Knopf, 1965).

their neighbors endlessly discuss the details of their cattle. An informant once recognized, with curiosity and, I think, affection, a cow that was being taken to market by a stranger; the cow belonged to his neighbor, who lived thirty or more miles from where we were working. I have analyzed in the appendix the genealogical data on the cattle belonging to Kambuya—a record of animals, their sources, their exchanges, their fates— more than seven hundred animals over a forty- or fifty-year period. I could never get a human Sebei genealogy more than three generations beyond the living one.

In these cattle-keeping societies, cows are not merely cows; in a symbolic but very real sense, they are people. Where each man has a "bull of the herd" that is to be slaughtered at his death; where there are elaborate songs of praise for favorite animals; where wives cost so many cows, and daughters will fetch so many more; where the price of a life is calculated in cattle paid as wergild; where the status of a man depends on the number of animals in his kraal—in such a place, the cattle raising dust on their way through the dry bush to water are not seen simply as a herd of animals. Basically, people are interested in people, and each man is concerned primarily with his relations with other men. But among the Sebei, as among other cattle-keeping people throughout East Africa, relationships are measured in livestock, the calculus of cattle is a tally system for the worth of men, the play in livestock is the essence of lifemanship. It is no mystery that attention is focused upon them. Thus the drama of Sebei life revolves both around people and around cattle, for the two are essentially one.

The paradox noted earlier—that the atypicality of the events leads us to generalizations—may be extended. My second purpose in presenting this material is to induce reflection on the nature of social behavior. The actions surrounding Kambuya's legacy, though not typical of Sebei, do raise the question of whether, on a very different level, they are not typical of mankind as a whole. I want to discuss this point here only sufficiently to provoke the reader into examining the events in this light, reserving for the closing chapter a more extensive treatment.

If we direct our attention away from the things that the ethnographer usually describes—the customs, the structuring of society, the specific symbols of wealth, the explicit rules of procedure—and focus upon the interaction of personalities, the preservation and furtherance of status, and the tricks by which these ends are satisfied, we find an intensely "human" document. That is to say, we feel at home, just as we do when we read C. P. Snow or John P. Marquand. This fact seems to me both relevant and important.

Because both the method of presentation and the purpose of the book are somewhat out of the ordinary, I feel it necessary to guide the reader in advance through what may seem somewhat remote and often obscure detail. I shall do this by first summarizing the events and then calling attention to the elements in the narrative which bear watching, from the standpoint of my second—my theoretical—purpose.

When Kambuya died, he left four sons by three different wives, a herd of more than two hundred cattle, a very old wife, and a series of economic obligations and credits. We enter the scene (chap. ii) a week or so after he has died. Because the senior son, Salimu, is away on some mysterious errand, the hearings on the estate have been postponed. Even though three or four elders have responded to the request to come to Kapsirika and help settle matters, Salimu has not been reached. We pick up gossip concerning Salimu's inopportune absence and some preliminary discussions of the problems inherent in the situation. Efforts are made to undermine the position of Salimu by questioning his motives, and these are later reflected in public discussions.

The real action starts when Salimu and his traveling companion return. We find Salimu engaging himself with the problem (chap. iii) and establishing the legitimacy of his journey and his competence to handle matters pertaining to the estate. Despite the impatience of the elders, who have now been in Kapsirika for about two weeks, the first efforts at formal hearings are abortive, because Ndiwa (Kambuya's son by his second wife) and Salimu himself fail to appear (chap. iv). During these dis cussions, however, many of the problems inherent in the situation receive public recognition.

The formal hearings are recorded in chapters v and vi. The first hearing is associated with the ceremony of smearing (chap. v), an anointing of the personal possessions of the deceased so that they may be taken by the heirs. Of greater importance in the day's activity are the public statements made by those who have a claim against the estate and by Kambuya's family concerning debts owing to the estate. Most of this session is devoted to a series of specific claims, often with opposing arguments and determinations, and it therefore functions as a kind of civil court. Chapter vi deals with the allocation of Kambuya's cattle to the several heirs; had there been heritable wives, these also would have been allocated. In this extended session we come to the confrontation between Salimu and his full brother. Here the basic decision is reached regarding the distribution of Kambuya's animals among the sons. This decision is not in accordance with established law, though it has the sanction of a traditional moot presided over by respected elders. Chapter vii presents some minor addenda and clarifies a few miscellaneous issues; it is a kind of denouement.

I have chosen to include another hearing as additional testimony to the kind of interaction that takes place in Sebeiland. It involves essentially the same cast of characters and takes place a few weeks after these other hearings, but it has nothing to do with Kambuya's death. It centers on a marriage by one of Kambuya's wards and the accusation of intent to do witchcraft initiated by a sister of Kambuya against the co-wife of her daughter.

Our primary interest in this account is not the background of custom, which I shall presently sketch, but the interpersonal actions in the social encounters. We see the attitudes of the Sebei toward their own customary procedures, with expressions of uncertainty as to just what the rules are, the recognition of internal diversity in custom and the attitudes these invoke, and, in one instance at least, the poking of fun at customary procedures. One is reminded of Helen Codere's examination of some Kwakiutl attitudes toward their solemn rituals.[12] We see also the diversity of personalities, of capabilities, of knowledge, and even of values among the actors, and how this diversity is a factor in the ultimate decisions reached. Finally, we see that events are continuously being manipulated by individuals seeking to satisfy their personal aims. Even custom is manipulated and redefined. The Sebei have a real and meaningful belief in witchcraft, and the fear of sorcery is ever present; yet accusations of witchcraft are flung about evidently for purposes of satisfying private aims in these social encounters.

It will be useful for the reader to have some details of Sebei culture.[13] The Sebei are a people belonging to the family of cultures generally known as Nilo-Hamitic, of which the Masai are the most famous exemplars; their close neighbors are the Pokot (or Suk), the Karamojong, and the Nandi. All these peoples are devoted cattle keepers, but all, except some of the Masai, also engage in the cultivation of some crops—aboriginally, millet and sorghum—with short-handled hoes. The Sebei, sometime in the recent past, came to the great mountain massif now called Mount Elgon, which lies on the Uganda-Kenya border. Here they came into contact with, and were pushed back by, Bantu-speaking peoples to the west, from whom they adopted plantains. Hence, the well-watered and fertile slopes of the mountain were increasingly devoted to farming, and the ratio of cattle declined. The settled life on the slopes of the mountain discouraged aggressive warfare and cattle raiding, but the Sebei's neighbors and cultural relatives continued to harass them, stealing their cattle and their women; consequently, despite their

---

[12] "The Amiable Side of Kwakiutl Life," *American Anthropologist*, 58 (1956), 334–351.

[13] A detailed ethnography is in preparation. An analysis of the law among the Sebei has been published (*Sebei Law* [Berkeley and Los Angeles: University of California Press, 1967]), to which the reader is referred for details of the legal machinery and substantive rules, including social affiliations, inheritance rules, and the regulation of contracts, which play a prominent part in the discussions of Kambuya's legacy.

advantaged situation, they did not prosper. One effect of this military action was that the Sebei abandoned the plains lying to the north of the mountain, leaving it as a kind of no-man's-land which they sporadically used for hunting and fearfully exploited for agriculture, always working in groups for mutual protection.

Before World War I, the British established a military outpost on these plains not far from Kapsirika, where the events here recorded took place. Under the shadow of this British armament, the Sebei began to return to their flat country; Kambuya was one of the pioneers. Eventually a subdistrict governmental headquarters was established; roads and lorries appeared; and increasing attention was devoted to farming, chiefly of maize cultivated with ox-drawn plows. The British presence did not entirely stop the raiding; indeed, there was a rash of it at the time we were among the Sebei, and some of the plains-dwelling families—though not those of Kapsirika—had begun to crowd into brush-fenced manyattas for mutual protection. I accompanied one retaliatory raid in an effort to retrieve a kraalful of stolen cattle.

The Sebei in general have a mixed economy of cattle and farming. Parts of the escarpment are almost covered with plantains, whereas in other areas farming is secondary. Farming remains so, despite the plow, in Kapsirika; it remains so to an even greater extent when we consider the social involvements, as opposed to the economic importance, of the cattle.

Sebei society was organized without separate political institutions: no chief, no established leadership, and no inherited office. A kind of central authority was provided by the prophet or seer, whose special mystic abilities gave him some secular powers; but prophets were outlawed by the British, and play no part in modern Sebei life. At the present time there are appointive chiefs with administrative and judicial functions sanctioned by the protectorate (now the Uganda national) authorities.

Indeed, the Sebei as an entity did not exist in a formal sense, but is a creature of recent political development. Formerly, there were several independent tribes, which, through ritual and the influence of the prophet and common language and customs, formed a loose federation or cluster. The tribes themselves had no political machinery, but were divided into autonomous geographical entities called *pororisyek* (*pororyet*, sing.), membership in which was formalized. These units were mutual protection groups; they recognized the existence of elders (*kirwokik*; *kirwokintet*, sing.), whose judgment was used to settle disputes but who had no vested power. There were also military leaders. These pororisyek were divided into smaller geographical units called *sangta* (*songmwek*, pl.), which I have translated as "village," though the people were scattered over the land rather than concentrated in a single place. These too had their elders, who presided over moots largely concerned with domestic affairs. All these elders, at both the pororyet and the sangta levels, were men whose judgment had won them the right to public respect; they were not officials.

Sebei society is also divided into agnatic kin groups called *arosyek* (*aret*, sing.), which can be translated as "clans," though the literal translation is "roads" or "paths." These units, named after their presumed founders, are permanent social groups to which each individual member has a perduring spiritual tie, though the members are scattered throughout Sebeiland (and beyond) and, now at least, never collect as a whole. A man's membership derives strictly from his paternity. The clans do not control property—neither land nor cattle—but when a death is to be avenged or compensated, each member is expected to contribute his energies or resources. Since the injured party may seek retribution through witchcraft, and since witchcraft works on the guilty clan rather than on the responsible individual, there is a strong psychological motivation for mutual support. The clans are divided into lineages (*kota*; *korik*, pl.; literally, "house") made up of the patrilineal descendants of the presumed sons of the founder. Members of a kota are in closer actual association; and thus the lineage has more involvement with the daily life of the individual, though not theoretically with the inner spiritual force. Each aret and kota has a head, the senior member of the senior line, but he has no true authority beyond the expectation that he offer leadership and preside over such meetings as may take place. As with the pororyet and the sangta, the clan and the lineage may hold a formal meeting or moot—called *kokwet*—to settle internal matters. In a sense, the meeting here is thus a kokwet of the kota of Kambuya.

Finally, there is the age-set, a group of men initiated during a particular span of time. Formerly it was, in effect, a generation; the initiations were held each six or seven years, and a set of three initiation groups formed an age-set, called *pinta*. Now, initiations are held every two years. The initiation is a long series of ceremonies undergone in early manhood (age eighteen to twenty), beginning with circumcision and ending with the formal induction into age-set membership and indoctrination into its mysteries and powers. The girls also are initiated as they enter womanhood; their initiation likewise involves circumcision—cutting away the labia minora and clitoris—and inducts them into counterpart age-sets. Among neighboring tribes these age-sets perform political functions, forming warrior and elder classes. Among the Sebei they have no such function, though age deference remains a strong sentiment and the ties to one's fellow initiates are close and enduring.

Most men own cattle, which are not only their sustenance but their wealth. Each man keeps or sells or slaughters his cattle, as he wishes. He also engages in exchanges, the contractual details of which are highly elaborate. These exchanges will be more fully described later; here we need only note that in the basic exchange, *namanya*, the rights to a bullock (normally for immediate consumption in association with a ceremony) are acquired in return for a future heifer, under contractual obligations that assure there will be a reproductive cow at some future date. Since Kambuya took part in many such exchanges (see Appendix E), and since diverse situations can impede the fulfillment of contract, the pattern led to considerable litigation. Some of this appears throughout the discussions. The Sebei also lend cattle, under a contract called *kamanakan*, in which the borrower receives the milk and blood from the animal in return for taking care of it. Animals held under this contract are spoken of as being in *kamanaktay*. Thus it is that the cattle in a man's kraal do not all belong to him; some are his own, some belong to others but are in his herd under the namanya contract, and others are there in kamanaktay. At the same time, a man may own animals living in the kraals of other men. Such a program has many economic advantages: it spreads the risk, makes cattle available to those with greater need, keeps herds to manageable size, and obscures the level of one's wealth from neighbors and tax collectors.

Inasmuch as we are dealing with the events surrounding a death, we should also take cognizance of inheritance rules. It is customary for a man ceremonially to anoint and give some cows to each wife. In a basic legal sense these animals remain his, but he cannot exchange or slaughter them without the wife's permission; even if she is divorced or dies, the cows[14] are to be inherited by her own sons and not by sons of her co-wives. The animals that a man keeps as his own are called *tokapsoy*. Thus Kambuya had animals that were tokapsoy and some that had been anointed for each of his several wives.

As a boy grows up, he acquires the cattle that will form the nucleus of his herd. His father pays the bride-price for his first wife out of his tokapsoy and perhaps from cattle anointed for his mother as well. The married son normally acts as his father's herdsman for a period of time, and keeps his animals together with his father's. As the next son marries, or after several years, he establishes a separate household. At this time the father gives him additional animals; these are his heritage, and he no longer has any legal claim on his father's tokapsoy, although he does retain a claim on the animals anointed for his mother. Consequently, as a man's sons grow up, each in turn serves as his father's herdsman until, in Sebei idiom, he is "chased out of the house" by being given his share of animals. The last son is

---

[14] The calves from such cows will have the same status. Indeed, the Sebei speak of a family (kota) of cattle, following the descendants of an original animal, including those obtained in exchange, trade, or even purchase with the money obtained for it or its descendants.

expected to serve until the father dies, at which time he takes over his father's herd as a kind of residual legatee. In Kambuya's family, Salimu and his half brother Ndiwa had each been given his share; Salimu's full brother Andyema was his father's herdsman, as the last son had not yet reached maturity. Under standard regulations, Andyema should have had all the father's tokapsoy cattle, holding a share of them in trust for the younger half brother.

The rituals surrounding death are simple. The burial itself is unimportant. (Formerly, the dead were set out for the hyenas to eat.) Three days after the death a bull is slaughtered and there is a feast. The personal possessions of the deceased are anointed with fat, and beer and the chewed root of a plant are sprayed on them by an elder; they are thus freed of the spirit of the deceased, and may be taken by the heirs. The ceremony is simple and unimpressive.

Since this book is essentially a document, I have sought to preserve its documentary character intact, though I have tried also to make it understandable through background descriptions and annotation. In addition to communicating about Sebei life, it will be available for other scholars to use for such purposes as may subsequently seem worthwhile. Because this is a document, it is important for me to describe as accurately and honestly as possible the circumstances in which it was recorded. No document is a perfect record of actual human events, and this is no exception.

The essence is contained in the record of a series of meetings, some formalized sessions and others informal discourse (though I must say that there was as little formality of organization in the one as in the other). At these meetings I sat next to my interpreter, Yovan Chemtai. He gave a running translation of the discourse, and I recorded in longhand, which I write with great speed and poor legibility. Between us, we usually identified the speakers, though sometimes we failed to do so. (In the text, an unidentified speaker is indicated by a dash: ———.) The documents were then immediately typed from my notes. There are occasional lacunae and questions of detail which are indicated in the text. Clarification on some points was sought later in conversations with the principals, but not all the problems were satisfactorily resolved—there is a limit on the burden the most cooperative of informants will take.

There are two essential questions regarding the validity of the document. First, is it an accurate record of what actually took place? Second, did my presence alter what would otherwise have occurred? To answer these questions it is necessary to turn to the general setting of the events here described.

This document is a by-product of a study being made of the cultural adaptation of the Sebei to different environments and economic modes. In 1954 I spent six months with the Sebei under a Fulbright grant. Out of this experience I subsequently evolved, with the aid of my colleagues, a rather elaborate research project on the ecology of four pastoral-farming tribes in East Africa, of which the Sebei was one. In addition to being director of this project, I contributed the study of the Sebei. The research program included the detailed analysis of two communities within each tribe: one in the farming sector and one in the herding area. Thus my time was split, first, between the directorship and ethnography, and, second, between the two local communities. Our base camp was on the mountain in the community where farming was paramount; our second was in Kapsirika, on the plains, where Kambuya lived and died. We spent two periods in Kapsirika: one in March–April, the second in August–November, 1962.

Labu, as I was called by the Sebei (for no reason I could gather; I have questioned dozens of persons for the meaning, fearing it has some derogatory connotation, but was told only that it means a friendly person, which by Sebei standards is not entirely a compliment), was known from Kitale to Mbale. My wife and I were on cordial terms with the politically important as well as the ordinary citizens. In Kapsirika we had been instrumental in getting medical help for an outbreak of meningitis, and so at the very least we were regarded as useful. We had known the principals in this drama for some time; indeed, the protagonist had given us a sheep in gratitude for our having taken his daughter (Kambuya's grandchild) to the hospital just before these events took place.

It is fatuous, in my opinion, to speak as anthropologists often do of good rapport, as if it is somehow simply good or bad. The ethnographer's relation to the tribe is a many-faceted thing, and friendship in one place may mean enmity in another. Although we were well known and "accepted," we had real intimacy with few Sebei. The Sebei do not seem to make close relationships; they tend to see all personal relations as instrumental. Love, warmth, trust, and even obligation do not characterize their attitudes toward one another, nor did these attributes characterize their attitudes toward the strangers in their midst. Our presence in all kinds of situations seemed to be taken for granted, sometimes with real or feigned pleasure and occasionally with evident annoyance. Concern tended to be evoked in the situations that were regarded by the Sebei as being sensitive to European influence: circumcision, because it awakened criticism of local culture; magical involvements or oaths, because Europeans had outlawed them; land disputes, because they might threaten title to land; ceremonies that held secrets protected from the uninitiated.

Our presence may have influenced the action in two aspects of the hearings. Accusations of magic were repeatedly made, although I am not sure how firmly they were believed. I felt then (as now) that these accusations were expressions of hostility and strategems in gaining social advantage rather than sincere accusations. It is possible, however, that they were more serious and had deliberately been muted precisely because of my presence, and that some of the delay and the night meetings at which I did not appear were probably efforts to clear the air in my absence.

Perhaps also a higher degree of "fairness" of decisions came about because of my presence; that is, efforts to hide, to deny, or to be arbitrary may have been curtailed just because the fates had decreed that precisely these hearings, of the hundreds that have been held by the Sebei, were being recorded. One of the younger brothers, expressing satisfaction with the decisions rendered, said he thought our presence was a factor in creating such fairness.

Thus our influence may have been to mute to some degree the expression of hostility and the maneuverings of self-interest —the most fascinating elements of the drama. I am inclined to think this was true, but to so slight a degree that it is irrelevant to the purposes of this document. Notwithstanding, insofar as this effect obtained, it had the tendency to lessen rather than to heighten the drama, to make some of our evidence unclear rather than overemphasized—to make this document an under-statement, as it were.

By the time these events took place, Chemtai had been my interpreter for a year. He had previously been a governmental court interpreter, and was both rapid and accurate. He had already done a great deal of this simultaneous interpretation for me. It is a skill that one either has or does not have, and he was excellent at it. He had a further quality that is relevant: he had no interest whatever in concealing from me the kind of things that many of the more sophisticated Sebei tried to hide. He made efforts to get the local gossip—whether about sexual affairs, magic, or secret rites—almost with a salacious interest. He had exactly the right degree of alienation from his culture; he was not ego-involved so as to want to maintain cultural "face," yet he did not look down on his less educated fellows as inferior; he was correct in his interpersonal relations, always, for example, carefully greeting his age-mates with the special gusto prescribed by custom. On the whole, he was a moderately respected and personally accepted Sebei, but he was not drawn in, or taken over, by the Sebei as against his employer. He also had endur-ance; one chapter here represents some six hours of consecutive recording. Ultimately, when his interpretations threatened to become sloppy and my writing totally illegible, I called a halt. What we could not reconstruct from informants later (we got the essence of the major speech from its maker) was lost, along with other discussions that took place in our absence.

How accurately did Chemtai render Sebei statements into

English? How completely did he cover what was said? On both scores I am reasonably satisfied. There are a few places where the translation makes no sense, where either Chemtai misspoke or I misheard or misrecorded, but the essential record seems accurate. There are a few obscure attributions of speakers, mostly among the minor characters in the drama. There are inevitable elisions, for the events were occasionally too disorderly to prevent speakers from overriding; some of the confusion natural to meetings is lost. Far more serious is the fact that some discussions took place, in groups or in pairs, in my absence; of these I have at best only indirect evidence.

I do not say this in any spirit of apology, but for the sake of scholarly accuracy. The interest of the document lies in its presentation of a sector of the life activities of a people, to give the reader a sense of participation in events from a different time and place. It presents, I believe, as accurate as possible a picture of the ongoing processes of this particular event, but the reader deserves my own assessment of its adequacy.

The artist may take liberties with life; the scholar must not. In a novel each act fits into a unity; it develops both character and plot, and in the end there is resolution. It is only fair to warn the reader that he will find no such unity in the pages that come. Events take place which can but barely be discerned; actions occur which have neither beginning nor ending; much remains enigmatic. I do not mean to make a virtue of this shortcoming, and I am aware that it does not make the text either easy or more valuable. When possible and necessary, I have made interpretations and annotations to help guide the reader through the activities that are here recorded. But in the end, it is not the understanding of each detail which is sought; rather, it is the total event that is important: the generality of human interactions in the context of Sebei life must claim the center of our attention.

Busiendity Kambuya came to our camp while we were still setting it up. We had moved down from the escarpment to make
investigations of the Sebei who lived on the plains north of
Mount Elgon. Kambuya was being led by a young man, who
held the end of his staff and walked slowly in front of him. He
was a small old man, dressed in a ragged kanzu; the most prominent feature of his attire was a large felt hat, battered and
shaped so that it peaked out in front like a coal scuttle and hung
low over his eyes, making it entirely impossible to see his face.
He cared little about being seen, and he had been blind for
more than thirty years. According to the date of his circumcision, which was 1910, he must have been between seventy and
seventy-five years of age. He was respected because he was old
and wise. I had already heard about Kambuya. The oldest resi-
dent of the plains area of Sebei told me that Kambuya was the
second or third man to come down to live on the plain, as Kambuya himself subsequently confirmed.

Mount Elgon rises out of the plains of eastern Uganda into
a great massive extinct volcano, but it is so large and so gradual
in its rise that it is not an impressive mountain. The plains below stand at an altitude of 4,000 feet, from which Elgon rises
more than 10,000 additional feet to the crater rim. The crater
is bitterly cold but not snow-clad. It is not a beautiful mountain
to look at, but it is a fine one to be on—it is all cliffs and deep
green valleys and rushing mountain streams with high water-
falls. The Sebei had discovered the mountain some time before
history came to this area, and had occupied the whole of it until
they were pushed away from some parts by the neighboring
Bagisu. Before the Europeans came, the Sebei used to plant

millet and sorghum fields on the plains below their mountain, going down in large groups and working together in order to protect themselves, less from leopards, lions, and other large animals than from the depredations of their more warlike, still fully cattle-keeping neighbors, the Karamojong and the Pokot. The Sebei say that at a still earlier time they actually occupied the plains, which they abandoned when the military operations of these warlike neighbors became unbearable. They retreated to the fastnesses of the mountain, where raids were at least less frequent and where they could hide their livestock and their women and children in the caves while they fought off the marauders as best they could. But this was long before even the arrival of the Swahili traders who preceded Jackson, Austin, Gedge, and other early explorers. The plains between the mountain and the Greek River, which runs in a westerly direction a few miles north of the foot of the mountain into an embayment of Lake Kyogo, became a kind of no-man's-land, claimed as the territory of the Sebei and used by them for their modest farming enterprises and for hunting, but not occupied by permanent dwellers.

Pax Britannica worked its way northward and eastward from the center of Uganda civilization and reached the outpost known as Greek River about 1912, when a police station was set up there. With the establishment of askaris in the neighborhood, a few bold young men came down from the mountain and occupied the plains, bringing small herds of cattle. Kambuya was one of the first of these pioneers. I estimate that he came down in 1914, when he was a young married man who had been circumcised for four years. He said he brought three wives, but that seems unlikely. Some 10 miles to the west lived the first of the pioneers, Mwanga Muganga, and to the east a similar distance, and nearer still to the Greek River outpost, lived Amisi Mwanga, both still active and wealthy neighbors. The grass had been little disturbed by the occasional wandering herdsmen or by the abundant game that dwelt there. It was an ideal place for a young man of courage to build up his herd. The lush plains were good for the cattle, and if a man could survive the mosquitoes and was not killed in a raid, he had an opportunity for increasing his wealth. The fifteen head of cattle that Kambuya brought with him increased to a hundred in the first five years.

When I asked Kambuya to whom the land had belonged when he settled, he said:

This is Sebei land, but it belonged to nobody. Our cows have been dropping dung on the river above here and urinating on it, and this has washed down here over the years, and therefore we are following that and settling anywhere. I came and found the area pleasing, just as you have found this camping place good for you. During the time of my father we used to come here to hunt; when I came here, people still came to hunt. Later the government introduced the system of growing cotton; then the people came down and tried to grow cotton and stayed with me. There is still a place called Kapamban, which indicates a field of cotton. This work started two years after I came down here. I was accompanied by Labu Kamwasir, who at that time also had three wives, and we lived together. He was married to my sister. He is now dead, but his sons and brothers are alive, and one of them is your neighbor here, Sabila Araplabu.

These pioneers were followed by others, until now the plains are so full that the people are beginning to worry about who owns what piece of land. Small herds of giraffe and zebra are reminiscent of former days. At that time there was little land-holding and less agriculture; the growing of cotton never became very popular in this extreme outpost, with its problems of transportation and giraffe (who are particularly fond of cotton plants) adding to the more usual difficulties of the farmer. It was, overwhelmingly, a period of cattle herding for these Sebei. In the past ten or fifteen years, plowed fields of maize and millet have become of increasing economic importance.

Kambuya was a rich man, though no one could tell it by looking. He had none of the trappings that we assume as a natural part of a man of substance. His clothes were dirty, old, and torn. His left arm was encircled with a simple iron ring of ancient Sebei manufacture. He wore the sandals made of old automobile tire casings which are the surprisingly comfortable and efficient footgear of the African bush today. His house was, if anything, poorer than most. He lived near the youngest of his married sons, in a separate house. It was a characteristic mud-and-wattle structure with a thatched roof. Aside from tin cups, aluminum pots of Indian manufacture for cooking, and a few other battered modern items, there was little in it that might not have been in his house shortly after he had moved down from the mountain, and considerably less of native manufacture.

Such, it might be said, was characteristic of Sebei men of wealth of Kambuya's generation. Most of the old men who had many cattle and much wealth—and some with many wives—lived in the same kind of circumstances that characterized the life of Kambuya. It is the younger generation that has taken to the consumer goods, surrounding themselves with modern dishes, tailored clothes, corrugated iron roofs, and the like, to distinguish themselves publicly from their neighbors. Not only do these old cattle herders present themselves in this poverty-stricken manner, but their conversation is also "poor-mouthed." They complain of having nothing, of being mistreated, of subsisting on an inadequate diet; and they demand of their neighbors, whether African or European, gifts of tobacco, sugar, or whatever consumer item they may fancy. This is old and established Sebei custom; it is as much a part of their way of life as is their circumcision ceremony or their beer drinking. I do not know precisely how many cows Kambuya owned, but his herd was a substantial one, and its value was great in absolute terms as well as relative to his fellow Sebei citizens. We have some measure of Kambuya's wealth in the details that follow.

At this first visit, Kambuya talked about the early days of life on the plains. He gave me some genealogical information about his ancestry, and we had a friendly talk amidst the unpacked boxes and partly finished thatching of the house that was being erected for our use. At one point, I was called away to supervise some detail, and when I returned I found him "tossing his sandals"—a form of divination the Sebei have learned from their Karamojong neighbors to the north. I thought he was doing this merely to pique the curiosity of his strange host, but I soon discovered that one of the men who had gathered around us was seeking to learn the whereabouts of one of his cattle which had not returned to the kraal the night before. This cow was about to throw a calf, and the owner was particularly concerned because the hyenas had been noisier than usual.

Kambuya held the sandals sole to sole in his right hand so that the plane of the sole was vertical to the ground, and then tossed them sharply upward and let them fall to the ground. Each throw was expected to be the answer to a specific query. Occasionally, the sandals were spit upon, presumably ensuring their validity. (Sebei told me that some sandals were very truthful but that others lied.) Sometimes, in fact, Kambuya did not seem to like the answer, and he picked the sandals up and threw them again before he answered the query. If one sandal had fallen over the other, it would have indicated that the hyena had the cow and was on top of it eating it. But one sandal was nested against the other, indicating that the cow had borne the calf and was lying down. If the sandal that represented the calf was bottom up, then that calf was black. On one of the tosses, the sandals were close together, indicating that the cow was not far away.

Kambuya refused my request to help me find a fountain pen I had just lost; I suppose his response was fair enough, since he asks no pay for his skill but is invited to partake of the feast when the cow is slaughtered. He also refused to tell me in what direction the cow was found; in all fairness, it must be said that the cow had calved during the night and was discovered not far from where we were.

Kambuya left our camp shortly afterward, led away by the grandson who was the apple of his eye. The grandson, the firstborn son of his own firstborn son, was a deep-chested, reddish, handsome young man of petulant expression. I found it difficult to appreciate the virtues that the father and the grandfather found in him. He had recently married and was living at his father's kraal, serving his father as herdsman. Though he seemed an indifferent herdsman, he was ready to participate in a raid; thus he had one of the outstanding qualities of old Sebei tradition—one that is rapidly diminishing with each succeeding generation. In recent years the raids by the neighboring Pokot and Karamojong, usually for the purpose of stealing cattle, had almost reached the point of warfare. Indeed, a few months later these raids became so numerous and so hostile that, after a number of persons were killed, many of the residents of Kapsirika and neighboring communities left for the mountains or other havens of safety. It was rumored—no one wanted to say it outright—that this young man had killed an enemy and was therefore a hero.

I saw Kambuya only two or three times while we were on the plains on this trip; I was busy gathering special information and was waiting for a more leisurely return visit. I did spend one afternoon at his house, getting information on his family composition and gossiping with him. I got to know his sons, particularly his eldest, Salimu, who was recognized throughout the community as one who knew the most about cattle keeping. My first personal evidence of his special knowledge came when I stopped at Salimu's house to gather information about family composition, livestock, and farming. Indeed, he was well informed on matters pertaining to cattle, and his prodigious memory was substantiated when he rattled off thirty-eight separate namanya arrangements.

A namanya arrangement is a contract freely engaged in by two Sebei for a trade in cattle. Essentially, a man who needs to slaughter an animal, or for some reason needs to have one that he does not have, contracts for the animal with a neighbor, a friend, or relative, or anyone with whom he is on amicable terms. In exchange he gives a heifer or the promise of one in the future. Actually, the arrangement is more complicated than this simple statement suggests. The man who wants to acquire the animal for slaughter is usually the person who initiates the arrangement. He may need an animal of a certain color for ceremonial or magical purposes and thus be forced to go to another's kraal; but in fact the Sebei consider it better to slaughter someone else's animal, and a man will therefore make the exchange even if he owns an appropriate animal. He offers to give one of his heifers in exchange; in the old days he might even have offered the next-born heifer of a young cow. This animal is not given outright to the other, but is returned when she has produced a heifer and when this daughter in turn is of an age to be served. Because the Sebei have no writing, these contracts are held in the memory of the individual. Entering into such an arrangement establishes a quasi kinship bond, called *tilyet*, between the two persons, who are expected not only to be polite to each other, to use the appropriate kinship terms of address—*tilyeñu*, "my kin-of-the-cow"—but also to invite their tilyet to drink beer and to partake of food on all occasions.

Such bargains involve not only cattle but other commodities as well. Chickens may be exchanged for goats, goats for cattle, and any of these for granaries of maize or millet or even food growing in the field. It is a standard contract, and every Sebei person of substance will have some in effect at all times; some persons have many. As I said, Kambuya's son listed thirty-eight for me at one sitting, and I can only assume that this was the full number.

At present, these arrangements seem to be rather casually entered into. (In the course of our narrative we shall have occasion to observe the negotiating for exchanges.) In the old days, however, entering into such an arrangement required an elaborate protocol, which Baita, another old blind man, detailed for me. I think it will help us understand some of the spirit of Sebei economic transactions and social intercourse if we stop to examine in detail what he said.

When you want to borrow an ox [Baita began], that man you borrow from will be your true friend. A person may own a cow that has been served, but needs an ox to slaughter for some ceremony. He uses this heifer that is to be born from the served cow to return for that bull. So he must seek out a man with an ox or a bullock. The man will invite him [or, rather, his emissary] in and feed him before any business is spoken of. The conversation may go as follows.

HOST: Ai, sir, as you have come here, what purpose do you bring?
VISITOR: I have come as a visitor of this house.
HOST: For what special business?
VISITOR: I would become a son-in-law.
HOST: A son-in-law of what? Of the house or of the kraal? [I.e., Do you negotiate for one of my daughters or one of my bullocks?]
VISITOR: Of the kraal.
HOST: If the daughter of the kraal [i.e., the bullock] is only one,

what shall I then do? (He says this however many he has.) As there will be only cows in my kraal, what animal will serve them?

VISITOR: You have many neighbors, sir, and they have many bulls; the one here will be nothing. Your cows and their bulls will meet in the pastures; who will want to separate them, for who can manage a bull with a cow?

HOST: You go, but may come back again.

VISITOR: Ai, I shall go and come with the man who wants the bull; I am the agent.

Propriety demands that the man who wants to slaughter the cow should not make the initial visit; instead, he sends his neighbor to do the bargaining. In Sebei custom, when a man wants to marry, his father goes to see the parents of the girl he seeks; in the bargaining, a neighbor represents her father. So it is with bargaining for a cow. Late in the evening or the next morning the agent reports to the man who wants to borrow the animal. The agent must go to him, not the other way about. He will report, "I went there, but the man is a very hard man; yet I think that he has willing eyes," and will tell him to return the day after tomorrow.

On the day promised, the agent and the borrower go together to see the owner. The agent is like a witness. If the owner is not present, they will go in and sit on the left of the door in that part of the house called *metsu*. Whether the man is there or not, the woman of the house will get up quickly and spread a cow skin for them to sit on. It indicates that the woman likes these visitors and that they will be given the friendship of the bull, will become tilyet. After they are properly seated, the husband greets the visitors and immediately goes out. Perhaps the bull the men want to borrow belongs to the woman [that is, has been anointed for her]. By her hospitality, the husband knows that the woman wants to establish a friendship of the cow. The husband may go out to supervise the crops or to stay in the house of the second or third wife. This is to show the feeling that the woman really has. She will go out and get a large stem of plantains and a small stem also. When she comes back she will drop the bunches at the door. She pulls off the hands, and throws them into the house. The husband is watching from afar, and if the woman does this, the husband knows that she is willing to give the bull and he will quickly give in to his visitor. When she has them all inside she will come in and start peeling them, and now she is ready to greet the visitors. Before she starts peeling, she will wash the cooking pot four times and she will be happy. So if the husband meant to refuse, he will know now to accept. She puts leaves in the pot and cooks the bananas.

When the husband returns, he will become very harsh, fussing about why the cows are still in the kraal when the sun is up, and the woman will say humbly that the herders haven't yet had their breakfast. The husband complains that the wife is too slow.

The woman washes her hands and divides the food: a basket for the visitors, a basket for her husband, a basket for the children, and a basket for herself. She washes her hands again and goes into the back part of the house and gets a big calabash of preserved milk. The woman cleans the gourd carefully for the guest. The woman must have a number of gourds, and if she likes the guest she will take the biggest one. When the woman is cleaning the milk, she pretends to scrape some bad stuff with a stick and scrapes it on her finger and then throws it away. Then she will give it to the guest, and he will try to shake it to stir it up, but he can't [for it is soured milk, old, thick, and a great delicacy]; so he will ask for a palm rib to stir it and will stir it very thoroughly. Then he will ask for something to share it with the borrower, but she will protest that she should get another gourd of milk; yet the agent, pointing to the other food that is already before them, insists that it is enough. So the woman gets an empty gourd that is smaller than the original one and gives it to the agent, who then divides the soured milk, putting the smaller amount in the small gourd. He gives the original gourd to the borrower and keeps the smaller amount because he is humbling himself and making the real borrower more important. The borrower is being very quiet and gentle because he is the one "who will marry the daughter."

They hold the calabash in the right hand by the strings and tip it with the back of the left hand to drink. They also eat their cooked bananas with the left hand. While they are doing so, the woman is busy. She gives fresh milk to the husband, saying, "This will do for you." She also pours some milk into open calabashes for the children. When they have eaten, the woman will send the children out, saying that it is time to get the cattle; the woman and children go out to herd, and the young ones to play.

When the guests have finished they return the baskets but they hide the gourds behind them. The agent would have finished his, but the borrower, who is now the "son-in-law," should not finish his. If he finishes that milk, he is not a true friend of the cow. Before returning it, the borrower must bless the remainder of the milk left in his gourd by spitting into it and rubbing the mouth of the gourd on his chin. Then he returns it, saying, "My relative of the cow." And now he starts the conversation, saying, "I did send this man to see you because I had such and such a reason for needing this bull." The owner of the bull might ask, "When do you demand the bull?" And he would answer, "Just now, today." The owner then asks the wife what she thinks, and the woman will say, "I have no power; it is up to you to accept." She is agreeing in the matter.

The husband will then ask, "Will this bull go alone?" It is not proper for the borrower to take the cow himself, and someone must drive it to his kraal. So the husband will tell his wife to go along and sprinkle some milk before the cow is slaughtered. As the woman should not use milk for this purpose out of a gourd from which milk has been given to somebody, she must wait until the next morning. So the next morning the woman will milk a cow. It does not matter what the color of the cow, but she will keep that milk separate.

The borrower will send his helpers to drive the bull to his kraal. In the morning the husband appoints one of his neighbors or somebody he trusts to take care of the meat that is to be returned to him as part of the price. The "meat" [as Sebei call a recognized portion] that he gets is the neck, half of the hump, the meat from the top of the ribs as far as the fourth rib, all from the right side of the animal.

When they take the cow, a rope is tied around the horn and around the muzzle so that it won't make a sound. Before the animal is slaughtered, the wife of the lender takes the milk she has brought. "Ai, tilyeñu," she says, "we will visit each other in peace; we will love each other very much. We do not want any quarrels. The girl has been given to you. Any hatred that we have among us is finished now." While saying this she sprinkles milk over the borrower's head so that it runs down only the right side of the man. Then she sprinkles milk on the bull, starting at the head and all along the back, so that finally some runs down the tail. Then she proceeds: "Ai, black bull, may your belly be good. It is we who have offered you. You are not stolen. Don't think a girl will grow until she reaches this far. Don't think to make a shield for a girl. You go peacefully." [These words refer to the fact that the bull has now become, for this family, a cow, for in time they will receive the heifer in return. A man does not make a shield for his daughters, but only for his sons.]

Now the animal is slaughtered, and those who were sent to get the bull will each claim a piece of the flesh from the owner. The meat from the right side will be sent back to the lender, but they will claim meat from the left side. The two men are each other's tilyet, kin of the cow; they address each other "tilyeñu" and show each other friendship and hospitality.

I have never heard such a formalized session; the discussions that take place nowadays are carried on in a most ordinary fashion. But these exchanges are a frequent and important element of Sebei economic and social life, and sentiments of friendship are expected to go with the transactions.

I was never directly informed by Kambuya how many cattle he owned. (The data in Appendix E, which do not purport to be all his cattle, suggest more than 200; see table 3.) The Sebei do not like to tell anyone how many cattle they have, partly because they have the same sense of personal secrecy about the size of their herds as we tend to have about the size of our bank accounts, and partly because they feel that to state the precise number would bring bad luck and the decimation of their herd. Nor would Kambuya detail to me the namanya deals in which he was currently engaged; he had the best of all excuses: he was blind, and could not know these things.

It was an excuse that one could not deny to his face, but manifestly it had nothing to do with the truth. Kambuya knew his cattle—each and every one of them. His herdsman (Andyema, the youngest of his married sons) spoke to me about the knowledge Kambuya had of his herd, admitting it was better than his own. Kambuya would stand by the side of the kraal gate as his cattle were returning from grazing and would ask about individual animals. He had a sixth sense about things being wrong, and unfailingly would ask about any animal that was limping or missing. It reminded me of a statement by one of my interpreters, who said that as a boy he had been herding his goats one day when a hyena took one of them. His mother, who had no notion how many goats and sheep were in the herd, noted the absence of the animal the moment she looked at the flock and queried him immediately as to its whereabouts. The memory was still painful.

Kambuya, though blind most of his life and though living in impoverished circumstances, was nevertheless a rich man by the most important standard that an old Sebei herdsman could bring to bear: he had a large and excellent herd of cattle. These he had preserved because they were his wealth, his substance, and his satisfaction.

CHAPTER III *Salimu*

Kambuya died the week before we returned to Kapsirika in August. Among the Sebei, a very old man who has really lived out his life and is no longer able to get about on his own is especially venerated. When he dies, his death is called *kelil*—a "sweet" death, a natural, not a magic-ridden, one. Though Kambuya was an old man, he was not so old that his death could be considered kelil; so he was put into the ground the day after he died. In the past, the body of a man who died a sweet death was not set out for the hyenas but laid out under a tree for his grandchildren and great-grandchildren to see and admire. Such a man has weathered the vicissitudes of a long life, and by magic contact brings the opportunity for a long life to those around him. He is not buried by his brother (which would be unlikely) or by his son but, unlike all other Sebei, by his grandchildren.

The Sebei get rid of the body as quickly and quietly as modern Americans do. On the third day after the death, however, there is a ceremony of cleansing. The heads of selected mourners are shaved, and the widows are released from hiding. They too are shaved, but poorly, to show that it is for mourning (all Sebei women used to have shaved heads), and those who partake of the ceremony are ritually cleansed. After this, a meeting is usually held to air the debts against the estate; the heirs to the wives are selected, and the cattle are allocated. An animal is slaughtered, and the possessions of the deceased are blessed by rubbing with fat from the animal and by spraying mouthfuls of beer on them; these too can then be taken by others.

But with Kambuya, the ceremony had not been completed because Salimu, the elder of Kambuya's sons by his first wife, was nowhere to be found. They had observed the shaving cere-

mony and had slaughtered an ox, though some apparently felt
that even this should have waited, but they did not smear Kambuya's belongings or hold the meeting about debts.

Salimu's absence troubled everyone. As Kambuya's eldest
son, Salimu was now the head of the kota, the extended household of the sons and grandsons of the deceased. Nothing could
be decided without him, and matters were being held in abeyance until his return. Messengers had been sent to all the places
for miles around where it was thought he might be—seeking the
wife who had run away with another man, trading for cattle
in the far eastern part of Sebeiland, or in the town of Mbale
seeking medicine for his illness. There were many rumors about
where he was, but none of them gave satisfaction. The messengers came back without Salimu and without any information.

Salimu's absence was as much a subject of gossip as it was of
concern. Many felt that he should not have left when his father
was so ill, though this judgment seemed merely to be wisdom
by hindsight. Others felt that his leaving implied that he was
the person responsible for the death; why else should he have
left at just this time? These sentiments were perhaps heightened
by the mysterious nature of Salimu's disappearance. Neither the
special messengers sent to different parts of Sebei nor the bush
telegraph that usually works so efficiently seemed to bring any
response as to where he was. As it turned out, he had indeed
gone far away, deep into Pokot territory on the Kenya side of
the boundary—but that gets ahead of our story. I was as anxious
for his return as anyone else, for I was aware that the problems
inherent in the allocation of Kambuya's cattle would give me
additional knowledge about the Sebei. I had a long talk with
Ndiwa, Kambuya's son by his second wife and next in age to
his half brother Salimu.

We are waiting for Salimu [Ndiwa said] before we do anything.
The chief says that the people keep giving false information about
Salimu's whereabouts. We will wait until Salimu's return before holding the final funeral ceremony. It is not true that I want to go ahead
without Salimu. Kambuya asked me to write down the debts before
he died, but I didn't do it. He had ordered a notebook and had sent

for Eryeza; but Eryeza delayed too much, and Kambuya died before he came.

The old man mentioned about a quarter of the debts to me, but not all. We must invite people who can help us divide the property. People came on the third day after the burial. They started to state their debts then, but they were told to stop and wait for the smearing ceremony.

If Salimu fails to show up for a long time, we must ask the old men to advise us what to do. We are too young to know about that. We will ask Amisi Mwanga and also another man from Bok named Zebroin Kaptyemoyok. These men are not related to us, but we are all from the same pororyet.[1] Also there is a man named Mwanga, from near Kapenguria. These are men of Kapcheptemkoñ pororyet. Mwanga is visiting here now.

Salimu has been very much liked by our father. Half of his cattle were given to Salimu as kamanaktay, and he has kept them since we were all very young. To get these back from him and divide them among ourselves is a very hard task. That is why we want the help of the old men.

I recognized that outstanding debts would have to be settled. But as each son is given his share of the cattle and "sent away" from home soon after he marries, I thought that the older sons would have their heritage and that this division would not present a problem. Not so. When I asked whether Salimu had not by now been sent away, Ndiwa said: "Yes, he was given his cows. These I speak of are kamanaktay to him, and should be divided. I have also been given mine." "But is it not the custom," I asked him, "for the unmarried sons to get the remainder?" "No, that is not so. We must divide the rest of the cows according to the wives and their sons."

In saying that they had to divide the animals according to the wives and sons, Ndiwa had reference to the basic principle of Sebei ownership: although all animals are held by the head of the household, a man will give each wife some cattle, which will go to her sons. Thus the cattle are divided according to the wives and the sons. Since the man does not smear all his cattle,

---

[1] When the Sebei returned to the plains, they did not establish pororisyek but retained their affiliations with the pororyet from which they came. Thus the elders represent the pororyet.

but holds some entirely for his own discretionary use, there remain some that are not previously allocated.

Kamanaktay cattle, as already briefly explained, are animals that a man places with the herd of another while retaining full ownership of them. It may be considered a loan or, if one prefers, the hiring of help, for the man who keeps the animals enjoys their milk, their blood, and their presence. If the animals increase over the years, the owner has a moral, but not a legal, obligation to share one or two with the man who has husbanded them well. A man may place his cattle with his close relatives— as Kambuya had done—or with others. They may be with a person who lives nearby or at a great distance. As we shall see, many of Kambuya's cattle were held by a Sebei relative who lived in the territory of a neighboring tribe, more than 100 miles away. The fact that Salimu had some of his father's animals in his kraal gave him no particular right over them, but it did give him the advantage of knowledge about the herd which his brothers did not fully share.

A day or so after my conversation with Ndiwa, Salimu's daughter-in-law came to see us, bringing with her Salimu's prepubescent daughter who, like my interpreter, was named Chemtai. We knew Chemtai from our earlier visit; we had watched her milking her father's cows and had found her an appealing, very sad, and lonely young lady. She often seemed to be the only one working around the kraal, and her circumstances were far from pleasant. Her mother had left Salimu and run off with another man, leaving her motherless. A daughter, under one of the strongest of Sebei tabus, may not sleep in the same house with her father, and so she was living with her brother and his wife.

At this time, Chemtai was in deep pain. She had been gored in the vagina by a cow she was attempting to milk. She and her stepmother asked us to take her to the hospital in Mbale. Fortunately, under the ministrations of modern medicine there, she recovered.

Shortly afterward, Salimu returned. We did not see him for a while, nor did many others; upon learning of his daughter's accident, he immediately (and with a concern somewhat out of keeping with the usual Sebei attitudes) went to Mbale to discover the circumstances surrounding the accident and to learn of his daughter's welfare. He arrived back in Kapsirika on September 7, a full two weeks after we had moved down to the plains and approximately three weeks after his father's death. To all of us concerned (for our various reasons) with his whereabouts, the wait had seemed much longer. Salimu's house was about a mile from our camp, just across the narrow Sundet River and slightly downstream. Early the next morning, in true appreciation of our good offices, he came to express his thanks.

Salimu was fifty years old. I was told that he had come to the plains on his mother's back when his father pioneered this country. He was a small man with sharp eyes, a rather narrow face, and light complexion. He was given to wearing clothes many sizes too large, emphasizing the slightness of his build, but his unclothed body clearly showed that he had been a man of considerable physical strength, now waning with the advance of years and ill health. Despite his wealth and like his father, he wore old and battered clothes, although they were more modern than those his father wore—usually a purple shirt, a pair of khaki shorts, and brown sneakers rather than the usual sandals made of tire casings.

As we sat in the thin shade of a giant thorn tree that was the focal point of our camp, he told me about his peregrinations. I do not remember all his wanderings, for I did not take notes on this conversation; I do know that he went deep into Pokot country to the small towns of Kacheliba and Amudat, where he sought medicine from European doctors, as he substantiated by showing me the hospital chits. As I look back on it now, I am certain that he took the trouble to show me these chits because he wanted to establish the purpose of his trip. I feel also that there were other reasons for his long and difficult journey, mostly by foot or hitchhiking or by the old, dilapidated, and uncertain buses that serve these outposts.

Salimu brought with him a man of about his own age and build, though somewhat more robust in health. This man had been his traveling companion, and there seemed to be a special bond between the two, a bond that created considerable gossip—not gossip of the kind one might hear in our culture but a perturbation over the special relationship with an outsider whose credentials seemed not entirely clear and whose purposes were suspect. The friend was an outsider, not from his own village, not from his own pororyet, not from his own clan. Why were these two so close? Why had they traveled together? Could it be that Salimu was learning magic from this man?

One's feeling about this friend was heightened by the peculiar enigmatic smile that characterized him. One could not help thinking that some devious purpose, some hidden reason not entirely proper, motivated his actions, that some special ends lay behind this constant companionship. Perhaps it was no more than an effort to engage in trade in contraband goods. (This indication was supported by my single personal meeting with Salimu's friend when he came one evening, privately and quietly, carrying with him a dirty print handkerchief in which a knot had been tied. Without benefit of interpreter he entered the thatched Sebei-built house that was our combination study and kitchen, and conspiratorially unknotted the handkerchief and carefully placed it on my small desk. In it were a few grains of gold, which he endeavored to sell me, saying that he could get me more if I should care to buy. Despite my lack of expert knowledge, I am sure that these grains were truly gold; but they were so small that when he inadvertently knocked them off onto the dirt floor, they were forever lost to commerce—legal or illicit.) Aside from lending an aura of mystery and deviousness to the scene and creating a doubtful basis for malicious gossip, Salimu's friend was not important to the events that took place. He was present at most of the gatherings, but he made no decisions about Kambuya's cattle. He lent color and texture to the proceedings, but he gave them no substance.

Salimu, as I said, came to our camp in the early morning. His narration of the trip—his vicissitudes in bussing and hitchhiking, his paying 10 shillings to a police driver for a lift in an official Land Rover, his experiences with European doctors, and his receipts for medicine—was all very circumstantial. It included no concern with magic, and there was, of course, an implicit denial that he was engaged in any way with native medicine. His presence drew others, including Siret and some of his sons, to our camp to hear his tale.

Salimu had seen his cattle only briefly before going on to Mbale (his kraal was about 2 miles from his house), and he became anxious to examine them, knowing they would be held for him and not turned out to graze until he arrived. Before we could get started, Siret began to press Salimu, saying that he had come to see him and had to be going soon, that he wanted to beg a bullock (that is, engage in a namanya exchange) from him for the circumcision ceremony for his sons and daughters. Salimu laughed at this request, saying that he was home all the time, thus firmly rebuking Siret for his unseemly haste and lack of manners. Siret, however, was not at the moment so much concerned with etiquette as he was with his own problems, which were severe. He had decided to perform the circumcision at a time that was not in keeping with modern government regulations. In my own ethnographic interests, I had interceded that he might have it earlier, but at this time he was not sure whether he would have, in addition to the considerable cost of performing the ceremony, the additional burden of the 500-shilling fine for holding the ceremony when not legally approved. Further, in the neighboring village Kobolomon was also preparing to have a circumcision, and he was known for his lavish slaughtering of cattle and offering of beer. Siret therefore not only had the problem of making arrangements in time to precede Kobolomon in the ritual but also that of putting on an adequate display of wealth. Thus, Siret was deeply interested in acquiring a number of animals to slaughter and to sell for money so that he could make the necessary purchases of grain for beer and food, sugar, and other requisites of a circumcision as it is done on the Sebei plains.

Receiving no proper answer from Salimu, Siret climbed into the Land Rover with us. We drove along footpaths and cattle trails for the mile or two to the base of the mountain where

Salimu kraaled his cattle. Here was an unusual homecoming. Salimu was seeing his kraal and his cattle for the first time in four weeks (except for a brief visit before he went to Mbale); he was having the first visit with his son, who was his herdsman, as Salimu had once been for Kambuya; he was interviewing his Ankole employee, who helped with the herding; he was arranging a namanya exchange; and, in addition to everything else, he was saddled with an ethnographer and his wife and their interpreters.

At this point, it is perhaps best to quote from my field notes.

It is about ten when we arrive at Salimu's kraal. The cattle are bunched around it, outside, as if waiting for their owner to return. Chemisto [Salimu's son whom we met earlier leading his blind grandfather], Chemisto's wife, the employee who is a member of the Ankole tribe, together with the fellow Ankole this man had in turn employed, were all present when we arrived. Coming with us, in addition to Salimu and his traveling companion, were Siret, a friend of Siret's from Sipi, I, and my interpreter Chemtai. My wife and her interpreter joined the daughter-in-law inside the house.

Salimu immediately walks into his kraal and looks over the cattle. He is told that one has a bad foreleg, which he examines most cursorily though the animal has a bad limp; he orders the calves separated from the cows, which is done with a minimum of efficiency. The calves are sent up the steep slope of a shoulder of Mount Elgon which rises behind the kraal; the cows go off onto the plains. While still among the cattle Siret keeps requesting an answer to his question, to which Salimu replies: "I don't have a bullock to give you, but there are plenty in Sebei. Why don't you ask somebody else?"

SIRET: I have gone to many. I have one, but I need another.
SALIMU: I have this bull, but I must sell it as I need money for my daughter Chemtai, who is in the hospital in Mbale. I plan to sell the cow that gored Chemtai. I have one of her bulls, which I will keep to remember that cow by.
SIRET: You should not sell that cow; you should kill it and let your daughter eat it while she is ill. If it were I, I would slaughter it and not look at her any more. [Meanwhile Salimu has walked off to look after his calves, and Siret turns to Chemisto.] Do you have any cow that is too old to produce or whose teats are bad and they can't be milked?
CHEMISTO: Don't try to tempt me. I won't answer you; you must ask my father.

We now walked a few feet up the side of the hill. Chairs were brought out, and we sat in the miserly shade of a small thorn bush overlooking the kraal and the house in which Chemisto, his wife, and the absent daughter Chemtai were living. Salimu was addressing his son and the Ankole herder at the same time. The Ankole was requesting pay for himself and for a fellow tribesman, who, as it turned out, was a friend who had come to help without permission or request from Salimu. Salimu merely said, "You have had the milk from the cows that I gave you to milk, and you have had the ghee to sell; I don't know what pay you are asking for." Salimu then explained to me that he had hired this Ankole man a month ago, that he had come to Salimu asking for work, that there had been no talk of pay; it was agreed what cows he would have for milking, that the milk he took was the pay for his work, and that the other cows were milked by Salimu's family. Salimu went on to explain to the Ankole that it was his own fault if he wanted to share the milk with a friend of his. Finally, he turned back to me and said with disgust, "I regard them all as women, these Ankole; if they do not do their work properly, one must send them away."

Salimu now turned to Chemisto, who had remained in the background, quiet, mostly looking at the ground, and asked him why, when he had gone to Teso country to invite some of the relatives to the funeral session, he had stayed so long a time. Chemisto answered that it was because he had no money. Salimu responded that he should have walked. Chemisto pointed out that the rivers were swollen from many rains and that he could not get across by walking. Then Salimu mentioned the fact that one of the calves had died, and asked, "Do you think that when a calf dies it will come back?" Salimu went on berating Chemisto, saying that he was now a man and it was up to him to look after his property. Finally, Salimu complained that Chemisto had failed to get the heifer from someone who owed them one—the heifer that was to be picked up from a namanya arrangement that had recently been made—and pointed out that it is up to the person to get this animal when he says he will do it.

Now Salimu, beginning to work himself up to a mood of

petulance and disgust at the problems of allocating responsibility to others, turned again to the herder to say that he did not think his Ankole friend was a proper person to herd the cattle. He was far too old, and could not keep up with the cattle; further, when Salimu was here before going to Mbale to see his daughter, he had found that the old man had left some of the cattle outside and Salimu himself had to go after them. Chemisto took this opportunity to be on his father's side, and came forward to report that the man had been milking the cows that were meant for the children and had not been giving the milk to the family. To this the herdsman replied that the children were too small to milk the cows. In response to Salimu's suggestion that he should milk them for the children, he merely laughed. I do not think Salimu took his own suggestion seriously. Then the herdsman complained that one of the cattle was very wild.

SALIMU: No, they are all tame enough; you are just afraid that one of them will kick out and spill the milk. [Then to us:] I know these people; if you keep the cows that are for the family together with those that they are supposed to milk, these herdsmen will get up in the middle of the night and milk the cattle that belong to the family, and the next morning the family gets nothing from them. That is why one must keep one's own cows separate from those that the hired men milk.

Salimu had some errand he had to do in the house, and I joined him. As we were walking through the late morning, Salimu turned to me and said:

I am not going to give Siret a bullock, even if I do have one. The last time he had a circumcision, he came to me for a bullock and he gave me a heifer; but all her calves died, and so he gave me a very small one outright [that is, not namanya; thus breaking the contract, which was his legal right but an unfriendly act]. I also had given him a he-goat, and he did nothing to return that, and I am not going to fix up his circumcision ceremony.

At this point I left Salimu to his errands and watched the herdsman preparing ghee. He rendered the butter and sold the liquid fat at about 3 shillings a bottle. While we were in the little hut watching him, he again complained about the matter of pay, saying that the milk was just the ration and that the Europeans gave both rations and pay.

SALIMU [who had again joined us]: You have failed to carry out your duty. When you came here, you never asked for pay. All people here work for milk only. If it is not all right, you will simply have to go.

ANKOLE: If that is the way you feel, take the milk and give me pay. The law has been passed that I must be paid. It is my duty to look after the lost cows or to pull a cow out that has fallen into a hole.

The matter remained unresolved. It was reasonable to assume that this pattern of bickering characterized the relationship throughout, that Salimu would give him nothing in addition, and that it was up to the herder either to leave the job for a better one if he could find it or to make up for the difference with some such form of chicanery as that mentioned by Salimu. As matters turned out in this instance, the herder and his friend were involved with a third Ankole in a very large piece of chicanery indeed. The friend was looking after the cattle of another Kapsirika man, who had taken his wife to Bukwa in search of medicine for her illness. The three Ankole ran off with the whole herd, the personal possessions that remained in the house, and even the goats and the dog. They were nearly out of reach of the district police before they were apprehended; the animals were returned safely (except the one or two that were eaten en route), and the Ankole were placed behind bars.

We returned to our one shady spot under the tree, where we sat and talked for a long time. Siret again pressed his case.

SALIMU: The last time, you refused to let me have one of your daughters. This time, please give me one of them for my son.

SIRET: These days the girls are too independent and decide for themselves. There are too many boys always coming around to see them and pet with them. [Continues after a pause.] Salimu, please consider my request with friendly feelings. Have you ever seen me refuse a cow when somebody wanted one? [I had, as a matter of fact, heard him make such a refusal the week before.] Already I have spent 400 shillings, and I have nothing. This circumcision is costing me too much.

SALIMU: The last time I had a circumcision ceremony I had to kill a bull that I liked very much.

SIRET: Yes, it is costing me much. If you have a cow that doesn't give milk anymore, give me that one. I still need four cows—two to slaughter, and two to sell for money. I wish I lived in Masop, where the people aren't troubled. As soon as the circumcision is over, they just walk away to find where the beer is. A friend of mine in Kaptum who had his girls circumcised had made beer, but when the time came he sold that beer and went out to find beer for himself.

These remarks of Siret's related to cultural differences between the Sebei living on the Elgon escarpment and those living on the plains, who are more thoroughly involved with cattle. Those who circumcise their children in the plantain-growing area do not provide the lavish display of food and beer after the manner of the plainsmen; indeed, many of them fail entirely to be hosts in accordance with prescribed custom. Siret was not exaggerating much.

At this point Salimu turned to the thoughts that must have been uppermost in his mind: the matter of his father's funeral rites, the debts to be paid, the debts to be collected. He said: "I don't like to see these young people despising cows. The animals should stay as they are, in one herd, even though the old man has died. I don't think these young boys know all the debts. There are forty-six cattle that have not been paid."

SIRET: That is true. Some of them may know a few, but not so many as you remember.

SALIMU [becoming reflective and ruminating over the problems connected with the estate of his father]: Mwanga took my father's bull and gave us a heifer as namanya, but she died and we had to ask him for another. This is still pending as an unpaid debt. My father went to Mwanga and asked for a bull and gave a heifer as namanya, but all her calves died except two bullocks and then one heifer. My father said, "I think that my cow was unfortunate; I would like to take those four animals back and give you a heifer for good." So he brought back those four original animals. As the animal had originally belonged to Ndiwa's mother, those four cows all belong to Ndiwa. But the mother cow escaped and went back to Mwanga's kraal, and it died there. But that was not Mwanga's fault, according to my father. But the

heifer that was given to Mwanga outright to replace those four
animals was a tetapsoy.[2] So my father went to Ndiwa and said,
"I must have the heifer from those four that were brought, as it
was exchanged for a tetapsoy heifer." So my father took that
young heifer, and Ndiwa kept the two bullocks that my father
had taken back earlier. This is something that Ndiwa may bring
forth, but if he does so he is wrong. That is finished. The heifer
that my father took back was given to his young wife, and neither Ndiwa nor I can claim it.

Let us pause here to examine this instance, which appears
again as the subject of the first claim, for Ndiwa did bring the
matter up as anticipated (p. 82). The above account covers two
transactions. The first was simple. Mwanga took a bull belonging to Kambuya and gave him a heifer; but, because she died, he
was required by Sebei contractual obligations to give Kambuya
another, which he had not yet done. The second was more complicated. In this instance, Kambuya took a bull of Mwanga's for
slaughter and gave in exchange a heifer that belonged to Ndiwa's
mother. This heifer had two bullocks and finally a heifer calf.
There was no clear reason why, in accordance with Sebei contract, this last calf could not have "released" the mother and
Kambuya have taken her and the two bullocks back and closed
the obligation. He chose not to, saying that the exchange was
unlucky; instead, he took all four animals and gave Mwanga a
heifer calf outright (that is, with no further claim or obligation,
an acceptable means of terminating a contract under conditions
reasonably viewed as inauspicious). But the mother cow, having spent her life in Mwanga's kraal, returned to it on her own
and died there. For this, Mwanga has no responsibility. Kambuya had, however, further complicated matters; although the
original heifer had belonged to Ndiwa's mother, the second one,
given outright, had been tetapsoy. Therefore, because Kambuya's original heifer had died (in Mwanga's kraal), he took
the daughter heifer from Ndiwa as replacement, leaving the two

[2] Tetapsoy is singular for tokapsoy, which are animals held by the husband without formal allocation to one of his wives. Kambuya had complicated the problem here by using a tetapsoy heifer to cancel the debt
originally contracted with a cow anointed for one of his wives.

bullocks with Ndiwa. This was proper Sebei procedure; otherwise, Ndiwa would have had nothing. As Kambuya subsequently anointed this heifer for his last wife, it should go to her son, the young Mangusyo.

SIRET [in an effort to bring Salimu back to matters of the present]: We shall solve that when the time comes.
SALIMU: My father did retain two cows that had belonged to Ndiwa's mother; they are now in the hands of the young boy who is caring for the kraal of my father. [It was thus that Salimu referred to his full brother Andyema, a man of about thirty.] These two cows are the ones that Ndiwa should use to pay his debts; if there are no claims, then he can take those two cows, but that is all. He has already taken all the calves from those two cows.

At this point, an old man arrived. He disclosed, upon being asked, that he had just come from a visit to a diviner on behalf of a neighbor who was suffering from pains in his joints and abdomen and thought he might have been bewitched. "But the diviner said that he merely had disease. He told me to prepare certain medicines and to kill a white hen and cook it with the medicines, and to put this in with the beer and give it to my neighbor."

SIRET [again trying to bring Salimu back to his business]: If you are doubtful about the payment, I could bring the heifer here for you to see.
SALIMU: How can you do that when I haven't agreed?

The conversation then took many turns. It was interrupted by the herder's bringing the ghee that he was selling to my interpreter, by their discussing the kind of wood that bows and arrows and arrow shafts are made of, and by many other things. A cry of alarm was heard, to which only passing attention was paid, though it brought up the matter of the alarm that was cried the day before. It was said that yesterday three lions had killed two cows a few miles below and that the zebra were leaving this country on account of the lions. This led into a long tale of a lion hunt that took place many years ago, the details of which I could not follow.

Chemtai, my interpreter, then led the conversation to another matter of rumor. He asked if Siret planned to have the leopard ceremony immediately after the circumcision. The leopard ceremony is the final item in the ritual cycle of initiation of girls, which starts with circumcision and ends with a highly secret ceremony in which the medicines (both practical and magical) are revealed to the initiates. Then their initiation is complete, and they are full adults. This ceremony usually follows circumcision by four or six months, and may be delayed even longer; nowadays there is a tendency to hold it soon after circumcision. Chemtai was motivated in this interruption because he knew of my interest in the matter. Siret agreed that he planned to have the leopard ceremony immediately. As he said, "Nowadays the girls get married too soon, and so it is necessary."

Increased laxity of sexual standards has pressed parents to circumcise their daughters at an ever younger age and to have the ritual as soon as possible in the hope that they will be married before they become pregnant, though there is no real stigma on either premarital sexual affairs or illegitimate birth. This turn of the conversation reminded Siret of another complaint about the younger generation. It had to do with Lasto, a man in his late middle years who had come to Kapsirika a few years before and who was very much involved in land and cattle disputes. He was manifestly disliked for his open efforts to further his own self-interest. Siret's son had married one of Lasto's daughters for whom Siret and Salimu had been bargaining rivals in behalf of their respective sons. Siret had won by not making a proper bargaining arrangement but, instead, by reaching an informal agreement with Lasto; now he was regretting the matter. Lasto borrowed two of Siret's oxen, and Siret was complaining that though they had not been part of the informal agreement, the bride's father claimed them as part of the bride-price and refused to return them. In this context, Siret again struck the note of envy of the ways of the mountain Sebei. "They have it easy to marry their daughters. They don't have to brew beer; they can just go to the shop and buy it. But those girls from the western side of the escarpment don't stay at home. If you marry one of them, she goes home to her parents and then starts petting with men."

This conversation about the waywardness of women from the mountain area continued for some time. Then Salimu, with reference only to his inner thoughts, said: "If you want to exchange a big bull for cows, don't accept two young heifers, for they will surely die. You should exchange for one heifer and for one bullock, and then they will multiply."

SIRET: Your father is dead, Salimu. You know that once somebody dies, all his cows will follow him if you are not careful. For example, Taradya was the richest man in this area. After he died, his sons lost the cattle, and now they are poor and must steal. The same thing could happen to this man named Juma.

SALIMU: Yes, that is true. Whenever I sell a cow, I must get money to get animals to replace them. In that way my father's herd will remain. It is also important to have cattle at different places. Noibei used to live near the Greek River. Last year the Karamojong raided him and stole his two hundred cattle, forty calves, and his goats and sheep. They even took the clothes off his children and his women. None of these things have been found, and that man had nothing. But he was clever and he had kamanakan arrangements with many Sebei and Teso people; so he went back and collected his kamanaktay cattle, and now he is as rich as ever he had been. He went to Teso and got forty of his own cattle back.

The final subject of our discourse that morning under the tree dealt with Salimu's son, Chemisto, who was sitting with us. Chemisto had been Salimu's herdsman, as is usual for the youngest adult son, but he was now in the process of separating his herd from his father's and establishing his own household, having been married for a couple of years. His herd was not large, but undoubtedly he would be herding many cows kamanakan for his father and perhaps his uncles. Salimu told me how Chemisto began accumulating cattle. He had had three cattle by the time he married. He had obtained the first one when he was a very young child. He refused to go anywhere near his grandfather, and so Kambuya gave him a bull to persuade him to be friendly. This was a kind of ceremonial friendship, and apparently it was effective, for Chemisto, who though not what one would call a sweet and gentle person, had been very patient with his old, blind grandfather. He acquired the second cow at the time he was circumcised, by refusing to put up his hands until he was offered a cow by his father. This is a customary form of gentle blackmail. It apparently expresses the degree to which the youth is master of the situation under his ordeal; in making these demands, he refuses to let the ceremony proceed until he has been bought off with an appropriate gift. It reminds one of those middle-class American fathers who offer material rewards to their sons if they make good grades. Chemisto acquired the third cow by refusing to wash from his hair the ghee with which he had been anointed at the close of the lion ceremony—the final step in the ritual cycle involving male circumcision. These cattle and their offspring were in Chemisto's kraal, and formed the basis of his herd; they were not used by him for his bride-price, which had been furnished by his father, according to custom. In addition to these cattle, Salimu anointed some cows for Chemisto's wife at the time they were married, and now intended to give Chemisto some more. In order to do so he was to brew beer, but this did not take place while I was in Kapsirika.

The next morning Salimu came to our camp again. This time we took the Land Rover through the bush in a different direction, driving to the home of Andyema, the youngest of Kambuya's three married sons, his last herdsman and caretaker. Kambuya's two small houses lay to the south, separated from the home of Andyema by perhaps 50 yards of withered grass and weeds. Andyema had only one wife (for which he received some criticism from his relatives) and so he had only one house and a small round house for the calves. His house opened onto the entrance to the kraal, which was large, for it held many of Kambuya's cattle. There was a large flat area with trees where the cattle rested in the shade; it had been trampled smooth and was dusty in the dry season, muddy in the wet. In the inadequate and shifting shade of two or three unprepossessing thorn trees, the events of the next few days occurred.

About three weeks earlier, the old men had gathered here to help resolve the problems of Kambuya's inheritance: the adjudication of claim against the estate, the determination of debts outstanding and payable, the allocation of the heritage of cattle, the resolution of disputes among the brothers, the reaffirmation of cultural values and social obligations, and whatever else might come up in the private kokwet that was to take place. I expected that the kokwet would now take place, but owing to the unexplained absence of Ndiwa and the compounding of delays so characteristic of Sebei, another week was to pass before the affair was completed.

"Kokwet" is the term for a council of any kind; "kok," for the place where such a council occurs. "Kokwet" has some of the generic meaning of the Swahili word *shauri*, but "council" is an adequate translation. In the past, the pororyet (region), the sangta (village), and the aret (clan) might hold a kokwet; now "kokwet" is also the term for a district council meeting. This one was a private or family kokwet.

What took place that particular morning was the preliminary review. It was a time for airing grievances, in effect a kind of dry run or dress rehearsal. Thus there is inevitably a certain amount of repetition in what follows, I think it better that the record be as complete as possible and that we understand the drama by seeing how it unfolds step by step.

It is necessary to introduce here some of the personnel connected with the kokwet, though the description of many participants is left until they play an important role. (See Appendixes A, B, and C for a list of major personnel and for genealogical relationships.)

No clear pattern was discernible in the roles the participants played. Just as there was no formal seating arrangement and no explicit leadership, so too there was no clear definition of elders versus family, of family versus outsiders. Some older kinsmen acted as elders; some elders said nothing or very little. Few attended every session; I could not record all the comings and goings. Occasionally some of the women would sit at the edge of the circle, but they said surprisingly little during the hearings. I cannot explain their silence; women are usually heard on matters about which they may reasonably be expected to have knowledge. They took leading parts not only in the witchcraft hearing that forms a kind of addendum record here (chap. viii) but also in discussions I heard elsewhere.

The three adult sons of Kambuya were present throughout most of the formal hearings and elsewhere except as specifically noted. Many other clansmen were present, principally Labu, who in Sebei reckoning was a brother of Kambuya. He was a small man, dressed in white kanzu and cap, a man of few graces and little authority. It seemed evident from the strong feelings expressed about some of his dealings that he was not highly regarded by the deceased or his descendants. He was, however, now the senior member of the kota to which Kambuya had belonged. Other clansmen included Salimu's son Chemisto, whom we have already met; Eryeza and Nablesa, sons of Labu; Noibei, a son of Kambuya's deceased brother Musani; and several others who played no important role in the hearings except insofar as they made claims on the estate (see chap. v). There were several men related to the family by marriage, including the man I call Teso, who was married to Kambuya's favorite sister Senguru, and Fagio, the son of another of Kambuya's sisters. Also present much of the time were the young sons of Kambuya's fifth wife, one (Mangusyo) by Kambuya, and one (Maget) by the brother from whom their mother had been inherited.

Three or four of the men might be best described as elders. One of these was Mwanga Kapkapkadyum, Kambuya's close friend; he claimed that they were born on the same day, were circumcised on the same day, and were members of the same pororyet. The pororyet is a territorial division, generally extending between two major streams. Pororyet membership can be changed, but usually a person belongs to the pororyet of his birth for life. The pororyet was the basic military unit, but, as may be expected, its importance has dwindled, so that the Sebei did not establish pororisyek when they migrated to the plains. Each man retains affiliation in the pororyet into which he, or his father, was born before he moved down from the mountain. Thus Kambuya's Kapsirika neighbors did not necessarily belong to his pororyet, and it was important to draw men from the appropriate pororyet to help make the decisions regarding his cattle. Mwanga was a shrewd-looking, sharp-faced old man who was very conscious of the role he held as an elder.

Another of the elders was Ndiwa Kapchepkwony, of Kapkoikoi clan. In my notes I came to call him Ndiwa V (for visitor) to distinguish him from Kambuya's second son; because I think this designation serves for identification better than his long second name, I shall preserve it here. Ndiwa V was a quiet man; yet when he spoke he did so with authority and, I think, a strong sense of fairness. I was told he was married to one of Kambuya's sisters, but it is not so recorded in my genealogical data, and I think she must have been a classificatory sister. He lived in Bukwa.

Kapsilut was a man of the plains and everything an elder

should be. He was a well-knit man who always walked about
with an excellent spear. This spear was one of two that had been
thrown at him by a Pokot during a battle but had missed its
mark by virtue of Kapsilut's protective magic. His steel-gray
beard was always trim and neat and clean. He held himself
straight. He was not afraid to lead the men or to harangue them,
and he was well informed in matters of custom. Kapsilut was not
present throughout the hearings, but when he was, he lent a
note of precedent by quoting proverbs.

Sabila Araplabu was a neighbor, rather poorer in cattle than
most of the older men. He had both namanya and kamanaktay
cattle from Kambuya. Sabila's father, Labu Kamwasir, was one
of the earliest settlers, and so Sabila was now known also as
Araplabu (son of Labu). This name of his established a kind of
joking, friendly relationship with me; the Sebei had named me
Labu, and thus Sabila was my "son." He turned this useful
friendship and rapport to small profit by demanding gifts from
his "father." Sabila was not a man of authority or stature, and
he said very little in the hearings, though he was usually present.

Salimu Kapchemei, a young neighbor, was present most of the
time. He was married to the older daughter of Tengedyes, the
sister to whom Kambuya and Salimu had given haven when she
was abandoned by her dead husband's sons. His older brother,
Seperia Kapchemi, was a local appointive chief, and brought
some official authority to the proceedings, particularly in the
division of the animals among Kambuya's sons.

While waiting for the session to begin, I talked briefly to some
of the men. They told me that Kambuya had mentioned some
people who should be present, particularly Mwanga. They began to complain of the long delay. "We have been here a long
time, waiting for Salimu. We want him to tell us his plans, as we
are anxious to get back home."

Salimu began asking Andyema about changes in the herd
during his absence.

Salimu [pointing to a certain animal]: What happened to the sister
  of that cow?

ANDYEMA: It has been taken over to ——'s [I failed to get the name].

SALIMU [pointing to another cow]: Where did this one come from?

ANDYEMA: It was paid by Wongai as part of the bride-price for our daughter.

The discussion turned to matters involving Kambuya's sister, Tengedyes, and her daughters. Kambuya and Salimu had helped these women in a way that emerges in the discussions that follow. A special kokwet was later held concerning Tengedyes' daughter (see chap. viii). At this point, Salimu was explaining the background to me.

SALIMU: Labores died in 1947. He had been married to Kambuya's sister Tengedyes. Labores had two daughters by her. These daughters were very young at the time. She had no sons at all. Labores had two other wives, who did have sons. In the house of my aunt Tengedyes there were more cattle than those other two women had. So when Labores died, the sons of the other two women mistreated her very badly so that she might run away. Nobody was interested in inheriting her. She was left to live alone in an old house, where she lived until it fell down. I decided to bring Tengedyes to my home with her two daughters. When they grew up, it was I who prepared all the circumcision. The first girl was married to Salimu Kapchemei [a near neighbor of Andyema's], who paid five head of cattle for her, of which one bull came to me as *kamama*. The rest went to the sons of the other two women. I was not given a cow for my guardianship. The second daughter was recently married. Seven head of cattle were paid for her. I was given one bull as kamama, but I gave that to Andyema. In addition, I seized one heifer to cover my costs for looking after those girls.[1]

ANDYEMA: Chemonges, the brother of these two girls, complained when our father was sick that they would like to take that heifer, but the girls' mother got very annoyed and said, "I should give this cow to my other daughter."

---

[1] The kamama is the animal paid in bride-price which goes to the mother's brother (*mama*). Kambuya actually stood in this relation to Tengedyes' daughters, but the relationship passes on to the sons of the mother's brother. Presumably, Kambuya stood aside and let Salimu take this animal; he had been generous. Where there is more than one daughter, the subsequent kamama go to more junior "uncles," as was true when Tengedyes' second daughter married. But the seized animal is a special demand.

SALIMU [with incredulous anger]: That is not possible. You cannot give the dowry to the daughter. I am the one who is supposed to take it. But this matter will be solved by the old men. It is quite impossible for Chemonges to have it, or for the older daughter of my aunt to take it. If Chemonges insists on taking this cow, then he must bring me his own heifer and take this one. Chemonges lives nearby.

ANDYEMA: Before our father died, he said that he was annoyed about this cow and that it should be given to Chemonges.

SALIMU: That is nonsense. It is quite impossible. If Chemonges takes it, what will cover my costs? It is a custom of ours that if one keeps somebody's children, one must get something for it. I am sure my word will be accepted by the old men.

OLD MAN [becoming restive and wanting to begin the kokwet]: We have sent for you here because we are tired of waiting.

SALIMU: Yes, that is why I have come. I have just stopped at the kraal to see about the cows. When I went with my younger brother to ask about them, he showed that he does not know them all. Andyema is always trying to take cows falsely, saying that they are his. One day he took one of my father's bulls by force; he kept it until he sold it for 500 shillings, but he only gave our father 30 shillings. Another thing: a bull exchanged for a heifer with black eyes. The one who made the exchange paid 30 shillings in addition. Our father said, "Let me have the money, and you, Andyema, have the heifer."

NDIWA V: What happened to your brother Ndiwa? We asked him to come up, but he has not. Why? I don't want to talk about these matters now, but I want to know when the ceremony will take place.

SALIMU: Yes, the time has come for this to be done. You have your family, and are anxious to be back. I think beer will be brewed on Tuesday. Tomorrow I am going to market to get some money so as to be able to treat my daughter. The beer should be brewed by that day. [It is now Sunday, September 9; hence he is suggesting the day after the morrow.]

MWANGA: If you say beer will be brewed the day after tomorrow, it is too long a time from now.

SALIMU: All right. If you think it is too long, let us do it tomorrow. I want once more to let you know that you should consider that the cows of the old man must not be dispersed; if one is sold, you should see why it should be sold.

MWANGA: Yes. It is now on your shoulders. You are placed on your father's stool.

SALIMU: I think you are right about that. The only thing is that this brother here never comes to see me when I am sick, and he is annoyed with me. The reason is that I called him a mere boy.

MWANGA: I think he is wrong. Surely you can call your own younger brother a boy anytime you want.

NDIWA V [to Andyema]: Are you annoyed now?

ANDYEMA: No. It is my brother who is annoyed.

SALIMU: The other thing that is annoying him: Andyema fought with Ndiwa at Salimu Kaptemei's home, and I didn't try to separate them as I was afraid they thought I would be taking sides. It was my son Chemisto who separated them. Andyema later came and objected because I didn't try to help him. And now Andyema is friendly with Ndiwa; but why should he be annoyed with me and friends with the man he fought with? Another thing with Ndiwa: we had a land case between ourselves and our neighbors; my father was my witness, but Ndiwa became the witness for the other party. This case went as far as the district native court, and during that time we were very annoyed at him for separating himself from the family. The case was, however, decided in our favor. After it was decided for us, Ndiwa was asked by the other party to kill a hen for us and to invite our father and me and then to take the bones of that hen to bewitch us with. But we learned of this plan, and that is why we are annoyed—it may be he who caused our father's death.

MWANGA: That is important. If the matter comes before the kokwet, each should say out everything the others have done wrong.

NDIWA V: This is the time when people should meet and speak frankly of one another's wrongs. I would suggest, as it is a very important thing, that we brew one or two tins of beer and that all of you be present and invite one or two people and air your difficulties. Then when most of the beer is ready and all the people come, you can repeat this story very quickly.

SALIMU: That is a good suggestion. If Andyema will brew the beer today, we can have this talk on Tuesday after I get back from the market.

ANDYEMA: Yes, I will do that today.

SALIMU: Ndiwa is married to people who had this land dispute against us, and Ndiwa built his house on the very land that was disputed. When he did so, his brothers-in-law came and took his wife and said to him, "You are a very bad person to build a house on the disputed land." So he went and built his house somewhere else so that he could get his wife back. [Salimu continued at some length to tell the history of the land case when Ndiwa went against his own father and brother in the local government court and again in the saza (county) court and finally appealed it to the district native court. He explained that the statements were read very carefully, that the witnesses were cross-examined, and that the court found that their evidence was worthless; so Ndiwa and his wife's people lost the case.] This man is still on the land that was disputed; but we have reported the matter to the chief judge, and I think he will be put in jail. Now, old men, that is how hatred came between me and my brother.

MWANGA: Always women! If you are two brothers, your wives will say all kinds of wrong things; then a brother becomes annoyed with his own brother, suspecting that what his wife says is true.

SALIMU [after telling the group about the demand of his Ankole herder for pay]: I told him we had made no arrangement for pay.

MWANGA: I think he is stupid. Was it you who sought him out in his own country?

YOUNG MAN: This herdsman complained that the cows that were given to him for milking are too few. He asked, "Can we get milk from cows without any calves?"

SALIMU [turning to the main business]: Please. I do not want this herd to be dispersed at all. Mind you, we must decide who will look after these younger brothers of mine. For me, I don't think Andyema is a good and trustworthy person—I am afraid he will use all the cows for himself.

The younger brothers mentioned by Salimu were the two sons of Kambuya's fourth wife. This wife was inherited by Kambuya from his brother in accordance with Sebei leviratic practice. She brought with her a boy named Maget, now of school age. It was Maget who stole the money that later enters the discussion. He had no inheritance from Kambuya; the cows smeared for his mother by her former husband would legally be his held in trust. The only animals designated in Appendix E, table 4, as going to him were from the bride-price, against which Maget's father had a claim. The inherited wife subsequently had a second son, Mangusyo, by Kambuya. She had also had daughters, but they do not figure in the account at all. Mangusyo, who was of preschool age, was Kambuya's youngest son. The guardian for the boys was their older brother; by custom it would be the residual legatee of their father, Andyema. Guardianship might have been disputed if their mother had still been alive; she would have been of an age to be inherited, and guardianship goes with the mother.

SALIMU'S COMPANION [returning to the earlier matter]: Another
    thing: these herdsmen aren't trustworthy. Somebody must be
    there when they return from herding the cattle to see if all the
    cows have returned to the kraal. But this Andyema thinks that
    he doesn't care. [Turns to Andyema.] It is your duty to leave the
    house early to find out if all the cows have been brought back.

SALIMU: Our father was a blind man, but he always sought to deter-
    mine if all the cows were returned. This boy here [referring
    again to Andyema in this demeaning manner] says that my fa-
    ther has given him very few cattle. His mother's house has cows,
    but Father didn't give them out to him because he is wasteful.[2]
    He should have a second wife. Siret came to me and asked me
    for a bull the last time he was circumcising his daughters. He
    gave me a heifer, but it has produced three calves, which all died.
    I asked him to take that heifer back and bring me another one.
    So Siret's son brought a very small heifer and drove away the
    original cow without my knowledge. That heifer was returned
    for good—it is not a namanya. This animal, even though Siret
    brought it to my kraal, belonged to my father, and he instructed
    me to give it to this young man Andyema here. I wonder if my
    father told him about it. It is his cow.

ANDYEMA: That is true. My father gave that cow to me. Salimu, do
    you mean to say that I refused to take it? I was just waiting for
    you to give instructions to your son [Chemisto, Salimu's herds-
    man] to give it to me. Otherwise I couldn't get it. I am not bring-
    ing it back until our father's death is settled.[3]

SALIMU: That is why I am telling you this. I am hiding nothing at
    all.

NDIWA V: How big is it?

SALIMU [pointing for comparison to a half-grown heifer that is in the
    herd at a distance]: It is big enough to pay as a bride-price.

MWANGA: Yes, you are my son. That is the way you should speak. I
    don't want you to hide anything in your herd.

SALIMU: Also, there are two other debts; my father said Andyema
    should ask for them—they are his cows.

NOIBEI: Naburei took one of our father's bulls, and our father took
    one of his. He hasn't paid; nor have we. If he wanted to pay,

[2] Andyema was not given his heritage, and Salimu is asserting that it is
because of their father's distrust. This is manifestly unfair, because Kambuya needed his son's services and was acting entirely according to tradition.

[3] Andyema is expected to initiate the request in such a situation; I did
not know whether he was covering for ignorance or laziness, but he could
not properly take it by speaking only to the young Chemisto, as he would
have to ask permission of Salimu.

that is all right; if not, then as each of us took the other's, we
will make an end to that [i.e., cancel the debts].

SALIMU: No. Our father has already paid his debt. Perhaps there is
another I don't know about, but the first one was paid. It is he
who owes us a debt.

ANDYEMA: Before our father's death Naburei's son came demanding
the cattle. Our father said: "Why should you be so hot for this?
I'll not pay until you have paid me mine." He said it is I who
must pay this, because the debt was contracted for my mother.
Naburei promised a heifer namanya, but he has never come to
show us the heifer.

SALIMU: I think we must make an arrangement, as we have said.[4]

MWANGA: Other people may come here and bring their claims falsely
to you, thinking that as your father is dead they will be able to
make false claims.

SALIMU: Yakobo took one goat and never paid his cow namanya.
Yakobo is happy to pay; I have seen him. There is another cow
at Chemelili's kraal. It is a white cow. If he refuses to give it to
us, then there will be a case. [Turns to Andyema.] You have our
two goats, which are not paid. You took the hens and never gave
me the goats namanya. You also took one he-goat.

ANDYEMA: Yes, I remember.

SALIMU: Our father sent me to Ndiwa to get a she-goat, but Ndiwa
just hid that goat. My father was very annoyed and said that I
have Ndiwa's she-goat here, but I didn't take it as he suggested.
Perhaps our younger brother wasn't told by my father—but I was
with that young man [pointing to a youth], and he can be my
witness.

YOUNG MAN: Yes, I remember.

SALIMU: I wasn't consulted about the arrangement between my father and my wife about my hens. Yet I have no objection at all,
even though I was not consulted. One of our younger brothers
[Maget] was at school, and kept running away and stealing small
things. One day he stole 500 shillings from my father. Nobody
knew it was he, and as he denied having stolen it, we did *surupik*.[5] After that, he admitted he had done it, and our father de-

---

[4] This discussion anticipates some of the more controversial claims (see
chap. v, claims 2–4).

[5] Surupik is a formal curse against an unknown thief or other miscreant
which brings death or disease upon him or his family. One does not know-
ingly do surupik to one's own family. There were repeated references to
this act, which was done when Maget denied having stolen the money; he
subsequently admitted the theft. The curse had to be removed by brewing

cided to brew beer and spit it on him. Andyema, was this ever done?

ANDYEMA: No.

MWANGA: You must do it as quickly as possible.

SALIMU'S COMPANION: Before you perform this ceremony, do you know where the thing that the money was kept in has been put? That is very important.

SALIMU: Yes, we know. Andyema knows where everything was kept. The boy who stole the money knows where he got it from.

NDIWA V: Last night when we were about to go to sleep we heard the people crying in the next house, and somebody said that Kambuya's widow had hanged herself, but she only had a disease that made her faint. It was a long time before she got up. After we inquired about the disease, they told us that surupik had been done some time ago. Therefore, this must be removed as quickly as possible.

ANDYEMA [endeavoring to take the offensive by bringing up another matter]: One day Salimu urinated in a gourd—I don't know what was wrong with him.

SALIMU [overriding]: Another thing: when our father was sick, people came and threw stones on his house, and we were told to do surupik against whoever was doing that. We didn't know whether it was a witch or whether it was a disease. If it was witchcraft, then he should die; but if it was a disease, then it should go away with the surupik.

NDIWA V: What about this urine?

SALIMU: This is not true at all. We were drinking beer in our house, and this young man and others were present. My father's young wife went out from where we were drinking beer and started to go home; this young man said that I had been having intercourse with my father's young wife, and I vigorously denied that. My father was annoyed, and started cursing me, saying that all my children should die, except Chemisto [his favorite grandson]. So I was annoyed, and I urinated in a gourd and said to my father that we should both spit on this. Then my father said it was the others who had given false information and it was they who had had intercourse with his wife.

MWANGA: I think the person who has been doing this is one of the brothers. Going back to the land case—it was Ndiwa who gave evidence on the side of the father-in-law, and it was he who gave

beer and blessing the boy. The blessing consisted of taking mouthfuls of beer and spraying it over the person, accompanied by formalized expressions of amity.

false information that Salimu was having intercourse with the
father's wife.

SALIMU: That's that. I remember one day Kambuya and I obtained a
cow for some goats. We each paid three goats. The man did not
give us the animal; so we took a case and were awarded a small
bullock by the court. We took it to our father's kraal. When it
grew up, Kurani took it and killed it for a visitor. He never paid
it back, and we took a case against him. So he gave us a small
heifer. Unfortunately, all the calves from the heifer died, and
we exchanged it with another heifer. This heifer that we exchanged for was given to Eryeza as kamanaktay, and Eryeza in
turn gave it to another person as kamanaktay. I was annoyed.
However, the heifer produced calves—one heifer and two bulls;
then it got sick and died. Somebody came and asked Eryeza for
one of the bulls to exchange as namanya for a heifer, and Eryeza
did this. But Eryeza had the heifer and never showed it. He sold
the second bull of this group for 200 shillings. Then one day he
got sick and asked my father for a bull for him to sell, and it was
given to him. He promised a heifer, but never gave it. He came a
second time, and my father gave to him again. Now this adds up
to three that Eryeza has which are not paid (see chap. v, claims
18–20). I think he is a thief. I should be sharing that cow with
our father because both of us paid three goats each. If Eryeza
had not wasted these cows, we would be dividing them by now.

NDIWA V: This matter will be settled in the kokwet.

SALIMU: I want these cows to come back.

Let us pause to unravel this case, as an example of the com-
plex arrangements and involvements that enter into Sebei cattle exchanges. It started as the acquisition of a cow in exchange
for six goats, half provided by Salimu and half by Kambuya. The
heifer to be returned for the sheep would be shared between
father and son. An animal could be shared by having one man
take the heifer, the other its first calf, and then alternating rights
to calves for the life of the original cow. In this instance, however, the man failed to pay; a case was taken in the government
court, and they were awarded a bullock. This bullock was exchanged for a namanya heifer, but the person again failed to pay;
a second case was taken, and the court awarded them a heifer. As
this heifer lost all her offspring, it was exchanged (presumably
with the same man) for yet another heifer. Now, finally, Salimu
and Kambuya had a cow from their goats. They gave this to

Eryeza as kamanaktay—that is, to keep for them in his kraal and utilize its milk, as explained above. Eryeza, in turn, gave the heifer kamanaktay to another man, which should not have been done without permission, and when the heifer grew up there, she had a female and two male calves before she died. One of the bulls was exchanged by Eryeza for a namanya heifer; this would have been proper had he informed Kambuya, but "he never showed it." He sold the second bull, I think with Kambuya's consent, though on this point the record is not clear. The three cows claimed from Eryeza were the descendants, in Sebei reckoning, of the cow obtained from the six goats. Stemming from the initial exchange, there have thus been two namanya exchanges, apparently one outright exchange, two kamanaktay arrangements, two sales, two court cases and their awards, and a debt of three cows owing the estate.

Eryeza was the son of Labu—that is, he was Kambuya's father's classificatory brother's son—but in native terminology he was also a son to Kambuya. He was educated, and had been a government chief; at the time of these events he operated a *duka* (small beer parlor and store) 10 miles away, in the community of Ngenge. He was a hypochondriac, much concerned with himself and his health. Whether or not he engaged in chicanery, either as chief or in relations with his fellow tribesmen, he clearly did not model himself after Caesar's wife. It was he who had been sent for by Kambuya to write down the debts, and it was he who had not shown up to perform this task before the old man died. Kambuya had been most kind to him, not merely for reasons of kinship but also because he was one of the few educated men in this part of Sebeiland and Kambuya's only fully literate close relative.

At this juncture, Ndiwa V asked for food; he wanted soon to go to the nearby village of Greek River to get beer, but he was told that there was beer available in Kapsirika. The conservation then took a somewhat different turn, for these old men began hinting for their share in the distribution of cattle.

MWANGA [quietly]: My friend has now gone into his grave. I am now walking alone on this earth.

SALIMU: I am going to introduce you to our younger brother, and say that you were a great friend of our father's and that he is to treat you as if our own father were still alive.

MWANGA: As I am living far away, I am visiting here.

NDIWA V: Our friend, the son of our mother, I have a different request. I would like you to give me one bull to sell, for I have difficulties. I know it belongs to the kraal [i.e., is in Kambuya's estate] and I have been talking to the herdsman, but he says I must go to you, their older brother. I think we can talk about this now.

SALIMU [choosing to ignore the request for the time being]: There is a man who has three cows. He has not paid for them. He is a man from Sipi, and I understand that he is here now.

ANDYEMA: Yes. I understand he has been hiding his cows and trying to avoid paying his debt.

SALIMU: One of these belongs to your mother and, though I ask about it, it is your cow. The second is the same. The third debt came about as follows: he ate [i.e., slaughtered] a sick cow and offered us a she-goat in return, as the cow was already sick. It is not yours, but belongs to these young children [indicating the sons of Kambuya's young wife].

YOUNG MAN: Arapbusyendity has a debt that he has not paid.

SALIMU: Yes—a long time. I think there will have to be a case for that.

NEWCOMER [whose name I did not get]: Yes. If you delay a long time without asking, these people will forget their debts.

SALIMU [addressing Maget]: Do you remember when our father promised you a she-goat?

MAGET: Yes, and he showed me which one it was.

[There followed some discussion that I could not record.]

MWANGA: We have been living here a long time, and what I have been hearing is that Salimu is a bad man and that he can't take care of his brothers; but from what I have heard from his own tongue, I think these are mere lies.

SALIMU'S COMPANION: We shall hear from the old men. The thing is that the brothers are afraid of losing their cows—that he will be hiding some. Andyema and Ndiwa never talked to their father as Salimu used to do, and that is why they are afraid [i.e., they are not in control of the facts].

SALIMU: Next time I will keep quiet and just ask my brothers to tell me which cows in my kraal belong to these brothers. I am not going to hide anything, but they also should say if they have cows belonging to my mother. And I have none of Ndiwa's, just Andyema's. Perhaps I may give Ndiwa some that are tokapsoy, because they should be reserved for the young boys. [Ndiwa V

and Mwanga agree with Salimu on this.] We must decide who
will look after these children.

NDIWA V: It is you who will decide that.

SALIMU: When the old man was still alive, I asked him to give me
some cows received as bride-price for his sister, but he got annoyed and said, "These were for *my* sister; you have your *own*
sisters to get bride-price from."

NDIWA: I have one cow that the old man said should be given to
Andyema, but Andyema should share it with Salimu.

SALIMU: How can a young boy be the head of a shared cow? [Shared
animals are administered by the senior partner.]

SALIMU'S COMPANION: Yes. It is quite impossible for the young boy
to be in charge of this cow.

SALIMU: When one of our sisters was married, we were given cows,
but Kambuya gave one to his brother. The drought came and
killed most of these cattle, and only two bulls were left. One was
exchanged for a heifer, and another was given to Andyema
when he was young. Turei asked for Andyema's animal and he
didn't pay for the namanya cow, and we had to take a case
against him. Then the heifer was seized by court order and given
to me. I brought it to Andyema—it is your cow, brother, keep
it as namanya. We exchanged the other bull from this sister for
a heifer, and it produced two bulls; the first one died, but the
second grew up. Eryeza came to me, saying that the diviner told
him that he should kill a brown bull. He took it, but his kraal
was raided by the Karamojong, and that bull was taken. Also,
the cow was killed by the drought; so I had nothing from this
sister. I went to Andyema and asked him to share his cow, but
he refused. My father said: "It does not matter—I will give you
another." But he did not give it to me; instead, he persuaded
Andyema to give me a bull. This was taken by somebody, and
I was given a heifer in return; but that heifer died. I was again
left without anything. My father said to forget it, that I had to
leave this matter alone. But somebody married one of our sisters
and gave us only two cows, and those cows died; so I got nothing
from that girl. If this young man [pointing derisively in his
pique] were a girl, I would have had a bull from him, but he is
a man. His only wrong is that he never does get married. If he
had wives, they could give me food and beer.[6]

_____

[6] He pointed to Kambuya's sister's son, unmarried though obviously of
marriageable age. This last remark was teasing; Salimu was complaining
that the young man was not a girl, from whom Salimu might have had a
cow as mother's brother, and that he did not have a wife, from whom
Salimu would get beer and food.

[Somebody—I could not determine who—asked about an unpaid bride-price for one of Kambuya's sisters.]

We can't collect now. She was the mother of this young man here—it was our aunt. He would say, "All right. Take back your daughter, for she is old now and useless."

NDIWA V: We have discussed many things, but not which animal is being killed for smearing. My friend who is dead was a rich and an important man. Why should his things be smeared with such a small thing as a sheep? It should be a cow.

SALIMU: Yes, that is right. But I think we should kill a ram for smearing, and the next day kill a bull for his friends to enjoy. Before my father died, he mentioned a barren cow that was to be killed; I think that is the one his friends should enjoy. I will conclude this matter by Tuesday night. Each day things vary.

With that, the meeting closed. It was not resumed until three days later, at which time it was again abortive, this time because Salimu remained away. As before, there was some airing of grievances and much discussion, some relevant and some irrelevant. I shall include all that I recorded at the time, except where it duplicates information given elsewhere.

The early part of the discussion was informal, clarifying points for me. It rapidly became transformed into a discussion of Sebei customs and procedures. I do not have a record of the speakers for this discussion, but that is not important as it does not involve interpersonal actions.

Noibei, they told me, was the son of Musani, an older brother of Kambuya. Because he was the son of the older brother, he was an important person to the kota, even though he was younger. Therefore he had to be present. He did not inherit, but he had to be given some cows because, before he died, Kambuya had said that he should receive some.

Kambuya had also mentioned his sister's son Fagio, and said that a cow should be given to him because one given him earlier had died.

Kambuya had many cattle, about fifty of which were kamanaktay. If Kambuya had a young wife, she should have been inherited by Chemisto (Kambuya's grandson) and not by Salimu. Chemisto called himself the brother of Kambuya.[7] Salimu

---

[7] I did not understand this statement; the grandfather-grandson kin term, *kuka,* is self-reciprocal, and entirely different from the word for "brother."

and his brother called all Kambuya's wives "Mother," but Chemisto called them "Grandmother." If sons of the deceased had a son who was old enough, he could inherit his grandfather's wives. But sons could also inherit a father's wife. This was a new practice; formerly, the next man of another kota—never the man's own sons—inherited the wives. The son could not inherit a mother who had grown sons.

Chemisto should have taken his grandfather's stool, to show that he was the one who inherited the property.

Labu, the father of Eryeza, belonged to Kambuya's kota and would act as chairman of the kokwet. Kambuya's father was the older brother of Labu's father. Kambuya's grandmother was of the same clan as Kapsilut, one of the elders present. Arapmanguriya, also of the same clan but of a different kota, would also be there; his wife was dead, and he was merely wandering about.

Siret was present, and was discussing circumcision. He was teasing that the Sebei delay circumcision, so that sometimes the father and son are in the same age-set. This was generally denied, and was in fact not true. Siret was a man of Bok,[8] and sometimes dissociated himself from true Sebei and at other times did not.

KAPSILUT: I can list three men who tried to marry before they were circumcised. The father of one of these men sent the girl back to him. The second lost all his children, but the third has children and is still alive. Subsequently they did surupik against people to stop them from marrying before circumcision, but lately our people have been neglecting this custom. Another old man married before circumcision; his wife has already lost three children, though she is now pregnant. One young uncircumcised man recently arranged to marry a girl. He was firmly refused by his relatives, but he remained insistent. When another man came and asked for the girl, her parents insisted that she marry him, but she ran away to that uncircumcised man. She got pregnant by him, and then the man was sent away to Kenya to be circumcised and was told not to return until the last ceremony of his circumcision, but he did so at the time his wife was delivering and he died right away.

OLD MAN: Aramatui [the son of Sebei's great prophet] and eight

---

[8] The Bok are a tribe closely related to the Sebei in language and culture, living on the southern slope of Mount Elgon; their customs differ slightly from those of the Sebei.

other people married before circumcision. When I was circumcised I had two children; nothing is wrong with these children,
and they have children by now.

SIRET: Among the people of Koin [a neighboring tribe south of the
mountain, speaking the same language] nobody is to be married
before circumcision. Also the circumcised women despise the uncircumcised boys and cannot even pet with them.

KAPSILUT: That is very new to me. I am a true Sebei. If I tell a lie, I
will have intercourse with my own mother. We never, never get
married before we are circumcised. [This seems contradictory to
what he had said before.]

FAGIO: There was a young man who was married before circumcision,
and his wife was pregnant. After his wife delivered he went to
see this wife, and the child died. There is a strong law that if a
man marries before circumcision, then he cannot see his wife
until after the final circumcision is performed. He has been sick
twice, but so far has escaped death both times.

KAPSILUT: All right then, if he dies, never say that he was bewitched
[i.e., his own actions have brought it on]. The son of my sister
did this. We wanted the boy not to be married, but he did not
obey. There will be one day when his wife goes away. He is the
boy who came and asked Labu [me] to see him when he was to
be circumcised.

The discussion then turned to marriage between a man and
the daughter of his pinta. A pinta is an age-set—men who are
circumcised at the same time, and thereby enter together into
an association of initiates. Three successive initiation groups
form an age-set; these larger units (formerly a generation) are
named, and follow a cycle of eight. Fellow members of an age-
set owe one another certain obligations. A man is forbidden to
marry the daughter of a pinta-mate; to do so is considered in-
cestuous.[9] In a discussion led by Kapsilut, the men began to
argue about the details of this regulation.

KAPSILUT: A man from south of Mount Elgon came here. He was of
the first Chumo pinta, and had a friend who was of the second
Chumo. This man of Chumo married the daughter of the other,
but claimed it was all right because one was Sebei and the other
was Bok. Therefore, the Sebei living in Mbai [on the western

---

[9] Among some of the neighboring tribes a man may show hospitality by
lending his wife to an age-mate. This may be the historic source of this
tabu, but the Sebei do not practice such hospitality.

escarpment] and Bok are those who have broken the Sebei customs.

NDIWA: One man of Koin was of the third Maina pinta [the Maina were the last group circumcised before European contact], and another man was of the second Maina. The second man arranged to bargain a bride-price for the daughter of the first one. When it was claimed that they were of the same pinta, he denied this, saying, "We did not wear the white paint or share the skin together." And so he married the daughter of this other Maina man.[10] In Koin they have a very complicated custom. If Salimu were a Maina man and had these two young boys, they would be circumcised now, and as Maina; he is treated entirely as Maina—enjoying Maina beer.

YOUNG MAN: What happens to people who marry the daughter of their own pinta? Do they have children?

KAPSILUT: Yes. I can represent this by two examples.

STEPHEN KAMWASIR: Once a man married the daughter of his own pinta, but he died right away. We should not blame a man for marrying the daughter of his own pinta. It is quite impossible to do this if the two men stood together, but it is all right if they are of the same pinta but were circumcised in different years. Returning to my neighbor: he had two wives who were daughters of his own pinta, and as a result one of them has no children at all. The other does have children all right.

OLD MAN: There was an old man who married the daughter of his pinta and he died. But what about Wandera?—he did the same.

To that someone replied, "Forget him—he is a man of the Teso tribe." This led to a discussion of Wandera, a rich, formerly powerful man who had been first saza chief of Sebei. He was often called a man of Teso (a neighboring tribe of entirely different speech) because his father's father was captured by the Sebei from the Teso in a raid. Somebody then turned to Siret and asked if the man could marry the daughters of Korongoro if he were circumcised in the same year with Kwaimet men but then had his pinta changed to Korongoro. Siret replied that that would be quite impossible.[11] Someone else said that as he now

[10] Each age-set, such as Maina, is divided into three sections, usually referred to by number, and representing a span of about twenty years. The essential argument is: Does the marital restriction apply only to those circumcised at the same time or to the whole age-set?

[11] The age-set names are the same in several of the closely related tribes,

gave the oath on the Korongoro pinta, a Kwaimet man could marry his own daughter.

KAPSILUT: When I was a circumcision initiate, I fought with others of my pinta and could defeat many others, but Stephano was strong enough to beat me down. Nowadays, the initiates don't fight with sticks as they used to.

My notes indicate that by this time it was 12:45 in the afternoon. The people were beginning to complain about the continued absence of Salimu and the two old friends of the deceased. They also felt that Eryeza should be present, although it was not necessary for his father, Labu, to be there. Someone said he was pleased to see Stephano Kamon there, because he was frank. When other members of the group objected that everybody was frank, he denied this, saying that some people sat in a meeting and said nothing. The talk then turned to other matters unrelated to the business at hand. Kapsilut was reminded of an exploit of his from years ago, when, in effect, he had bested both the Europeans and his friends.

KAPSILUT: Remember when we refused to have our cattle inoculated and we were fined 400 shillings? At that time many people said they would refuse. Because everybody was afraid to speak, I asked, "Who will speak up to the district officer." Three men said they would speak up. I told them they would be afraid. I said in my heart, "When you white people come, cast your eyes down and don't be afraid." When that white officer came, none of these people spoke up. So I stood up and asked him if he came to hurt us or to save us. He said, to save us. I said: "Do you remember every year we furnished maize? Where is the maize now? There has been a drought. What will our cattle eat when they are inoculated now?" The officer excused himself, saying that he had been on safari; but I said that there should be a person to replace him. Then the officer said, "Are you refusing to have your cattle inoculated?" These three men stood up, and they were the ones who were fined, but I escaped the fine.

---

but they have come out of phase, so that the men of Bok may have been circumcised in the Kwaimet pinta whereas the age-comparable Sebei were Korongoro. A man moving into another tribal area would be ceremonially transferred into the age-appropriate pinta. Here the men were facing one of the problems this circumstance raises.

STEPHANO: Europeans behave like lions; if one man speaks up, that man will suffer. People should give different views, and then they will be satisfied.

KAPSILUT: The Miruka chief who tried to put me on the list [to be fined] has been dismissed, and he is now suffering.

STEPHANO: Some years ago, when we stopped our cows from being inoculated, we were advised by a chief as to what to say. I was the one selected to speak. When the veterinary officer came to us, he was driving fast and was very annoyed; I feared that if I wasn't supported, I would be taken to prison. Very many people gathered together, and he asked us to go to the meeting hall, which was overflowing with people. I stood up and said: "This is December 31, and tomorrow will be the new year. Do you realize that this is your last inoculation, as all our cattle will die because there is no grass? You should come back next year when there is enough grass." The officer asked if all the men agreed. They said yes; we all dispersed, and there was no inoculation. Nowadays, if somebody talks like that, the chiefs right away put people in jail. Kapsilut's friends should not have been fined—it was the chiefs who mentioned these names to the officers.

It was now one o'clock; someone mentioned that the sun had already turned. It was too late to start the discussion. Kapsilut remarked at the absence of a meeting, and wondered what was the matter with the people here. Stephano asked about the importance of the man from Kapenguria (Mwanga), and Andyema answered that he was claiming a cow from his friend.

STEPHANO: I blame Salimu. That is simple. We have been waiting for him for many days, and now we are still waiting.

KAPSILUT: I heard from Salimu that Kambuya spoke of Mwanga as his great friend and said, "I think I shall give him one cow." If you agree it is all right, you should give him a cow. But if you refuse, the gift is not compulsory.

There was now much discussion (it was nearly 1:30) about the missing Salimu, including talk about his companion and such remarks as, "What kind of magic are they sharing?" Criticism of Salimu was expressed; I felt that his position would be impaired by his absence. In the midst of this discussion the two old men, Mwanga and Ndiwa V, friends of the deceased, arrived. After a while, Mwanga spoke up about the meeting.

MWANGA: You old men—so many have come here—you have been
saying that you have been waiting for Salimu, but I don't think
that you should wait; you should start the hearings. There is a
proverb that says, "Even if a girl who is to be circumcised has
not shown up, yet the people dance." That encourages the girl.

KAPSILUT: No, that would not be right.

MWANGA: You should start the discussion now. You should discuss
now and explain to Salimu after he comes.

KAPSILUT: What do we discuss? What do we know of Kambuya's cattle?

MWANGA: You know about these things; you have all been discussing
these matters.

SIRET: Both of them [Salimu and Ndiwa] must be here so that they
can hear each other's voice.

FAGIO: Salimu said we should discuss nothing until we were all present. Ndiwa was not present, and we postponed. We should not
discuss except in the presence of all. That is why we asked for
beer to be brewed so we could all have a talk. This is not beer for
the public. Tomorrow is for the public, and that is what we decided. Eryeza asked to be present—that is why we didn't have it
yesterday.

NDIWA: I am sorry that I did not come the other day. I was taken to
see a cow [presumably for an exchange]; I thought it was near,
but it turned out to be very far away.

FAGIO: I want this discussed when everybody is here so that nothing
will go wrong. Everybody is waiting for Salimu as he is the one
to introduce everything.

SALIMU KAPTYEMEI: The other people are all here—everybody but
Salimu.

FAGIO: The sun is about to go in its house. What kind of meeting is
this? Let us just wait until the sun goes down.

OLD MAN: We can't have this discussion when the sun is about to
be leaving.

ANDYEMA: What kind of friend is this that Salimu has? He has been
staying with him a long time. Perhaps he is teaching him how
to bewitch.

MASAI: When I had my land case with Salimu, he was staying with
Salimu and teaching him how to bewitch me. The Muslim diviner told me he was teaching Salimu how to bewitch. Then that
friend went away. That diviner got 500 shillings and chickens.
He demanded 70 shillings and some few coins. He can tell you
who is planning to bewitch you.[12]

---

[12] Masai Arapchungeywa was a big, fat man, sullen and self-seeking. He
was called "Ishirini," the Swahili for "twenty," for some exploit of the

————: You had better ask him to come back, because this will stop
  the bewitching.

————: No, he is just threatening people.

————: The Muslim tells the truth. He mentioned that Burgeywa was
  bewitching people, and Burgeywa became shy then. This Muslim diviner has been outspoken with people. So many people
  have sold their cows, only to be told wrong things by diviners.

STEPHANO: What is the good of giving a paper telling him he is coming? We have been waiting, and perhaps by now he is beyond
  Greek River. Who can tell?

At 2:35 Salimu finally arrived. By now there were about thirty
people present. Salimu, for reasons that I could not understand,
remained rather remote. His greetings were most perfunctory.
Nobody asked why he was late. They continued discussing ex-
traneous matters, such as, "This man here is of my pororyet,
and is the oldest here." They were apparently trying to make
conversation, which continued for about ten minutes.

STEPHANO: Mwanga, you say there is something to be solved—what
  is it?

NDIWA V: This is not for the pororyet but is a private talk.

SALIMU: There is nothing here to discuss. I wanted Mwanga to have
  a talk with you, but everything is for tomorrow. If the young
  brothers have something to say, they should speak up then.

STEPHANO: I think that what you have said should be the end. It
  should all be done tomorrow.

MASAI: Yes, all the important matters should be discussed tomorrow.

NDIWA V: The last time, I said that only we three were to sit together
  and have our discussion, but we would bring the main points
  tomorrow before the pororyet. That is what Eryeza said. These
  people should be here tomorrow.

KAPSILUT: That is right. The claims should be for tomorrow.

SALIMU: Kapsilut, listen to me. People will come with false claims
  that my father has taken some animal and not paid it back. Perhaps some people have taken something from our father but
  have not paid him back—people don't stand up and mention
  that.

KAPSILUT [angrily and incredulously]: Can I come here from Greek

----

past. He was the father of one of Ndiwa's wives, and had the land case
against Kambuya in which Ndiwa had taken his part. He was originally
from Bok, but had lived in Kapsirika about twenty-five years. There were
mutual accusations of witchcraft between him and Salimu.

River and claim that Kambuya had taken my cow? Those who
do that are thieves.

MASAI: Let us disperse, you people who are waiting.

MWANGA: If anybody has a claim or anything to say, come back tomorrow.

At this point we dispersed. Before leaving I had a talk with
Salimu, who told me that the following were the main things
that were to have been discussed but had now been left until
the next day.

First, I was going to ask my young brothers if the deceased had
told them how many debts are outstanding for us to collect, and to
give the names of people individually; and if they failed to mention
all this, I have to add what they have not mentioned. Second, I
wanted to find out what outstanding debts existed and what demands
we will have to pay, and if there are some, which of the brothers are
to pay which debts. Third, we must discuss the cows to be given relatives. Fourth, who is to be invited tomorrow? Others may come, but
these are not important—only those who are invited. Fifth, we
should decide which cows are kamanaktay and namanya, both outside and inside our own kraals, that is, both those we have belonging
to others, and those of ours which others are holding.

There had not yet been any official hearings, for both these
discussion sessions were abortive. Nevertheless, much had taken
place, and a review is worthwhile. Most important was the fact
that basic grievances between the brothers had been aired.
These included Ndiwa's defection from the family in the con-
test over land; the dispute regarding sexual relations with the
young wife of the father; the theft of money by the stepbrother
Maget and the curse against a family member; the fear that Salimu would conceal some of the cattle owned by the father but
kept in his kraal. Meanwhile, at another level, there had been
communication too. Salimu had demonstrated his knowledge
of the animals, reiterated his brother's incompetence, and won
over the elders by his show of openness. Andyema had endeavored to undermine Salimu's position by reference to his urinating in the gourd and other suggestions of sorcery. In sum,
the nature of the confrontation had been revealed without the
sanction of a formal hearing.

When we arrived at the now familiar setting—the sere grass, the thorn trees scattered among the three or four houses, the cattle lowing in the background waiting to be released—we came upon a scene that held no promise that anything of importance could ever take place. Two naked children were running about, and women could be seen doing their chores. Chairs were brought out to us and placed under the trees, and from time to time a man appeared holding an old marmalade jar from which he was drinking *waragi*, a distillate of native beer. It became clear that a long drinking bout had taken place the night before. We had not been invited. This was just as well, as it was difficult enough to record the discussions in daylight and when everyone was sober. Perhaps Salimu's absence yesterday and Ndiwa's earlier were efforts to eliminate the ethnographer, and the issues raised lightly had been examined more extensively in my absence. Yet I am not certain, for I was privy to enough quarrels, accusations of witchcraft, wrongdoing, and the like to make it seem unlikely that any basic problems were being kept from me. I will of course never know. I went over some of the details of the night's discussion with Salimu and others, and include some of these remarks in the text. According to such statements, the discussion of the preceding evening had largely revolved around the handling of Kambuya's money, which had to be accounted for and properly divided.

We had been sitting about an hour, and, though people began to gather, there was no evidence that anything might happen. Suddenly, Salimu, Eryeza (who acted as scribe), and a few others gathered under a tree away from where we had been sitting. After all this waiting, the formal hearing began, unannounced, unceremoniously.

As I came over, they were discussing the acquisition and allocation of the cash that had been the subject of last night's argument, reexamining the information Eryeza had recorded. Salimu was claiming that he had received 1,300 shillings, of which he had given Noibei 700, Andyema 200, his father before his death 100, and Paulo Sayekwa 100. With the remaining 200 shillings, he had purchased a cow.

MWANGA [interposing]: Did you collect the deceased's personal belongings and put them aside?

SALIMU: I don't know about that, but we must find a ram [for slaughtering and anointing the belongings].

OLD MAN: It doesn't matter about the ram. All we need is the root of the moykutwet.

ERYEZA [shocked]: That is quite impossible.

[Discussion of the ram weaves in and out of the discourse.]

NDIWA V: These things should have been arranged yesterday.

ERYEZA: You thought this was a simple thing, but it is a big problem that is to be solved.

SALIMU: Please, Eryeza, on the list that you have written, did you write everything together, or did you put things down separately?

ERYEZA: No. I put the whole amount on you, but I divided as you told me last night. Last night you said you sold a cow from Andyema's kota for 300 shillings.

SALIMU: Yes. Go on.

ERYEZA: You said you gave your father 400 shillings.

SALIMU: Yes. Go on.

ERYEZA: Also that your father took 400 shillings for a *moyket*.[1]

KAPSILUT [addressing Teso]: It is difficult to find a ram to smear the properties with. Of course there is one here which could be killed; but its mother produced twins, and a ram belonging to such a family cannot be killed for the ceremony.

TESO: That is quite impossible. It cannot be killed.

ERYEZA: There are 300 shillings that you have not explained. What happened to them?

SALIMU: I got that money from a cow that was given to my father for crying when his mother died. There are 100 shillings that I have

---

[1] A *moyket* is a work party. Most work in the fields is done by a group, the host providing beer, and sometimes food, to the workers. Because Kambuya had no wife who could prepare the beer, he probably had to purchase it.

already consumed and must pay back. This cow was given to our mother, and belongs to our kota.

There were three different sets of money for which accounting was made. The first discussed was the sum of 1,300 shillings, for which the following details were later supplied by Salimu. The money was obtained from two oxen from Salimu's mother's kraal and from one cow that had belonged to Maget's mother. This cow had brought 200 shillings, but 100 of these were given directly to Kambuya to meet his personal needs. This money was distributed as follows.

700 shillings given to Korout, who subsequently died; the debt was inherited by his sons.

100 shillings paid to Paulo Arapkurei; the cow that will be collected for this will go to Maget.

200 shillings used to buy a cow that became one of Kambuya's tokapsoy, which Salimu will claim for his own.

100 shillings asked for by Kambuya before he died and given to him to spend.

200 shillings used to purchase a cow from Ndiwa Kapsiret; the cow has not yet been delivered, but when it comes it also will be tokapsoy.

SALIMU [returning to the matter of the needed animal]: If one of our neighbors has a ram, please help us. We have many debts to pay. We will give a ewe that will be for good, not namanya.[2]

ERYEZA: Salimu has mentioned how many cows he has had without any hiding of the information, so that there can be no complaints. If anyone has questions, please ask now.

NDIWA: There was a big gray bull in the kraal which Salimu sold for 550 shillings, and I want to know what happened to that.

SALIMU: There was a man named Araptambet who had two heifers for sale for 350 shillings each, and so I gave him all of that 550 shillings. I sold another cow for 250 shillings, of which I gave 100 [150?] to this man; with the rest of the money I bought another cow. That cow has multiplied, and has three calves.

It was later explained that the two cows obtained from Araptambet would go to Mangusyo and that the third animal would go

---

[2] The family was generously offering a ewe for the ram outright rather than in a namanya arrangement, which is the more usual exchange between a male and a female animal.

to Salimu, who had contributed the remaining money for the purchase.

NDIWA: Yes, I know. But even if it belongs to your kota, you should let your brothers know about it too.

SALIMU: When my father took his young wife, he took one of my cows and paid a bull to me. I exchanged this big bull that he gave me for two heifers, but one of these has died. The other has reproduced, but the cow died, leaving me only one granddaughter from that cow.

NDIWA: Is that true, Andyema?

ANDYEMA: Yes, it is.

MWANGA: It is right for you younger brothers to complain if what Salimu says isn't true, but otherwise you should agree.

NDIWA V: You know very well that Salimu has taken over from your father and is now the boss, sitting on your father's stool. You should be frank about everything here, or else you will just go on complaining.

SALIMU: Now I am standing up here. I think you brothers know the cows that belong to your mothers. Let me know which ones they are.

ERYEZA: Is there any money hidden by Salimu which he has not mentioned?

NDIWA: I am satisfied about the money.

ANDYEMA: I am satisfied too.

ERYEZA: This is the last day to speak. There will be no complaints later.

MWANGA: Perhaps there is something you are being shy about today.

ERYEZA: No, I think they are all speaking out.

NDIWA: I have been hearing rumors that my young brother has been complaining that I have been given some money and some cows by my father, but last night he found out that I had none.

SALIMU: I know all the cows belonging to my mother.

ANDYEMA: Ndiwa, what you say about money is true. There is a brown cow that you sold, but I am not satisfied about what happened to the money from that.

ERYEZA [exasperated]: Now you are saying that you aren't satisfied. We discussed that last night, and learned that Ndiwa had 700 shillings, and discovered what happened to everything but 20 shillings of that. Some of that 700 shillings came from the cow you are complaining about.

ANDYEMA: What do you mean, this money has been allocated? I want to know just what you got for that cow.

SALIMU [pointing to Eryeza's copybook]: Yes, there is a list written

down there. There was another—a bullock with a white tail. Andyema, how much did you get for that?

ANDYEMA: That was at Ngenge market. I got 340 shillings for it.

ERYEZA [addressing Andyema]: You say you got 300 [sic] from the
cow you got from Sabila. You got another cow from Chibuyu,
which you sold for 300 shillings. That makes a total of 800 shillings, of which 100 were given to your father. Of this money, you
[Andyema] have agreed that Ndiwa has 700 shillings, and you
find that, of the remaining 100 shillings, Chemonges has been
given 80 as a loan, which he is to repay to you.

ANDYEMA: I know about that 80 shillings given to Chemonges, but
what about the 200 shillings given to Ndiwa Kapsiret?

ERYEZA: Yes, Kapsiret has admitted he has that 200 shillings.

ANDYEMA: All right then. I am satisfied.

ERYEZA: Are there any other questions to Ndiwa?

ANDYEMA: No, that is all.

Later Salimu accounted for the money as follows.

300 shillings for one cow belonging to Mangusyo's mother.
500 shillings for three cows belonging to Salimu's mother.

These 800 shillings were distributed as follows.

100 shillings to Ndiwa for taking care of the money, despite the fact
that none belonged to his mother.
100 shillings paid out on Kambuya's debts.
100 shillings distributed among Kambuya's sisters.
100 shillings given to Mwanga, Kambuya's friend and pinta-mate.
150 shillings to Andyema.
150 shillings to Mangusyo.
100 shillings kept by Salimu.

SALIMU: Ndiwa is supposed to have 1,600 shillings. He raised this
money from three cows. I want you to tell which cows came from
what house. One of these was from my own house, for which he
got 600 shillings. For another cow he got 125 shillings, and that
one belonged to Andyema's house. This was an exchange for another cow, and this cow produced a bull that was sold to . . .

ERYEZA [overriding Salimu]: I think you are confused. Last night
you allocated how much money you got from each cow.

At this point, Eryeza read so rapidly from his notes that I
could not record it. I was subsequently told that 1,300 shillings
came from the sale of two oxen that belonged to Andyema's

mother and that 300 shillings came from a cow belonging to
Mangusyo's mother. The money had been kept by Kambuya
until the boys tried to steal it, and then it was given to Ndiwa.
The money was returned to Kambuya, who subsequently bought
cows with it. When Eryeza finished reading from his notes, the
discussion went on.

SALIMU: What is the balance due?

ERYEZA: The balance is 50 shillings, which Ndiwa has to pay.

NDIWA: Of these 50 shillings, I gave 10 to Kamudyer for him to go
    to school, and this amount was never returned. I told the old
    man that I had given 10 shillings to this boy. Therefore I have
    only 40 shillings to pay. I must pay this; I can't hide it. This
    excludes the 700 shillings we have already discussed. These 1,600
    shillings were raised from the sale of animals, but when the old
    man was sick he gave me 700 shillings. With those 1,600 shillings
    each of us bought some cows, which are now in the kraal.

ERYEZA: Andyema, last night when we were discussing these mat-
    ters, you were not paying any attention—that is why you are
    asking us to repeat what was discussed.

ANDYEMA [hotly]: All right. There is no reason to repeat.

SALIMU: All right. When you were finding out how much my father
    had spent, some people mentioned by themselves what they had
    taken. The rest of the money has been lost because we do not
    know who has taken it. I would like to postpone this discussion
    for the time being. I would like you to find the ram right now.
    Neighbors, you should help us. Even you young boys here can
    give us a ram.

FAGIO: Not I. I offered one, which was used when they threw cow
    dung on the grave.

TESO: It is your time, Ndiwa, to find the ram.

NDIWA: No. I tried last time to find one.

TESO: No, Ndiwa. You have one. Give it to us.

NDIWA: If I offered the one I have, I will have no rams to serve my
    ewes.

SIRET: You have been arranging this a long time, buying beer and
    everything. You should already have arranged for this.

MWANGA [addressing Masai Arapchungeywa]: "Ishirini," do you
    have one?

MASAI: No, I have none.

SALIMU: Eryeza, you have one. Let us have it.

ERYEZA: You two sons of the deceased have refused because you
    have none to serve your ewes. What about your furnishing one?

SALIMU: There is one here, but it has no horns. Therefore it is impossible to kill it for such a ceremony. [There is general assent.]

ERYEZA: Ishirini, please give us a ram.

MASAI: Their own sons have refused. The sons should offer a ram.

ERYEZA: All right. If you give me that ram without horns to serve my sheep, I will give you the ram that I have.

[This meets with general approval; there is further discussion about who would transport the sheep from Erycza's kraals some 4 miles away.]

I will not accept a ewe instead, not even for good, because my brothers refuse to let me have their rams to serve my ewes. Therefore I want to exchange the ram for a ram.

NDIWA V: I think we have discovered that you sons are very stubborn about helping your brothers. I think that for this rich man a cow should be slaughtered.

MWANGA: No. Send somebody right away for the ram.

NDIWA V [astonished]: This man has refused a ewe and has taken a ram.

SALIMU: That is up to him.

ERYEZA: I am determined that it should be this way.

KAPSILUT: You take the ram for the time being, and later you can claim the ewe.

ERYEZA: That is all right. But first I want to take the ram before I take the ewe.

NDIWA: Do you remember, Siret, the last time you took my ram and I was without one, and when I asked people to lend me a ram to serve my animals, they all refused?

SIRET: Take a bicycle right away and get the ram. If someone goes on foot, he won't be back before two o'clock, and that will be too late.

NDIWA: Who will perform the smearing?

[Someone suggested that Kapsilut should do it.]

KAPSILUT: I refuse. It should be done by a Maina man.[3] Leave me alone.

SALIMU: The man who has been asked to do the smearing is not here.

KAPSILUT: Eryeza, can't you do it?

ERYEZA: No. The old man was my father [sociologically, not biologically], and I am too young to do it.

---

[3] That is, a man of the Maina age-set, one age-set older than Kapsilut. I do not believe that he was correct about this; indeed, it was not subsequently done by a Maina man. I think Kapsilut's remark was a polite refusal to get out of a slightly onerous task. Someone then asked whether there was a Maina man there, but there was none.

SALIMU: Going back to the matter of property—I have mentioned
  that in this kraal each son should say which cow he owns.
SIRET: No, you want to talk about the ram.
MWANGA: No, let us go on. Maget's property should first be set aside.
SALIMU: No.

At this juncture, without any forewarning or any change of
pace in the discussion, the claims against Kambuya's estate began. I have separated these claims by numbering them, and am
offering them as they were presented, with certain addenda obtained from subsequent annotation. These followed one another
in quick succession, and were not recorded by Eryeza.

Claim 1. Ndiwa claims cows as Salimu anticipated (see also p. 46)

NDIWA [standing up and addressing the now rather large group of
  men—thirty or forty—who have come to present their claims
  and listen to the cases]: There are three cows that I want to
  speak about. When we lived at Nobokutu, two cows were sent
  away as kamanaktay. When I was going to arrange for my bride-
  price, one of these cows was to be given to me as dowry; but this
  cow got its tail cut, and I could not use it as a bride-price. So
  my father sent me to Amisi Mwanga to get another cow. My
  father was difficult about giving something until he was ready.
  One day I asked about that cow, but he said that he had been
  keeping it to pay a debt for my mother's house. That was the
  third cow. I have been told that Salimu says that this cow belongs to another house. I want to learn about that.
SALIMU: I know about only two animals. It is true that the old man
  has debts. He had to keep the cow himself; if someone went to
  Ndiwa to collect one of my father's debts, then Ndiwa would just
  say to that man: "My father is alive. Why do you come to me?"
  Only two animals remain. He gave a cow to Amisi [in a namanya
  exchange], but the calves died except one [?] bull and one
  heifer. Our father went to Amisi and said, "Give me this cow
  because it doesn't have good luck in your kraal." So he got this
  cow and its two calves, and he gave Amisi the heifer outright.
OLD MAN: From which kota did that heifer come which was given
  to Amisi?
SALIMU: This heifer belonged to these young boys, and was not
  from the kota of Ndiwa. Unfortunately, it died there, and our
  father said that that was all right—"I already have had two cows
  from it." Ndiwa took the bull that Kambuya had brought back,
  and he castrated it. The old man gave the heifer to Amisi to replace the cow he had already been given.

NDIWA: This was tokapsoy of the old man.

SALIMU: No, this came from Atori's house [the house of Mangusyo's mother].

ERYEZA: May I know if this cow was anointed for Atori, or was it just in her kraal?

SALIMU: These cows were given to Atori, and when she died they went to her son's guardian; they were not tokapsoy.

KAPSILUT: Is the argument that Ndiwa wants the cow of Atori?

SALIMU: Yes. Did you hear our father mention giving this cow to Ndiwa?

STEPHANO [who has just arrived]: Do you know if this cow that was given to Amisi belongs to Ndiwa?

SALIMU: You have come in too late.

[Ndiwa explains the background of the discussion to Stephano. Other remarks were not recorded.]

NDIWA: I used the money I got from this animal to take my father and mother to Mbale to the hospital, and with the remainder I bought a heifer.

SALIMU: Yes, and you now have that cow in your kraal.

STEPHANO: Did this cow produce a calf?

SALIMU: It produced a black calf.

NDIWA: It never produced any calf.

SALIMU: It produced a black calf that died.

STEPHANO: We are cattle keepers, and some of us have more than one wife, and the wives know their own cattle. Are you arguing about this cow, or are there others? This heifer that was exchanged with Amisi—was it in the hands of the old man? I feel strongly that this cow belongs to Ndiwa.

PAULO: Stephano, don't be confused. The cow given as namanya was Ndiwa's; but that cow died, and so the old man gave another that did not belong to Ndiwa's mother's house.

SALIMU: The reason the old man kept this cow was to reserve it to pay the debts of Ndiwa's mother. Ndiwa has two cows to pay these debts with. Chemonges Labores has one cow to be paid to Ndiwa.

At this point, someone whose name I did not get said, "You have already solved this."

Salimu, in his subsequent recapitulation, told me that goats were exchanged with Amisis Mwanga for a namanya cow. This cow had two bulls and then a heifer. Ndiwa sent for the bullocks and the mother cow, which had released itself by producing the heifer. When this cow reached Ndiwa's kraal, it ran back to Amisi's house, where it died; so the family was left with only the two bulls. As the cow belonged to Ndiwa's mother, these two bulls were given to Ndiwa. Ndiwa had felt that this cow was a tokapsoy when he raised the complaint, but he was informed that it was in fact a cow belonging to his own mother, and he got the two bullocks without question. Salimu said that Ndiwa was quite satisfied with this solution, which Ndiwa, who was present, confirmed.

We have three versions of this situation; they differ in detail but not in matters of first importance. Ndiwa had known that the heifer given to Amisi Mwanga was his mother's animal, and he was to use it for his bride-price. The difficulty arose when Kambuya decided to break the namanya arrangement and to give Amisi a heifer outright and chose for this purpose either a tokapsoy heifer or one already given to Atori. (One version has it that the heifer born of the namanya animal was given to Amisi; another, that it was replaced by one already belonging to Atori and that therefore Atori would get the heifer.) But the major legal points are clear. Ndiwa got the two bullocks because the original animal came from his mother, but the heifer went to Kambuya (and then to Atori's son) to replace the one given to Amisi to close the contract. Kambuya suffered the loss of the original animal that died.

Claims 2–4. Naburei is accused of hiding his debts

The second claim was made by Naburei, a brother of Labores, who had been married to Kambuya's sister. This relationship is not a close one, but he and Kambuya would call each other "Brother-in-law."

NABUREI [rising]: I am the second one to be paid.
NDIWA: You have to prove your case.
SALIMU: Naburei, our father took your goats and has not paid. But how many debts have you not paid to our father?
NABUREI: I have no debts. I paid the bull back to your father.
SALIMU: You brought a bull back, but the Karamojong stole the cow and the bull; therefore you have to pay them.[4]
NABUREI: I don't remember.

---

[4] As appears later in the discussion (see Teso's speech, p. 86), this is a cryptic reference to a namanya exchange in which Kambuya received a

SALIMU: There is another debt. Your father took our father's bull and promised that you would pay it, but you have never done so.

NDIWA: Before our father died, he said, "I have Naburei's debt, but never pay him unless he pays his debts to us."

NABUREI [with asperity]: All right, if you want to hide your debts!

FAGIO: You say that you have sent your son to collect a cow from my grandfather. I asked Kambuya about it. He said that he had sent Naburei back, saying, "I want him to pay the debts he owes me first, as it was he who has taken my bull." My grandfather was ill at the time. He said that Naburei must pay our debt first and then you pay him, and the person to pay that debt is Ndiwa.

OLD MAN: We are all Sebei people. We must always tell the truth.

KAPSILUT: I can give you a proverb. A man may deny having killed a person, but he cannot deny his cattle debts.[5] Naburei, you are denying for nothing. The story these people tell is true.

NDIWA: I talked to Naburei's son. He said that if a man pays a heifer in a namanya exchange and that animal is stolen by enemies, then that closes the debt.[6]

OLD MAN: He is wrong. If a cow has been stolen by enemies, that is not Kambuya's fault; it must be replaced by his exchange partner.

TESO: You are quite wrong, Naburei. You must pay.

NABUREI: You say that the debt belongs to my father; yet the old man never told me about it.

SALIMU: I want to make this clear to you. This cow was asked by your father to be slaughtered for your older brother, who has died. Your father said it should be paid by you if your brother died, and so it is true that you must pay it. It is quite clear that you must pay us our cow, and then Ndiwa will pay you.

KAPSILUT: All these sons of Kambuya who are sitting around here— have they said anything about Kapsilut's taking their father's cow? That proves that what they say is true. They are not giving false testimony.

---

heifer that was subsequently stolen along with one of her calves before she had reproduced the heifer calf that would release her. Naburei is expected to replace the cow but not the bullock, which Sebei contractual understanding recognizes as already belonging to him.

[5] This is a literary exaggeration; according to Sebei custom, no man can deny having killed someone, for he would suffer a fatal disease if he did not purify himself.

[6]This was an argument over the nature of the contractual obligation. There is no doubt that Naburei was wrong, that there was an obligation to put a reproductive cow in the kraal of the trading partner, and that the stolen animal had to be replaced.

SALIMU: Naburei, you have two debts: first, the bull you paid which was stolen; second, the one that was killed for your brother.

NABUREI: I will never pay, and I will never ask any more.

At this point, the third claim was opened, but in the middle of that discussion Teso expressed dissatisfaction with the resolution of this case and returned to it. In the interest of clarity, I shall complete this discussion and then turn to the third claim.

TESO: You say that Naburei has paid a heifer and that that heifer was stolen by the Karamojong. The heifer paid to Kambuya produced a bull and a heifer, and when the young heifer was ready to be served it also was stolen.

ERYEZA: Have you not been satisfied with what was discussed?

TESO: You paid the cow and got one bull back, and the heifer and her mother were stolen; thus Kambuya was left with nothing. Why can't you pay this debt first and let them pay yours?

NABUREI: No. I will pay nothing. I have lost and Kambuya has lost, and that is finished. What I strongly object to is the matter of the animal's being slaughtered for my brothers, which I am being asked to pay.

TESO: Haven't you understood what this young man [referring to Fagio] was told by his grandfather?

NABUREI: I don't know when they discussed all this.

SALIMU: Labores [the brother of Naburei] and Kambuya were great friends, but one day the old man's grandson seduced Labores' daughter. Labores came and took his cows[7] from the old man's kraal by force. Kambuya took a court case against Labores, who was fined 5 shillings for taking the cows without permission, and with this their friendship died. Remember? Kambuya came to you, and one of your cows attacked him. Do you know what he came for?

NABUREI: Just to pay a visit—nothing important.

FAGIO: Naburei denies for nothing. He has two cows and a goat to pay. He is trying to hide this debt because he sees that Kambuya is dead. One of the cows is a white cow.

NABUREI: I agree to having taken the ram.

————: I saw the cows being taken by Naburei.

NABUREI: I agree on that. Fagio knows all the debts beloning to his grandfather.

SALIMU: Pay only one cow.

[7] Presumably cows belonging to Labores himself; very likely the ones under dispute.

NABUREI: All right, I will pay one. But please consider about my
   cow. I have been refusing because you have added a cow that
   was never taken. I find it is difficult to understand; you say it
   was my father who killed it for my brother, and now you say it
   is on me.

————: It was your father who killed the cow, but it is you who inherited that debt.

ERYEZA: Do you mean to say that if a father had a debt the son will
   refuse to pay it?

NABUREI: I want to be clear. Do you mean I will pay one and you
   will pay me?

SALIMU: No, you have three to pay. Pay one, and we will forget the
   rest.

NABUREI: If that is true, I refuse to pay.

NDIWA: It was I who was to pay you, but it is to Salimu that you
   should pay the cows that you owe.

Here is a straightforward confrontation that will probably be
taken to court by Salimu. Both parties recognize that Kambuya
owed Naburei an animal to replace one that he had paid earlier
and that had failed to reproduce. Salimu later claimed that Naburei admitted his full indebtedness to Kambuya while he was
alive but is now refusing to admit it. Salimu said that the cows
and goat that Naburei owes were a claim that Kambuya inherited from his brother. Naburei admitted to only one of the debts.

Claim 5. Megawit claims a ram that died

The claim of Kubayi Megawit involved a ram. I did not record the form in which the claim was made, but, according to
my later notes, Kambuya gave a ram to Megawit and took a ewe
(namanya) in return. According to Megawit's understanding, the
ewe had produced the ewe to release her and a ram, and this latter, along with the mother ewe, should have been returned.

ANDYEMA: It is true that Megawit took our ram and paid a ewe and
   that that ewe produced another ewe and a ram. Unfortunately,
   the mother ewe was killed, and the ram fought another ram and
   got its horns broken, and the flies laid eggs on that sore place,
   and from this it died—and that was the end of that family.

MEGAWIT: You people never reported to me that this happened. Its
   skin was never shown to me.

TESO: What you must do is bring another he-goat, and they will

give you another ewe, and that will close out the debt. That will
cover the cost of the meat eaten by the hyena here.

MEGAWIT: No. You are telling lies here.

ISHIRINI: I agree with the man from Teso. Can you see any of the
ram's family here?

MEGAWIT: I am not going to bring a ewe. I will bring a he-goat here
and ask for my ewe, and that will be the end of the debt [i.e., will
eliminate the namanya contract].

This seems to be precisely what Teso had suggested; yet Teso
continued as follows.

TESO: Do you say that Kambuya ate that ram of yours?

MEGAWIT: What is your decision? I asked you to consider about my
sheep that got lost here. You have said that the ram was killed
by worms. How big was it, and what happened to the skin?

ANDYEMA: There was no skin—I just threw it away.

ERYEZA: Andyema, you know that if this ram belongs to somebody
else, you should keep the skin.

SALIMU: All right. I think this matter is clear. His sheep died here,
and nobody ate it. We are the ones who lost. We will not ask anything, and he is not to ask anything.

Despite Salimu's subsequent discussion, this case remained
enigmatic. I felt that Megawit was not being treated fairly—as
Megawit himself felt. Aside from failing to preserve the skin as
evidence, which is an explicit expectation in Sebei law, Salimu
seemed to have rejected even Teso's recommendation that they
cancel the namanya by exchanging he-goat for ewe. Perhaps the
resolution lay elsewhere. Megawit was a man of Koin; he had
a Pokot wife, and was letting her brother and family live on his
land. The Pokot had been raiding the Sebei frequently, and a
few weeks later Megawit was accused of aiding the Pokot in
these raids. But this is conjecture; nobody made overt reference
to this situation during the hearings or in subsequent discussions, so far as I know.

Claims 6 and 7. Two resolved claims

The next claim was made by a person who said that he had
taken a bull from Kambuya and had given a heifer. This heifer
had produced two heifers and a bull calf, and the claimant took

the bull back along with the original cow. This cow was lent to another man, and then ran away from him to Kambuya's kraal. About this, Salimu said:

That cow has disappeared completely. You come at another time, and I will take you to where this cow was lost. The first two calves died, and you demanded that he bring a heifer to him for good, but you left both of them here. They each produced a heifer while they were here, and so you apparently had forgotten the matter. One of these has disappeared completely. There is only one cow that you have to claim. That will be paid by the man where the cows are kept in ka-manaktay. This cow always escaped our kraal and went back to that other man.

This decision was agreed upon.

A second person, whose name was not recorded, claimed that Kambuya had taken his goats and asked Salimu to pay this debt. Salimu agreed that he made the exchange with goats that he had originally obtained from Kambuya but that he had meanwhile paid his father, so that presumably the debt was against Salimu.

SALIMU: With respect to your debt, clearly understand that we are going to pay it back.

Claims 9 and 10. Arapsitaki claims some goats and owes some

ARAPSITAKI: I took Kambuya's goat. There was not enough milk in the she-goat I gave as namanya, and so she was returned to me. Kambuya took another goat and promised me a she-goat as na-manya. I came to Kambuya, and he gave me a second one; when I paid him, the ewe produced a ram. Of course I do have his two goats that I owe to him, but Kambuya had three of mine which he has not paid. He paid one, but it got sick and I had to re-turn it.

SALIMU: It is true that our father took a big ram, intending to ex-change it for a cow, and was given a ewe; but he was kind enough to keep this ewe as namanya instead of obtaining a cow. The other I took from him. The third goat that Kambuya should have paid was eaten by a leopard. I will pay for yours, and you pay one, and that will solve the debt.

ARAPSITAKI: I failed to mention one that your father killed for visi-tors from Bumet.

SALIMU: I think that this man is not lying. What he says is true.

KAPSILUT: Are you arguing on what he is saying?

SALIMU: No, I don't think this man can tell lies.

KAPSILUT: I am happy to hear that.

SALIMU: As for me, I suggest you have two to pay, and we have three to pay. I would like to pay only one and forget the rest. Why pay back and forth?

KAPSILUT: All right. You give Salimu one she-goat, and that covers the debt of two, and let him give you a she-goat to cover two and another she-goat as namanya to cover the other one.

ARAPSITAKI: Yes. I am happy with that.

Claims 11–13. Paulo claims a goat and pays two

PAULO: The old man took my goat, which he gave as a gift to Eryeza, and gave me a she-goat as namanya. When it produced a kid, both the mother and the young one were eaten by hyenas, and therefore the debt is again due me.

SALIMU: Yes, but what do you owe Kambuya?

PAULO: Yes, I have to pay Kambuya a goat. That goat belongs to your mother.

SALIMU: That is true, but you also took our hens and never paid a goat for them.

PAULO: I had been told by the old man to pay other people.

SALIMU: No, that is now owing to us. Have you paid it?

PAULO: No, I have not.

SALIMU: You owe that goat. We agree that we should pay yours, but you should pay us.

To this Paulo agreed. The goat to Eryeza was a gift by the old man. Eryeza had asked for help from him when he acquired his last wife, and the sons were honoring this obligation.

Claims 14 and 15. Salimu demands payment from Masai, a classificatory brother

The next claim was initiated by Salimu against Masai, who stood in the relationship of brother to Salimu; according to genealogical information, the great-grandfathers of these two men were brothers. They belonged to the same lineage.

SALIMU: Masai has two goats to pay. We exchanged a cow namanya for goats, but he has failed to pay two of them. That namanya cow has produced a bull, and Masai has been hiding that bull. However, that cow has cleared itself with a heifer, and she is

back in the kraal.[8] We want him to tell about the bullock—
the one that is the son of the heifer we gave namanya.

MASAI: It is true that the heifer produced a bull and then the heifer
that released her and then a third calf—a bull—which died. There
was another bull, a black one, which is the one we hid at Mai-
mei's kraal. There was still another bull; that one went back
with its mother. This cow produced four calves, one heifer and
three bulls, plus the one that died. It went back with a young
calf that is still suckling.

FAGIO: Yes, it is true that when the original heifer came back, it came
with a small bull. Kambuya said that the bull was not the proper
one, and he gave it back to that man.

ANDYEMA: This man kept the cow a long time, until when my father
was dying he told me to go and collect that animal. This man insisted on keeping it, but I managed to get it from him. But he
gave me the wrong bull. When I was driving it home, the bull
did not follow the cow but just went its own way, which shows
it was the wrong bull; so we had to return it.

MASAI: No, the bull belongs to that cow.

——: What happened to that bull?

ERYEZA: It died. You know you have to pay that. It died in your
kraal.

MASAI: All right. There must be a case. You say the bull belongs to
you. If there are witnesses to say that the bull you took was not
of that cow, the case will go against me.

——: This bull that these people claim is theirs—is it still in your
kraal?

MASAI: No, it has been stolen by enemies.

NDIWA: Please—it is wrong to hide such property. All the neighbors
will prove that you have it.

MASAI: This matter should be tried in court.

The case was summarized later by Salimu as follows. Kambuya exchanged goats for a cow namanya. Masai had given only
four of these, leaving two to be paid. Kambuya gave him the
heifer, which produced a heifer and was thus released. When the
cow was sent for, there was a young bullock to be returned with

---

[8] The namanya contract provides that the heifer given in exchange be
returned when she has produced a heifer calf (though should that calf prove
barren or be killed without reproducing, it would have to be replaced).
However, any bull calves born to the exchange heifer return with the
mother. The issue involves one such bull that was not returned.

it; though Kambuya had been told that this bullock was white, Andyema was given a black one. Therefore Kambuya sent that black one back and told Masai to give him the proper calf; meanwhile the black one died after it was brought back. So Kambuya's estate claims that proper calf as well as the two goats. Masai does not agree, but the neighbors concur that he is hiding this. It is another impasse.

Claim 16. Masai tries to collect an ancient debt

MASAI: When our sister eloped with Erisa, Kambuya went to that man and took three cattle from him. Among them was one bull that was taken by another man in exchange for a namanya cow. This namanya produced a heifer, and the old man said: "You should wait. When this heifer reproduces, you can have a cow." But Juma took this cow and exchanged it for a big bull from the Karamojong. I am claiming that bull.

SALIMU: I don't know anything about this. Do you old men know this? We did not make this exchange.

MASAI: I may be wrong about the person who made the exchange.

————: What color was the cow?

MASAI: I was young, and live too far away; I do not know.

NDIWA: It was a gray bull taken by Mwanga, who paid for it.

SALIMU: These people are telling lies. They don't know. That cow was paid in exchange for goats.

NDIWA: No, that was another—not the one I mean.

SALIMU: The one I mean was exchanged for goats. It produced a heifer, but the calf that was to release the mother was sick, and Kambuya said not to return the mother yet. This heifer produced a bull, which was taken by ————, but it died. It produced another, which was also given to ————, and the heifer exchanged here.

NDIWA: No, that was another one. What Masai says is true. It is another cow—not the one you have just discussed.

SALIMU [deep in thought]: You sit down and let me think. [There is a long pause while Salimu sits with chin in hand.] When he says that cow was brought by Kambuya, he is speaking false. By that time Kambuya was blind, and it was I who brought the cows to Nabokutu. It is true. The man was given a bull, and he gave a heifer in return; the heifer produced, but the calf was eaten in the bush, and all that family died.

MASAI: My father came to Kambuya and said, "Do you mean that I get nothing?" And Kambuya said, "When I get a calf from the heifer, I will give you one." But I have had nothing.

KAPSILUT: All right. The only solution is that when Kambuya's daughter is married he will give you one bull.

MASAI: No, that is another thing. If his daughter marries, that is another thing.

KAPSILUT: When your daughter was married, did Salimu ask for a cow?

MASAI: I have another claim.

KAPSILUT: No. Solve this one first.

SALIMU: It is up to you.

KAPSILUT: When your daughters marry, give him a bull.

NDIWA V: If these people were friendly, they should discuss this as brothers. But as it is before the kokwet, what Kapsilut says is right.

TESO: How did this cow come to the old man? Was it as part of the bride-price?

MASAI: This cow we claim was given to the old man as kamanaktay [i.e., it was received as bride-price but given over to Kambuya to keep].

MWANGA: We didn't know it was kamanaktay. Therefore Salimu could not give him a cow.

STEPHANO: Kambuya and this man's father are [classificatory] brothers. So when his father was going to marry, Kambuya gave him cows for a bride-price. So when his daughter married, Kambuya claimed a cow in return. So that cow is not kamanaktay, but is the return of the father's bride-price.

ERYEZA: Kambuya had helped his relatives, and he later complained that the daughters of the women for whom he helped pay bride-prices should give him one cow.

STEPHANO: This is a simple thing to be solved. I would say nothing further needs to be considered; this was solved by the man's father and his brother [Kambuya].

MASAI: No, it was kamanaktay, not a part of the bride-price.

SALIMU: We aren't going to pay this. [Turns to the old men for support.]

KAPSILUT: I know this story. This man's father had no cows, and asked for help. So Kambuya helped this man's father because he was poor. That is not a debt. Therefore I want you to be satisfied. Your father was poor, and had help from Kambuya; this cow was given to Kambuya because he was happy for the help, and you should not claim this at all.

MASAI: I didn't know anything about that.

STEPHANO: Who kept these cows for you?

MASAI: It was my father who did this.

STEPHANO: Then your father should claim this. He knows what he did.

ERYEZA: You said your father brought some cows to Kambuya. When he took them back, he left one bull behind. Do you know why?

MASAI: No, I don't know.

ERYEZA: How old were you by then?

MASAI: I was very young, but I remember.

FAGIO: Do you know that small heifer?

SALIMU: No, that is another family of cows. This animal was left in the kraal a very long time ago. This cow is completely finished.[9] It is up to you old men to decide what you think.

FAGIO: Masai is just delaying, talking of other things. He should sit down. It has been a long time since we moved here from Nabokutu.

ERYEZA: You say the old man had promised that if one of his daughters marries he would get a cow. But they were married a very long time ago. Why didn't you ask the old man?

FAGIO: Do you mean Salimu took an animal from that cow and paid it for bride-price?

MASAI: No, I am just claiming for my cow.

SALIMU: When our father brought that cow, were you circumcised?

MASAI: No, I was still too young.

SALIMU: You say Kambuya promised to pay a cow from his daughter's bride-price, but they are all married and have grandchildren. [This is not literally true; there are daughters remaining.] Where were you? You already have two wives; why didn't you ask for the bull for your bride-price?

MASAI: We were friends, and I didn't like to trouble him. What is the decision on the cow?

ERYEZA: This is finished. Do not come back and ask for it.

MASAI: This is not the end. I will take further steps.

The Sebei say, "A debt never rots"—there is no time clause in the Sebei cattle contract. Time, nevertheless, despoils human memories, and in this case the heirs of the two parties to an exchange had clearly differing concepts of the nature of the obligation incurred. The one viewed it as a social obligation initiated by Kambuya's original generosity; the other, as an economic transaction involving a legal obligation. It was impossible, in view of the death of both principals and the absence of documentation, to find where the truth lay.

Claim 17. Masai claims a cow that was left too long as namanya

MASAI: I have another claim. Kambuya took my bull and paid a red

---

[9] That is, there were no animals of this line remaining in the herd.

cow namanya. When it got to my kraal, it became sick and was returned. A second cow also got sick and was returned, and so we asked for another bullock instead.

SALIMU: He came to my father and asked for his bull. My father asked me for one, and I gave it to my father; then this man didn't take his bullock but left it in the kraal. It stayed there until it died. I am still asking Kambuya for my namanya heifer for the animal given to you.[10]

NDIWA V: That is correct.

ISHIRINI: Have you ever asked Salimu what happened to the bull?

MASAI: No, I never left this bull with Salimu. I took it to Araplabu's kraal, but it ran away to Salimu's kraal.

———: So you left it there, knowing it was yours, and it died.

STEPHANO: It was just a bullock. How can you claim a bull?

MASAI: No, I was going to give a she-goat and ask for a bull.

STEPHANO: That is a matter of asking them a favor.

KAPSILUT: How big was your namanya heifer?

SALIMU: There were two calves that followed this one, which was already old enough to have a bell tied on it by the time it died.

KAPSILUT: Then it had been long enough. Your claim cannot be considered.

MASAI: I am satisfied on that, but I claim for the bride-price paid on my sister [his previous claim]. We are all brothers, and you should give me a cow from this family.

SALIMU [rhetorically]: Are any of the cows from this family still alive? [If there are no descendants of the particular cow, then the claim is not viable.]

MASAI [with resignation]: When your sisters marry, you should give me a cow.

The case hinged on a fine point in Sebei contractual obligations. Masai had wanted to abandon the namanya contract by taking a bull from Kambuya after two attempts at getting a viable heifer had aborted. Kambuya used one of Salimu's animals for this purpose, which Masai placed in the herd of Sabila Araplabu. The bullock returned on its own to the herd of Kambuya, where it remained until it grew "old enough to have a bell tied on it," and two subsequent calves were delivered by its mother. Though Masai did not take possession of the animal, the kokwet ruled that he had ownership, that the loss was his. But Salimu

[10] Salimu was here referring to a claim he had against Kambuya's estate stemming from his part in the transaction.

retained some doubts; he subsequently said that the matter might be brought up in court. Even more to the point, he added, "Had he come and begged for a replacement, we could have given him one." There is in Sebei contractual obligation a point beyond which legal responsibility does not extend, but frequently a moral responsibility remains viable. Such moral responsibility is, however, abrogated when a legal demand is made.[11]

Claims 18–20. Eryeza accounts for his debts to Kambuya

Eryeza, it will be recalled, was a classificatory son of Kambuya, a literate man who had a small store in nearby Ngenge. Salimu detailed his complaint against Eryeza at an earlier session (pp. 62–63), in which he expressed certain doubts about Eryeza's integrity. There were several complications, and later Salimu said that although they would not demand return of some of the obligations if he paid the others, they would claim all of them in court if he did not.

SALIMU: Eryeza, how many cows of Kambuya do you have?

ERYEZA: He gave me one cow. He asked me to sell it to treat myself for my disease. He said, "You take this cow, and I will ask you to pay only me; you will not have to pay my sons."[12] He gave me another cow that belonged to Chemgut.

SALIMU: True. Go on.

ERYEZA: Kambuya went to my father to collect his debts, and asked me to get the cattle in his kraal and to keep them kamanaktay in my kraal. One of these cows produced a bullock; when it grew up, Labu, my father, took it. When Kambuya learned this he was annoyed, and said that I should not have given it to Labu. Labu gave the bull to somebody else, and that man refused to pay until we had to take a case; the court seized the heifer and gave it to me. After I got it, all its calves died. So I explained to Kambuya, and he said I should sell it, which I did. I bought a heifer with the money, and it had produced a heifer and a bullock by the time I was arranging the marriage to my second wife. Kambuya gave me the heifer to use as bride-price, but before I gave

[11] See my *Sebei Law* (Berkeley and Los Angeles: University of California Press, 1967), chap. 11, esp. pp. 198–199.

[12] As I understand this, Kambuya kept it possible to claim the animal while he was alive, but it should not be claimed against the estate. Salimu subsequently said they would not ask Eryeza to pay it back.

it to my father-in-law its mother died; so Kambuya stopped me from paying that heifer. I remained with that bull and heifer. [Salimu later said that Eryeza would have to pay this one back.]

SALIMU [coming to a matter he had raised in an earlier session (pp. 62–63)]: Eryeza came to our father on behalf of Lekali and asked for goats; so I paid three goats, and my father paid three goats. These were paid to Lekali, not to Eryeza. Lekali refused to pay until we took a case and the court seized a bullock from him for us. We placed this as kamanaktay in Eryeza's kraal. —— asked for it to slaughter for a work party, and we had to demand repayment again through the court, which seized the heifer [as namanya, presumably] for us, which later produced a heifer and a bull. That bull was taken, and still he didn't pay. We asked Eryeza to get it for us, and that man paid him a bullock. Eryeza took this bullock and sold it without our knowledge; when we asked him he said that the man had not paid, whereas Eryeza had in fact collected it.

ERYEZA: That is true, but the old man told me the goats belonged to Kambuya himself. I didn't know that some of them were Salimu's.

SALIMU: Eryeza has three cows to pay.

ERYEZA: I am not going to hide anything. Don't blame me. I have been sick all the time. The family of these cows are still there, but they always escape back to my kraal when I take them home.

SALIMU: Another bull I am not going to ask Eryeza to pay—he took it, promising to pay 80 shillings, but that money was stolen on the way to the market. My father said that we won't ever ask him to pay because of his bad luck.

ERYEZA: This cow that we have been claiming for goats—I did not know they were Salimu's.

KAPSILUT: How many cows do you owe?

ERYEZA: Three.

NDIWA: What Salimu claims is right. He paid three of the goats. Salimu is entitled to take one cow, and two remain as tokapsoy for the old man.

Claims 21 and 22. Two claims without question

At this point two men got up in quick succession and claimed debts which I did not manage to record. Salimu told each of them to sit down, adding: "Your debts are well known, and there is no question about them." One of these men was Kapsiret, no kin to the family. When Kambuya was sick just before his death, he obtained an animal to cure himself. "We pointed out that he had just got that cow and that it is obvious that he got it and that he should not stand up and make a claim so soon." Then Salimu remarked, "There are few in Sebei who can agree when somebody dies; people always try to deny the debts of the deceased."

Salimu said of the other claim, which was made by Arapbera, also no kin: "We bought a cow from him and had a debt left of 40 shillings. We paid 20 shillings of this on that day, and still owe him. This is also a recent purchase. The cow cost 140 shillings and we had already paid 100 shillings."

Fagio came in and announced that the Bumet man had refused to perform the ceremony and that it was necessary to find an old Maina man to do so. The matter was, however, not discussed at this point.

Claim 23. A debt due without question

SALIMU [turning to Arapchepkoiny]: I claim 60 shillings. You promised to bring a heifer, which you haven't paid. You gave a heifer, but it was too wild; we couldn't take it, and the debt is still outstanding.
ARAPCHEPKOINY: I agree to that debt.

Claims 24–27. Arapbera makes a claim for his brother and is reminded of other debts.

This claim was being put forward by Arapbera Kapkurit, a man from Atari, on the mountainside. His father was dead, and he was standing for his brother, who should have come.

ARAPBERA: I claim that when you were living in Nabokutu with the old man he took 20 shillings, which he hasn't paid.
SALIMU: Yes, I agree. It was not you but your brother who gave it. If you are standing for your brother, let me tell you about his debts. He took a ram, promising a bull, and there are two goats to be given him in addition.[13] He hasn't paid that. He also owes for three goats and for a bull for his father, who was sick. He did pay a heifer for the last bull, but it died. Therefore he has our four goats, which he hasn't paid, and we have his three goats.[14] I sold

[13] That is, a ram and two goats were exchanged for a bullock.
[14] The four goats owing to the estate presumably included the ram (the word was probably *warek*, which is used as a collective word for goats and

a black cow at the market; your brother asked me for 19 shillings, which I gave to him. These 19 shillings have not been re-
paid, and those 20 have not been paid. Your 20 shillings are
known. Do you remember the other debts?

ARAPBERA: Yes, I remember them.

Claims 28 and 29. A debt is claimed and a debt is forgiven

SALIMU: Arapkwarat has 70 shillings to pay. He promised to pay a
cow, saying that it was in Bukwa, but he never paid.

ARAPKWARAT: I know about the 70 shillings. Kambuya gave me this
money to pay my taxes. I asked for some money, and he said let
us go and sell a cow. We stayed in the same house—three people
together. In the morning I saw the money just lying on the
ground, but the other fellow said not to tell the old man his
money had dropped. Later Kambuya gave me 20 shillings. I had
already taken 60 shillings.

FAGIO: No, it was 100 shillings.

ARAPKWARAT: The 20 shillings were given to me by Kambuya as a
friend—not to be paid back. I was given another 10, so it all comes
to 70 shillings.

SALIMU: All right. Let us forget the 20 shillings. I was there when the
old man gave that to him to buy clothes.

ARAPKWARAT: No, the old man gave me 30 shillings in Bukwa and
later gave me 40 shillings; it is 70 shillings that I owe. I don't
think you should ask me for this money because I have been your
father's herdsman for a long time.

It was agreed that there were two separate debts; the first
would be demanded, but the second was to be forgiven on the
basis of friendship.

Claim 30. A youth claims for replacement of a namanya cow that died

This claim was initiated by a very young man; I am not certain whether he had been circumcised yet or not. He was the
brother of one of Ndiwa's wives. He was in an unfavorable
position, but, as we shall see, the matter seemed to have been re-

---

sheep but is literally "goats") plus the three mentioned. The three goats
owing to Arapbera's brother included the two to be paid if the bullock
was produced in return for the ram, plus a payment of a goat that was
made when a namanya animal died and was replaced.

solved—or at least given full consideration. Neither Salimu nor
Ndiwa seemed to have been told of this debt; possibly Kambuya
was himself unaware that the debt had not been cleared, for, as
Eryeza explained, the heifer given in payment had died.

ARAMANGUSYO: My father told me that when Ndiwa was arranging
for the bride-price for my sister, Kambuya asked me for a cow to
pay. He came and asked for a bull to pay taxes. Kambuya paid
for the first cow.

SALIMU [incredulously]: I don't think he is right about asking for
bride-price for Ndiwa, as Ndiwa married his sister. How can
Kambuya ask for a cow from the people he is going to pay it to?
The second was taken, but it has died.

———: Why did you leave your mother behind? She knows much
more about this.

NDIWA [correcting his brother]: The bull was taken to pay part of
the bride-price. I sold the bull for 100 shillings, which went to
my brother-in-law and another for buying sufarias [aluminum
pots] and the like, and this was given me by Eryeza here.[15]

SALIMU: Do you remember the cow, from which we took one of the
calves? What was that for?

ARAMANGUSYO: I don't know.

SALIMU: That was given to pay back for the bull my father took for
taxes.

ARAMANGUSYO: No, that was another cow. It was the one that bought
the granary.

SALIMU: That is the one.

FAGIO: You are wrong. You should bring your mother here—she
knows about these things.

ERYEZA: They had a bull for taxes, and a granary for a heifer. Both
of these have been paid. The granary is finished. The bull was
paid, but the heifer died. That is what they have agreed to pay.

———: Go ask your mother to explain all this to you. You were still a
raw child. Your mother has been milking these cows, and knows
what is what.

KAPSILUT: This man isn't satisfied. I ask you to consider his claim
when his mother comes here.

The discussion then became somewhat confused. Sabila inter-
jected more about the matter of the ceremony, saying: "Let us

[15] A man cannot borrow from the man to whom he is going to pay the
bride-price, but in this instance he did make an exchange with him for
an animal to sell so as to get money for the purchase of the clothes, vessels,
and other things that now entered into the marriage exchange. It was the
only clear instance of Salimu's being successfully contradicted.

get a man from Chumo pinta to perform this ceremony. The Bumet man is a bad man, and should not ever have been asked. Perhaps someone is afraid that they will have to share the meat with Kambuya's widow, but there are no widows to share with."[16] More information, which I did not get, was given about Aramangusyo's case. It made all the men laugh because of his naïveté.

> TESO: There is a claim against that boy. Kambuya offered to kill a goat but, instead, asked that Mangusyo [the boy's father] keep the goat and let it multiply, but he never heard any more about it. Chemisto should go and collect that goat.

Salimu said subsequently that the mother came later.

She claimed one cow and money. The cow was for a bull that Kambuya had taken. The cow that was given them namanya had died; they are claiming for a replacement, and we will pay that debt. I asked the mother to bring witnesses and also the person who brought the old man to her [as he was blind, someone always had to lead him], and we will discuss this matter. So, until she brings the witness, we will not pay. My father did not mention it, and Ndiwa doesn't know about it.

This is a good example of a case where the facts must be proved but the legal responsibility itself is not in question.

Claims 31–36. Diverse claims quickly handled

> SALIMU: I think there are other people who owe Kambuya, but I do not like to mention their names as they may deny their debts. What do you have, Stephano?
> STEPHANO: I have 30 shillings. I would have paid this, but my brother-in-law Andyema said that he would pay it for me. But if he won't, I am prepared to pay it.

Everyone thought it impossible for Stephano to ask his classificatory brother-in-law to pay his debt.

> KAPTYEMEI: I have 20 shillings belonging to the old man.
> SALIMU [to Chesurei, Kambuya's sister's son]: What do you have?

---

[16] Widows who do not have grown sons are inherited, but Kambuya's remaining wife was old. If there are widows, the person who performs this ceremony eats a feast with them and their children and engages in ceremonial intercourse with the widows, a practice known as "cleaning out the ashes." From other situations, I gather that men consider this act onerous.

CHESUREI: I killed his bull, and he killed mine—that is all.

SALIMU: I am not asking about those; you have a kamanaktay bull in your kraal.

CHESUREI: Yes, I have a bull kamanaktay. We have agreed not to pay each other back for the two heifers who died.

They slaughtered each other's bulls, and Kambuya and the other man both paid each other, but both of the heifers died. So the debt has been crossed off—"We tried to pay, but they have died." The bull that was kamanaktay was tokapsoy and would go to Mangusyo, the youngest brother.

SALIMU: Labu has 100 shillings.

LABU: No, you should say 60 shillings.

SALIMU: Of course, he asked his son Eryeza to give us a heifer na-manya for 40 shillings. Eryeza gave us a heifer, but his father became very angry and said that this family of cows produces only twins and demanded it back. And therefore, as we gave it back, the whole 100 shillings remain as an outstanding debt.

Salimu later added that as this man had many cows belonging to them, they wanted money for this particular debt. The other cattle were not mentioned in the meeting because Labu had already agreed to pay them.

OLD MAN: Do you know about the 60 shillings I owe?

NDIWA: No, that was given to you outright.

At this point they returned to the problem of finding someone to perform the ceremony of anointing the belongings of the deceased. They seemed to think that it should be a man from the pinta to which Kambuya belonged, but there were only two such men left in this area, and neither was present at this meeting. There was some joking about how to smear for the last man of the pinta; no one seemed to have an answer.

Claims 37–39. Sabila Araplabu must replace a namanya heifer

SALIMU: Sabila has taken our bull and paid a heifer as namanya. This heifer has produced a heifer, but, unfortunately, both have died. This debt is now outstanding.

SABILA: I agree. Whenever I have Kambuya's cows, they all die.

SALIMU: Some people are unlucky. I should like to tell you which brother it should be paid to. Andyema is the one. Also, Sabila has a he-goat he has not paid.

SABILA: I was going to pay a she-goat to Kambuya, but he said it was
    too small. I agree that I must pay that goat also.
SALIMU: The goat is to be paid also to Andyema.
SABILA: I claim that Kambuya owes me two goats.
SALIMU: We agree about that. Andyema is the one to pay you. As
    you owe him one goat, it remains for Andyema to pay you the
    one.

Salimu turned to some debts outstanding on persons who
were not present. Mentioning a name I did not get, he said:
"This man, who is not here, owes two bulls that have not been
paid. One of these bulls the old man had given to my wife, and
so it belongs to me; but the other one will be given to Ndiwa."

Someone asked Eryeza about a debt Eryeza owed him, to
which Eryeza replied with great dignity, "Are you bewitching
me by asking about my debts when we are discussing those of a
dead man?"

This closed the discussion. It was now after one o'clock. The
ram had been brought back about half an hour earlier. There
was further discussion about who would do the smearing; after
some argument, Sabila's brother agreed to do it for 20 shillings.
At about 1:20 the ram was slaughtered by having its throat cut,
and then it was skinned. The tail fat and the contents of the
lower intestines were reserved for the smearing. Kambuya's
spear, beer straw and its holder, sandals, shorts, sleeping skin, an
enamel cup, two bracelets, neck ring, and bedstead were brought
out. These articles were smeared and then spit upon with
chewed moykutwet root and beer. All this took but a few
minutes, closing the ceremony.

We were told that on the next day the brothers would divide
the stock in Kambuya's herd. With this information, we left.

A brief summary of the legal action in this session is in order.
The discussion dealt with about forty items. (It is sometimes
arbitrary to assign limits; should mutually canceling obligations
be treated as one claim or two?) About twenty-two different persons—some closely related, others hostile nonrelatives; some near
neighbors, some living at a distance—participated. Some of the
issues were complicated, others straightforward; some required
merely a nod of agreement, others led to an impasse and to

threats of court action. Nor were these the totality of Kambuya's contractual relationships. Only one matter was raised with Labu, Kambuya's classificatory brother, but "other cattle were not mentioned in the meeting because Labu had already agreed to them." The cattle genealogies given me by Salimu (see Appendix E) listed eighteen debts, some of which were recognized as uncollectable. There was a clear implication that many obligations had been quietly resolved, as no issue or question was involved.

Further, we must take note of the fact that although claims *against the estate* had to be made at these hearings or the individuals might have had to forfeit them, claims *by the estate* were not necessarily made at that time. Most of the latter were made after a person had made his claim(s) against the estate, although Salimu did initiate some. He initiated none against persons who were not present, though he suggested that such claims did exist.

A summary of the action shows much more owing the estate than was owed by it. Among the transactions discussed, ten concerned bulls, six owed to Kambuya and four owed by him; seven concerned heifers or cows, five owed to Kambuya and two owed by him; thirteen concerned a total of twenty-one goats or sheep, eight (thirteen animals) owed to Kambuya and five (eight animals) owed by him; and ten claims concerned money, of which all but two were owed to the estate. Kambuya was a rich man, and it is characteristic of rich men of Sebei to use their property in exchanges that are profitable.

Most of the claims were recognized as valid and proper, though not always without extended discussion. A few obligations were treated as gifts. In several instances of disagreement, the kokwet seemed clearly to have rendered a decision by seeking out the relevant evidence and applying established regulations. Thus in one of Naburei's claims, responsibility in the event of theft determined the kokwet's action; in another, the recognition of debt inheritance was brought to bear. Naburei did not accept these decisions, and he might have a basis for court action; but the kokwet seemed to have sustained Kambuya's family. Again, in Masai's case, it was ruled that Masai had left an animal unclaimed in the kraal so long that Kambuya could not be held responsible; in another case, cognizance was taken of ancient events surrounding Kambuya's getting an animal. In one instance (claim 30), the kokwet insisted on the re-examination of an issue; but in another (claim 5), it took no action despite the failure of Andyema to preserve the skin as evidence.

On the whole, only three claimants seemed to have been dissatisfied with the actions taken: Naburei, Megawit, and Masai. There was evidence in two of these cases which suggested a pervasive ill will between the parties; in the third, there was no such evidence, and Masai was of the same clan as Kambuya. In sum, the results of the day's work indicated an impressive use of Sebei custom to resolve the myriad potential conflicts that arise out of the continual negotiations in cattle and other property which characterize Sebei economic behavior, and particularly that of this cattle-rich family.

We returned to Andyema's house with Salimu and others at nine the next morning and found a number of men already there. This time there was no waiting. The men immediately gathered under a tree and started a discussion, which was still going on without interruption, even for beer or food, at half-past three, when Chemtai and I left, exhausted.

MWANGA: We have been staying here for a long time. Let us settle this matter. All you people who slept here throughout the night, what did you people think or dream during the night? Yesterday we discussed at length, but one thing was omitted; it must be solved today, because if you leave here without solving it, you will be blamed by the old men who are not here. There is one thing: the tokapsoy have not been discussed. The son who is in charge of the tokapsoy should state how many cows he has and which we should divide, to prevent quarrels in the future.

NDIWA V: I agree with what Mwanga has said. But I don't think we visitors here should interfere with these boys unless there is some complaint. If they mention some disagreement, then we should speak. I think these sons are friends, and I think they know how to divide among themselves. We cannot force them.

MWANGA: No, we must force them. Some of them mentioned here yesterday that the old man had been bewitched, and that is also what must be solved.

NDIWA V: I object. We should not interfere in their discussion. As to this bewitching, perhaps that is just mere lies. You are talking Koin custom, but among us we don't do this. [It is not clear whether he means they do not do witchcraft or they do not discuss it, but it is quite clear he wants to minimize the existing conflict.] Among the Sebei people, if somebody dies, after the third day of burial they perform the funeral rite; and if the man is rich, they kill a cow on that day. I object that yesterday nobody mentioned the bewitching until last night when they got drunk.

[Mwanga brought forth a proverb to which Ndiwa V responded, but unfortunately I could not record it.]

NDIWA V: Who is going to offer the bull to be killed? I have inquired about this, and some say Labu, the brother of Kambuya, should offer the bull; if not, it should be Nablesa, his son.

———: No, the animal was killed on the third day after burial.

NDIWA V: You should not have killed it during Salimu's absence. I myself think that was a mistake. Some here say that if Labu or Nablesa kills a bull, he is cursing the descendants of the deceased. My father died recently; and when we performed the mourning, we discussed who should kill the bull. People said it was not to be we four brothers who should kill the bull. At last it was agreed that one of us sons should do so, and that was all right. You who say that the sons were wrong to kill the bull on the third day were mistaken. I don't find that you were wrong. Perhaps this is a Bok custom. We Sebei people, when somebody dies, we don't wait for the sons to come back.[1]

SALIMU [hotly]: What you are speaking of here is just mere nuisance. Nothing good can come from it. This animal has been killed—do you want to bring the bull to life again? And nothing will be killed today. Let us go on to another subject. The person who criticized killing the bull is mistaken, and I think he is a man of Bok.[2]

FAGIO: I think Salimu is right. It has been done, and let us forget it.

STEPHANO: I quite agree with you.

SALIMU: Yesterday we spoke about the outside debts, and now we come to the tokapsoy. I am not the one to mention them. I want my brothers to mention them; if I do so, they will say I am hiding some.

MWANGA: I quite agree with you. I want you to speak out frankly to avoid future complaints among yourselves.

SALIMU: As for me, I have come back and found my father dead. I blame my brothers. I don't know how my father died, for when

---

[1] The speaker was objecting to there having been a bull killed at the appropriate time without the hearings, but was approving the idea that the slaughtered animal should have come from the sons rather than from the collateral relatives of the lineage. On this point of custom, I have no further information.

[2] Bok and Koin (referred to in an earlier speech), neighboring tribes closely allied in culture and language, are much intermarried with Sebei; many people from one tribe live in the territory of the other. The speakers were asserting that the customs they did not follow, or did not choose to follow, were characteristic of their neighbors.

he was alive, they went to my father and said the cows would be hidden by me.[3]

LABU: I want Nablesa [his son], Ndiwa, and Andyema to come and mention how many tokapsoy are here.

SALIMU [heatedly]: Keep quiet! Why should you invite Nablesa here? He has no cows in any of our kraals. Nablesa had a cow in this kraal, but when he was arranging to marry he exchanged it for a big bull, and therefore there are no cows of his in our kraal now.

NDIWA: All right. Let me try to mention the cows I know. As our aunts[4] are here today, they can support us.

MWANGA: Where are they now?

SALIMU: Why ask them here? We need them here only if there is an argument.

NDIWA: There was a cow that came from Kamatu. I didn't take one of those cows. Of the four sisters of our father, no bride-price cow was given me except one, which I was given when Kambuya was about to die. Our father had given Kamatu a she-goat, and she multiplied to six and was exchanged for a heifer. Kamatu had a boy who used to live here, and our father asked him to bring the cow to us, which he did. From that I received no calf. I want to add another . . .

SALIMU [overriding]: Let us finish this first one. With respect to that cow, what you say is right. Those goats had belonged to our father alone. But he has a debt owing to a Nandi for a cow that produced no calf, and he demands to be paid. Before we consider this particular cow, I want somebody to stand up and say he will pay this Nandi. Perhaps you have paid this debt while I was away.

---

[3] It is clear that tensions were high from the beginning. Two of the elders had clashed, and the issue of accusations had come forward out of the previous night's drinking. Also, Salimu was putting his brothers on the defensive by asserting that they must expose their knowledge of the herd and by reiterating his insinuations regarding witchcraft.

[4] The "aunts" were Kambuya's sisters. The tokapsoy would be discussed in terms of the ultimate source of each "family" of cows, starting with the cattle received as bride-price from the several sisters. In actual fact, the women took little or no part in the discussion, for reasons that I did not understand. Sebei women are not loath to speak up; and the men, though in many ways dominating their women, do not refuse them permission to participate in discussions. In the following, there are places where it sounds as if all the cows had been settled and that everyone should be ready to go home, when suddenly a whole new group of cattle are brought up—a new "family" of animals obtained from a particular source. Unfortunately, I was not always able to determine the sources exactly; the references were too cryptic, and later efforts to clarify were unsuccessful.

ANDYEMA: No, the cow has not been paid.

SALIMU: Therefore the person taking this cow must pay the Nandi debt. Our father took this cow in 1937.

STEPHANO: What Salimu says is correct. The one who takes this cow must pay the Nandi.

Salimu later discussed the details of this transaction:

Kamatu was given a she-goat as namanya, and our father did not take the goat back until it had multiplied to six. Kamatu wanted to keep the goats and offered instead a bull, given outright and not in namanya exchange. This bull was then exchanged for a heifer. The bull was lost, and the man demanded another but was refused. Yet Kambuya said that if his debt partner brewed beer for him, he would then give him another bull. Meanwhile, the heifer Kambuya received grew and produced a calf that died; that cow is now still in our kraal. It is necessary that we go to the home of Teso and find out if there is a bull belonging to one of us sons that can be given to the Nandi; if the bull belongs to our house, then that person takes this heifer. I have been thinking that I may keep this cow until it multiplies, and then divide it among the brothers. This will not be considered until we divide the cows that Teso is holding for Kambuya as kamanaktay.

The next speech was made by Teso.[5] He had spoken before but up to this point had said little. In this context however, he becomes a more important character, and it will be useful to know something about his background. He was an elderly but not an old man, and seemed to have been closer to Kambuya than any of the latter's relatives were, except perhaps Salimu and Teso's wife, who was Kambuya's favorite sister. He was a pleasant, easygoing man, who was all the more obvious for the bright red sport shirt he was wearing at the time. A colony of Sebei was now residing in Teso territory. Teso had many of Kambuya's animals as kamanaktay, and the payment to the Nandi, who also lived among the Teso, would be made from among these animals. A kokwet similar to the one we witnessed was due to take place at Teso's house, to allocate the many animals Kambuya had in his kraal; I tried to organize it before my departure, but

---

[5] Teso, whom I so nicknamed, was a Sebei living in Teso country. He had many of Kambuya's animals at his home, but these were not generally discussed at the hearings. The payment was to be made from these animals for convenience, as the Nandi to whom it was owed lived nearby.

without success. Teso seemed to have known the details regarding Kambuya's cattle as well as any man except Salimu, and in this discussion his voice took on added authority.

TESO: Yes, concerning the Nandi debt, the old man told me he had taken a cow from Arapto a long time ago and that if Arapto should come to me, I should pay this debt for him. One day I was invited by this Nandi to Soroko where he lives; there he mentioned this debt of Kambuya, and he asked me that when I came here I should ask Kambuya for it. I later saw Kambuya and gave him the message from that Nandi. Kambuya said: "That's true. Tell him I'll pay him, and if he comes to you, pay him if you have a heifer." It happened that Arapto came to me three days after I had seen the old man. When he came, I took him into my kraal and showed him my kraal [i.e., pointed out the animal for him]. He said that that would be all right; yet he didn't take the cow, and it is still in my kraal.

SALIMU: If you paid that debt, that is another one altogether. Our father has taken goats from Arapto as well; when he comes, he should be paid.

TESO: This is clear—the one entrusted with this cow should pay the Nandi. Please take care of this so that we can go on to the next decision.

LABU: Salimu, go on with other cattle.

SALIMU: We have been stopped; we must first finish this one.

STEPHANO: These cows are too many! We can't finish this today.

SALIMU [proceeding to set forth some of the problems, despite his earlier insistence that his brothers should speak up first]: What you mention, Labu, is about one bull. We gave you a bull, and you gave our father a heifer; and that was an outright exchange. It got sick for two months, and then it recovered. Mangusyo was a careless herdsman, and the cow was left behind; it fell into a hole and during the night it was eaten by a hyena. My father, when he heard about that cow, yelled angrily, "What happened that you closed the gates but didn't count the cows?" And he beat me, even though I said it wasn't my time for herding. That cow died, and so our father paid another cow to Arapto. My father sent me to Kamwasir to buy a bull. I don't know what he used it for, but this cow is still unpaid. I saw one bullock paid as bride-price for one of his sisters. It was given but not paid.[6]

---

[6] I suspect that the transitions in this speech were not so abrupt as they appear, and that these were all transactions that reverted to the Nandi debt; but the references were too cryptic to make this clear. I understand the last sentence to mean that the specific cow had been indicated for payment of bride-price but had not been delivered.

At this point, there was some side play between two of Kambuya's sons, who were joking with one of their sister's sons. The latter was the only child of the sister for whom a bull had been paid. They were saying that if he had only been a girl, they would by now have had something in return from that animal.

SALIMU: I had a big bull; my father gave me a heifer for it, and it had two calves. The udder of one calf dried up; the other calf I kept. This heifer was received for a bride-price. I got it in exchange with my father; I did not receive it from him as a gift.

LABU: There is another cow you have not mentioned.

SALIMU: I have mentioned them all. It is up to my brothers to criticize.

STEPHANO: That is true.

NDIWA: What Salimu says is quite correct.

LABU: The cow named Olomon—what happened to it?

SALIMU: That cow produced a heifer which was given to me. The second heifer was paid by Kambuya to Arapsakuta for a bullock he had taken. That cow produced, but most of the calves died. One calf did live, and was paid on a [namanya] debt. Then she returned with one heifer, but then the mother died, leaving only the one calf. One day I saw our father asking Chemisto to come to him; our father said to him, "Here is a cow I am giving to you." And Chemisto brought it home. If you have cows received for our aunts, please mention them. I know only the cows I have in my kraal.

Salimu later expanded on this situation. The cow Olomon had been obtained as a namanya exchange. It produced, as well as the heifer that released it, a bullock that should have been returned to Olomon's owner. Kambuya, however, used the bullock for namanya exchange with another man, who still owed the heifer to Kambuya when he died. Salimu asked that this man pay the debt directly to Olomon's owner, for it was his bull. I believe this to be the cryptic claim 6. Meanwhile, the heifer that Kambuya received had reproduced, and that young animal had been given to Chemisto.

LABU: Have you mentioned everything?

SALIMU: Yes, I have. I think you heard what Ndiwa said.[7] From this

---

[7] We must remember that these were discussions where much was readily understood between the speakers, as in a family conversation. They moved from one case to another without transition; this speech appeared in my notes as a single paragraph, but there was here a shift from discussing the

sister of Kambuya sitting down here by us, there is one cow left. Kambuya said, "You must divide it after my death." Another cow came from the bride-price of Sumoita. It produced a bull and a heifer, and these are in my kraal. The mother was attacked by rinderpest and died. The bull grew big, and I exchanged it for two heifers. One of them produced three heifers, and then it died. But I took the other to my kraal and later gave it kamanaktay to Arapsigoria. It produced a heifer, and I took that heifer to Kambuya's kraal and not to my own. It died of black quarter fever while it was pregnant. One day my father sent Andyema without my knowledge to Arapsigoria's for that kamanaktay cow, and it is in Kambuya's herd. I have one cow of this family.

NDIWA: I am happy to hear that.

SALIMU: For this sister, only a bull and a heifer were paid. —— took the bull, and —— took the heifer. [I did not get these names but presume from the context they were Andyema and Ndiwa.] A diviner told my father to slaughter a bull for his sickness, and he killed that bull. The heifer produced a heifer, and this heifer produced a bull. Now Ndiwa's mother had no food, and so our father bought a granary of millet for her with that bull.

NDIWA: I am satisfied with that.

SALIMU: There are now four cows of this family. Another tetapsoy was received from Lengesi when she married; it is now in Kambuya's herd. That is all I know we got from Lengesi.

NDIWA: I know a cow named Chemutwo, which our father said was in Salimu's kraal. Father said he had given Salimu a bull; and before he died he said that as he had no young wife to be responsible, he wanted Salimu to divide that cow.

SALIMU: Do you know how many I have?

NDIWA: No, I don't know.

SALIMU: There are two: one is in my kraal, and one is here in Kambuya's. I gave a bullock to Fagio, and he exchanged it with Siret. That namanya cow is in my kraal. It produced two heifers and one bull. My father said one should go to Andyema; our father took the bull and paid off a debt. You know that my father had refused to allow Chemisto to come near him. One day my father asked me to brew beer, and when I did brew beer he was happy. He asked Chemisto to come near him, and he asked me to give one cow of that family to Chemisto; so I gave the other heifer to him.

NDIWA: There was another cow at Kabruga.

---

cattle obtained from one of Kambuya's sisters to discussing those obtained from another. The notes did not indicate which sister was being discussed, and it was not possible to make a subsequent determination.

SALIMU: You are less concerned with that one. Kambuya took that cow, and it produced a bull. Somebody took that bull and paid a heifer namanya for it. That heifer that released the namanya produced a heifer and then died of rinderpest. That daughter produced three heifers, and then she died. All these cows died except one, which produced two bullocks and a heifer; and now there are just these four.

ANDYEMA: This is quite a different cow. It is not the one we got from Sumotwa.

SALIMU: True, this is quite a different one. The family of that cow you speak of now had a big bull, which I sold for 400 shillings; and after I came home from the market, I bought a heifer for 220 shillings from Eunice Mwanga with the rest of this money. This cow had been awarded to Eunice by the court from Arapchiwo, and he later came and stole her from my kraal. I took a case against him, but I didn't get her back. So I went to Eunice and asked for another, and was given one. This cow produced a heifer. Because these two cows cost 420 shillings, and the 20 shillings extra were my own, my father said I should have the heifer she produced. From the heifer my father gave me, there are two heifers and a bull calf. My father was sick, and the diviner told him to show a bull to his *oyik*.[8] I gave it to him, and it is now in his herd. Our father had a bull, and I gave him one of the heifers as namanya; it produced a heifer calf and was given back to me. My father said to give Ndiwa that calf. There was a cow called Seta that produced two calves, a bull and a heifer, and these are here—they are tokapsoy.

NDIWA: Our father said that your brother had hidden some of the cows that came from Kapchebugoch.

SALIMU: How many were at his kraal?

NDIWA: I don't know.

SALIMU: There were two. One was Namasero. It was given to Kapchebugoch namanya to pay a debt. This one stayed there, and the calves died one after another until only one heifer was left. The one remaining was a brown cow, which Kapchebugoch sold for 300 shillings. Kapchebugoch died, but his sons said that their father bought three cows with that brown cow. But I don't know where his sons are now. In that family there was one cow left in Kapchebugoch's kraal. It had no milk, and its calves all died. At

---

[8] Oyik are spirits, normally of the dead. A Sebei was concerned with those of his clan because they might harm its living members, who were expected to make frequent sacrifices and libations to the oyik. But in this instance the animal was merely kept in the kraal for the spirits to admire.

last our father got annoyed with it and exchanged it for a heifer, which was brought to my kraal; after it produced two calves, it died of rinderpest. The heifer became barren, and I sold it—this money was mentioned yesterday. One bull of this family is in my herd, and one heifer also.

STEPHANO: Is what Salimu says true?

NDIWA: That's right.

When Salimu later discussed this transaction with me, it seemed more complicated, but the end result was the same. He told me: "Ndiwa complained that I was hiding this cow. My father had gone to Kapchebugoch and got a bull, which was enjoyed in our house [i.e., was used for a feast for the family of Salimu's mother]. The heifer Namasero was given as namanya for Kapchebugoch in return. Namasero produced a heifer, which would have released her; but as Kapchebugoch is my mama [mother's brother], he asked if he could keep that cow and enjoy its milk, and I allowed him to do so. He kept Namasero until it had multiplied to nine in addition to itself. So I asked for these, and I brought all nine of them back. When Ndiwa complained, I asked if he remembered the cow Namasero that was given as namanya. 'Do you remember what house it came from—was it not our mother's house?' By this, Ndiwa was defeated. By the time these cows were brought back, Namasero had died. Out of this nine, two died of rinderpest, and one was sold because its milk dried up. Kambuya also sold another bull. My father took three to Andyema's kraal. Father sold one, but I don't know what happened to the money. So Andyema took those two, and I took the other two. One heifer and one small bull came to me."

ERYEZA: There are eight cows in Malinga's kraal which have been hidden, and Petero brought one.

SALIMU: That is finished. You will never get that back.

Salimu subsequently explained this as a case of an uncollectable debt—and one so recognized. The circumstances were as follows. "Kambuya gave a cow to my mama [mother's brother] Malinga. It produced two heifers, and I was sent by my father and brought those two, leaving the original cow. Then it produced four more calves, and I thought that, as the mother cow was getting old, I should go to bring her home. Therefore I went to Malinga, and he said, 'Please, you had better take the mother of these cows as she is old, but leave me one of the young cows which has a calf so that I can enjoy the milk.' So I took three cows home and left two animals there, a cow and her calf. That cow that I left there has multiplied to eight, and then my mama died. His son sold all the eight cows and migrated to Bugisu district. Eryeza reminded me of this case, but I said that we had better forget that, as that man is too poor to pay them back. That debt is simply written off. If I took a case against him in the courts, I couldn't get any cows from him anyway.[9] If he had a cow—or if he gets some—I may ask him for just one to cover the whole debt."

NDIWA: Some cows are in Chongeywa's kraal.
TESO: Forget that. You will never get a cow from him. You are joking. I tried to talk to these people, and was almost beaten by them. Chongeywa's eldest son, who is dead, knew about those cows, but all these remaining sons are now denying the matter entirely. When I went to them, they sent me back to Salimu.

This second bad debt was subsequently explained by Salimu: "My father bought four heifers and kept them at Chongeywa's kraal. He was living in Teso district and he had no permit to carry cows across the district boundary, and so he left them there.[10] In 1948 I went to Chongeywa's, and his son showed me twelve head of cattle from those four heifers. Chongeywa was not present, and was later told by his wife, 'Our son has pointed your calves out to your tilyet.' Chongeywa was annoyed with his son, and fought him and bewitched him to death for showing these cows to me. In January, 1960, I went to Teso district and saw Chongeywa himself. I asked about my cows and he said, 'I have no cows here. There are only eleven, but I won't give you

[9] Under Sebei law the entire progeny of a namanya animal, except the heifer that released her, belong to the man from whom the namanya came. Modern courts, however, tend to award the owner only the animal originally exchanged or its equivalent.

[10] Governmental regulations control the movement of cattle to prevent the spread of disease.

those.' And he said he would give us some he had in Sebei, but when I inquired at the kraal where he said they were being kept, these people said he had already taken the cows back to Teso district. I returned and found him sick, and so I returned home as I couldn't ask about a debt when a man was seriously ill. Then I got sick myself and I never went back. Then I was told that our tilyet Chongeywa had died. Chongeywa has a son, and I think we should take a case against him. We can't identify our cows; if we get only four, it doesn't matter. Sumotwa says that Chongeywa's son sold most of their cows. I am going to ask him, and if he becomes difficult, then I must take a case. I have witnesses."

MWANGA: If somebody dies, there is much to be solved. Therefore I ask you to divide the cows peacefully and happily.

SALIMU: One cow not mentioned was in my mother's house, and it is mine. The cow was sold for 60 shillings, and I bought a namanya heifer named Keri. It was brought to Kambuya's kraal, and it is mine.

STEPHANO: That is known. It is your mother's cow.

SALIMU: There are three cows named Muki, Bosyi, Chesabiñ. The grandmother of Bosyi was acquired for an elephant tusk. The family of this cow was our father's tokapsoy.

The circumstances of this particular cow offer some highlights of Sebei culture. The original animal was obtained indirectly by elephant hunting. Kambuya's father owned the poison used on elephant spears. He gave some of the poison to his brother's son Burich. Burich and Kambuya's father went elephant hunting, killed an elephant, and brought the tusks back. One of these tusks went to Kambuya's father in payment for the use of the poison, and the other was taken by Burich, who had speared the elephant. Both men exchanged their respective tusks for cows (probably with Swahili traders). Kambuya's father obtained a cow named Chepkwedye, which in turn bore a heifer named Kamateybon. This cow was given to Kambuya by his father; but before Kambuya actually took it, its mother died, and Kambuya's father took it back until it in turn had a heifer—Ngatimet. This heifer was given to Kambuya's brother Mangusyo, who smeared her for his second wife. There are three cows left from this family: Chesabiñ and her daughters Muki and Bosyi.

1. The plains area at Kapsirika, Mt. Debasien in the background.

2. Pointing out the tokapsoy.

3. Andyema Arapkambuya.

4. The bull of the herd belonging to Ndiwa.

5. One of Kambuya's daughters-in-law milking.

7. Salimu examining a calf.

6. Salimu arguing with young men over the number of cattle.

8. Pointing out the tokapsoy.

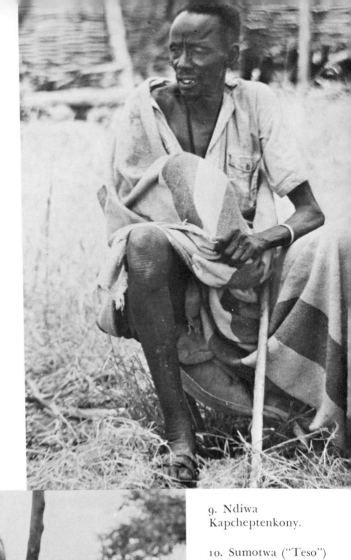

9. Ndiwa
Kapcheptenkony.

10. Sumotwa ("Teso")
Kambalyanya.

11. A neighbor.

12. Salimu scoring a point in discussions.

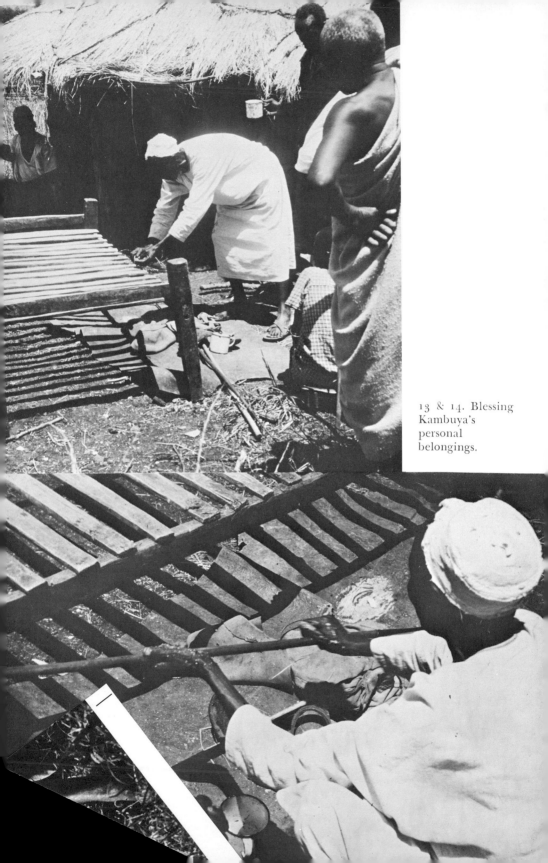

13 & 14. Blessing Kambuya's personal belongings.

The case illustrates how deep in time and how detailed in circumstance is the memory of these cattle.

NDIWA: What about the cow for which you took a case against Melala?

SALIMU: Do you remember the cow that was killed? In 1937 Sabila and another neighbor moved to Cheseber, and one of these men had a debt to Kambuya. He said he was going to Kabruron but he was not going to take our father's debt, and so he gave him a bull. Now Kapsulel asked our father for this bull, and it was given to him. Labu came and asked for it and then gave it to Araptege to sell for him. Araptege sold it for 46 shillings, but Labu was annoyed because he was given only 40 shillings, and so Labu told Araptege that he must pay this debt, which Araptege did. The cow paid was Somu, and it produced three heifers —Tolelyo, Keri, and Sirwei. These were all kamanaktay, but the man who was keeping them told us that no cow was left except Sirwei, and he had made his clan marks on the ear of that cow. So I went to his herd and found his son herding them and asked him privately to show me the herd. But he was also hiding that cow. So I called out, "Calf of Somu, calf of Somu," and that calf came of its own accord. [Laughter.] I returned after a few days and asked for Sirwei and found that he had paid it for his own debt, but that calf returned to the kraal where it had been born. I became annoyed and took that calf and placed it in another kraal. Next time I brought Somu and Tolelyo. He tried to take a case against us, but the chief gave evidence on our behalf. I also told the court that the earmarks of the cow were ours, and that man was asked why he should make earmarks for our clan, for which he had no answer. Before that case was heard, that man cut off the whole ear of the cow. By this time we had taken four cows of this family, and the case was decided in our father's favor, but the court ordered Kambuya to leave one of the cows with the man who was herding. Before he brought the cows back, he bought some beer and he put the tail of the cow into the beer, trying to do magic on them. Two of these cows became barren, and we exchanged them for some heifers, and all these and the cows of this family are in this herd and belong to our father [i.e., tokapsoy].

NDIWA: There is a cow at Chesori's kraal. I think that one belongs to our father.

SALIMU: That cow was given to Musani. That cow was very wild. Many people had been trying to take it, but they couldn't handle it. One day Kapkelang came and asked for it, and my father said,

"All right, you take it," and it went with him happily, and everybody was surprised. He paid a heifer [namanya] for that cow and it produced a brown cow and went back to its owner. That brown cow went to Ndiwa, who now has it.

Another three tokapsoy belong to the old man. One was a bull that I sold and got a heifer, which is now in my kraal. One was taken by our brother Eryeza, but he hasn't paid for that. So in this family there are four: I have one, Ndiwa has one, one is with Chemurei, and one Eryeza has. All right. I will keep mine, Ndiwa will keep his, and the two bulls—one should go to Andyema, and one to our young brother Mangusyo. [There is general agreement to this division.] One of our sisters was married, and six cows were paid, and it was I who brought the cows and gave them kamanaktay to ———. The father was very annoyed with one of the cows, as we were given a weak heifer, and it died. Among these six, our father gave one to Ndiwa, which he paid for his second wife. My father gave me one.

FAGIO: You should remember to ask the brothers if they are satisfied with what you are saying.

SALIMU: One was given to me, and one was given to Andyema, and one was given to Mangusyo. Now mine died, Andyema's died, Mangusyo's died, and Ndiwa paid his for his wife. There remain only one heifer and one bull. I went to my father and said that I was left with nothing from this marriage. Our father gave me a bull, which I exchanged for a heifer; but all the calves died except for one bull. Eryeza was sick, and he was advised to show a bull to his oyik. He was given one, but it was stolen by the Pokot and is gone. Our father went to Turu and got another cow and gave it to Andyema. I returned again to my father and said that I had nothing from our sister; so he said to go to my brother-in-law and ask him for another cow [to replace the weak one that had died], and he said he was happy to pay one more, but he has not yet done so. That is the end of those cows. Of these cows, one was given to Noibei, one to Mangusyo, and one left for the young children.

NDIWA: I want to explain the four cows. One to Noibei is right; one to me, which was paid for bride-price; he gave me another, which died of rinderpest; and another, which I kept, and it multiplied —this cow was brought by Andyema.

ANDYEMA: No, by Maget, not by me.

[There follows a break in the record, indicating I had missed a speech or two.]

SALIMU: I misunderstood you. I don't know about the cow given to me and I gave to you.

NDIWA: There was one, but I don't know which it was.

SALIMU: There is one cow Father gave to me and said I should give it to you. It was given to you a long time ago.

STEPHANO: It is up to you. If you don't like it, Ndiwa can give it to Salimu's son Chemisto.

NDIWA: Gentlemen, I have two debts to pay to the old man [i.e., to Kambuya's estate]. I took a bullock, Mur, and sold it to buy a maize mill. There is another that I haven't paid. I have taken three others that I have paid to him. I had a cow I gave kamanaktay to Masai Arapchungeywa. Later I sold it, and I came by here on the way back from the market and I gave my father 60 shillings, which he has not paid back to me. Another thing—I had a bullock in this kraal, but my father used it for a debt without asking me. Another cow, Alengekong, belonged to my brother. Do you know where it is?

STEPHANO: That's right. One of your cattle was killed [as a kind of sacrifice] when Andyema was sick.

NDIWA: One of the kamanaktay cows belonged to my mother. When Salimu married Stanley Salimu's sister, Stanley came down here and stole our father's cows without permission, and we haven't said anything.

STEPHANO: That's right. People just used to drive away cattle when you stole[11] a daughter. Salimu, could you divide these cows among your brothers?

TESO: The cow that Ndiwa is complaining about— is he right?

SALIMU: Yes, that's true. Arapkuru took a bull belonging to Ndiwa's mother and gave a heifer. It produced a heifer and went back to its owner. I had a bull, and my father asked me for it when Ndiwa was circumcised in 1942, and I gave that bull to him. That debt is still outstanding. Who is to pay that?

NDIWA V: Yes, Ndiwa, it is you who must pay that.

ERYEZA: Kambuya killed that bull for his pinta-mates, not for the friends of Ndiwa. It should come out of the tokapsoy.

---

[11] Elopement is a customary mode of marriage in Sebei; in the old days it was really wife capture. The Sebei now frequently establish liaisons without making any arrangement with the parents of the girl. Normally when this takes place, and apparently always in the pre-Europeanized days, it is followed by a bargaining session carried on very much as if it were before marriage. In recent years, however, sometimes the brothers of the girl and their friends steal as many cattle as they can from the kraal of the boy's father. Usually the number is roughly comparable to the brideprice, and subsequently they sometimes bargain, especially to retrieve the cattle that do not belong to the husband or his family but are kamanaktay animals in the kraal. This happened when Salimu married one of his wives.

To celebrate the circumcision of Ndiwa just twenty years before this conversation, Kambuya had killed an animal and fed his age-set mates, in accordance with Sebei custom. Now the question is, should the repayment for that animal be made from the cattle that belonged to Ndiwa's kota, or should it come from the tokapsoy?

SALIMU: Who am I going to ask to pay me? I asked my father about it, and he said, "You wait until you can get one from Ndiwa's kraal."

TESO: To us Koin, if people are invited, they come with animals. [I.e., gifts are given to the circumcised young man, and therefore it is his house that incurred the obligation.] It is quite obvious that Ndiwa must pay him.

NDIWA: There is no argument about this. We will divide the tokapsoy, and I will pay one to him.

SALIMU: I want you to pay from your own cows, but not from what we divide.

FAGIO: Do you remember that the bull that was killed for Ndiwa had one thigh broken and could not be eaten? You must give a she-goat for the thigh that was thrown away.

SALIMU: Yes. I will give a she-goat, and he will give me a heifer.

FAGIO: Ndiwa, you must pay the debt out of your own herd, and not from the tokapsoy given you.

LABU: I think one cow belongs to Nablesa [his son].

SALIMU: Nablesa is here.

NABLESA: What do you mean? I have no cow here.

This was the second time that Labu had tried to propel Nablesa into a position of heritage. Nablesa was Labu's son, but in Sebei kinship terminology he would also have been called "son" by Kambuya. Salimu objected the first time, but he need not have bothered; he was a young man who cared little for cattle. He had wasted his cattle—had refused to take even minor trouble to build up his herd. He was like a ne'er-do-well son of a New Englander, consuming his capital. Nablesa did not want more cattle. The desire of most Sebei to get all they can in any situation is adequately demonstrated in this document, but Nablesa was an exception, as this speech indicated. He really did not want to have any cows from this herd; he did not want to have cows at all. He was once married, but his wife left him and he seemed quite satisfied with the bachelor life.

LABU: I remember one day the old man said to me that he had a cow he was hiding from Nablesa because he didn't want Nablesa to know, as he always wastes his cows.

TESO: Could you describe its color?

LABU: No.

ERYEZA: I remember that the old man told me that there is a cow to be paid for Chelengat, who is the daughter of Nablesa's aunt [father's sister], and it is his cow. Nablesa was asked to give the daughter of this woman 20 shillings, but he refused to pay that money. The old man kept the cows.

SALIMU: The daughter came and asked for 20 shillings. We were all present, and Nablesa was asked to pay. But he said, "You keep your cow," and refused to pay, and my father asked me if I had money. I gave her 30 shillings and was given the cow. Later, the old man bought it from me for 300 shillings, and it is now in his kraal.

LABU [to Nablesa]: You give Salimu the 30 shillings and get the cow.

NABLESA: I never asked for that cow. Have you heard me complaining?

SALIMU: If he agrees to pay the 30 shillings, what can be given to him? The cow has already been bought by my father. However, there is one thing: we must consider Nablesa as he is the one who put our father in the grave. We should give him a cow for crying.

FAGIO: Remember that my grandfather said that when I die, give my brother [Noibei] a heifer; so I think he is entitled to one.

STEPHANO: Concerning the cows—are all of you here satisfied with the way they have been divided and mentioned by Salimu?

Ndiwa and Andyema agreed that the division had been satisfactory. By now it was eleven in the morning, and the council had been meeting for about two hours. It now turned to the discussion of money. Ndiwa had gone into the house and brought out some money, and he counted out 810 shillings and gave them to Salimu. Salimu examined the money and then put it down on the ground in front of him, where it remained for the rest of the session.

SALIMU: You remember that I paid out 20 shillings for the man who smeared our father's things. [Agreed.] This money did not all come from one cow. It should be 850 shillings.

NDIWA: From the 850 shillings, I spent 30 shillings for sheets to wrap the old man and 10 shillings for beer for the old man, and this is the balance.

There was further discussion about the money, and then the
men returned to the matter of the cattle. Obviously, the distribution of this money was troublesome. It had come from the sale
of several animals from different houses, and I suspected that
they did not know just where it had come from. At any rate, they
meditated over it for some time.

The discussion now turned to matters regarding Tengedyes,
Kambuya's widowed sister, whom nobody wanted to inherit.
She was then an old woman, and the second of her two daughters
had just been married. Salimu, who had cared for these three
women for many years, had taken, in addition to the animals
due the mother's brother, a cow to compensate him for his generosity. The Chemonges in the following speech was a brother
of the two girls, but by a different mother.

NDIWA: I am afraid that Chemonges is not present, but I received
    some information yesterday when I saw old man Arapkorit, who
    said that Chemonges wants to take his heifer. I asked, "What
    kind of cow can Chemonges have in this kraal?" This is the cow
    that Salimu has been feeding the sisters of Chemonges with.

SALIMU [annoyed]: Arapkorit is a stupid man. When these girls were
    young, Chemonges gave them no help at all. Why should this
    cow go to him?

ERYEZA: Let us wait for Andyema to come back, because 80 shillings
    are missing which, it was said, he was given.

SALIMU: Who paid the money for the bull that we got from the man
    living on this hill? The bull got lost; the money paid for this cow
    was from goats. Going back to the cows received for our sisters—
    there is one in my kraal which was given Chemisto by his grand-
    father.

ANDYEMA [returning to the matter of money]: I told you yesterday
    that the cow from Sabila brought 300 shillings, another from
    Arapmalinga brought 300 shillings, and another black cow
    brought 200 shillings.

SALIMU: These 40 shillings are the balance of the 1,600 shillings.

ERYEZA: Andyema, did the old man give away some of this money?

NDIWA: We should also count the money given to Moto.

SALIMU: No, that was a long time ago; this is money from cows sold
    recently. There were 80 shillings given to Chemonges.

ERYEZA: No, it was 100 shillings. Andyema already said that he took
    three cows and got 300 shillings each, which is 900 shillings. The
    150 shillings from the last bull sold and another 100 shillings,

were given to Arapsitaki. I think you know each of these cows
and where they came from.

[Salimu and everybody sit thinking quietly about this.]

SALIMU: Let us consider the person who killed the first cow, the *kintet* [the animal slaughtered three days after death].

NDIWA V: Didn't you settle this at that time? Who was present to
solve this matter, as Salimu was away?

SALIMU: This is to be given to the man who killed it, but this cow
cannot be given in bride-price or in kamanaktay.

NDIWA V: If somebody is given a cow for burial, he can give it kamanaktay, but with this one he cannot.

NDIWA: The Karamojong used to rush over here when there was a
burial; they got rich from that. [Laughter.]

ARAPBURITY: Some other people are waiting for others to die so they
can obtain cows.

FAGIO [taunting]: It is your fault. You always make excuses not to
bury people. [Much laughter.]

OLD MAN: There is an example. A man living in Riwa, who is a
Koin man, died; and when the man who had buried him was
drinking, he mentioned how the bull he was given for that burial
had grown, but the people there said he should keep quiet, for
he should not brag about an animal given to him for burying a
man.

NDIWA V: Labu is to be given a heifer for crying for this brother.
And Nablesa is to be given one for burying the father, and these
should come from the tokapsoy.

STEPHANO: If this had been in Sipi, everything would have been decided by now—just divide the plantain field, and that is all.

The men were getting tired. Decision making had gone on for
a long time, and stretched ahead of them indefinitely. The last
remark expressed this sentiment by drawing attention to the
absence of cattle in the farming area of Sebei. What followed was
an exchange of remarks about attitudes of the mountain people.
The asperity that perhaps comes naturally for people of different
cultural orientations, however slight, was sharpened by the current situation in Sebei. The neighboring Karamojong and Pokot
peoples were engaging in much cattle raiding across the border,
stealing from herds and sometimes massacring households of
people. A few months before this session the situation became so
bad that many people literally left everything they had, except
their stock and what they could carry on their backs, and moved

up on the mountain for protection. Most of those who left were
not Sebei, and all the Sebei had by now come back to live on
the plains. There remained, however, a not unrealistic sense of
impending danger, which created anxiety. At the same time, the
mountain people not only failed to offer any assistance to the
plains people but they also ridiculed the Sebei living on the
plains, treating them as being foolish for living in these danger-
ous conditions. That was the significance of Salimu's ironic remark that followed shortly.

FAGIO: These Mbai people! Somebody in Masop[12] died, and the sons
   of the deceased went out to plow their field; and when they were
   asked to bury their father, they said, "Wait until we are finished
   plowing." When they came back they buried their father and
   then went off to find beer, leaving only the eldest son.
———: People there behave just like hyenas.
SALIMU: People from Masop live in peace. They say, "Subay" [the
   standard male greeting], and ask, "How are your cows, and how
   are your enemies?"
ERYEZA: I went to a beer party in Masop, and there was a man of
   Kamichake clan who tried to send me away. Somebody defended
   me, saying that these people from the plains have been fighting
   our enemies and therefore I should have my chance at beer; but
   the Kamichake man said, "Who asked them to go looking for
   these enemies?" [All with much laughter.]
SALIMU [returning to business]: Andyema has been asking about
   some cows from the family of Chepkware. I should like to explain. Our father gave me one heifer and one bull and the same
   to Andyema. Unfortunately, both Andyema's heifer and my heifer died. I sold my bull and bought two heifers, which are now in
   my kraal. The rest of the cows that have not been mentioned will
   be divided with my brother, with no argument at all.

The discussion that followed had to do with a particular
family of cattle that had been given by Kambuya to the mother
of Salimu and Andyema. The genealogy of this line is repro-

---

[12] Mbai is the subtribal area that is the center of plantain cultivation,
where cattle are scarce. *Masop* is a term for "uphill"—by extension, the
people living above on the mountain. There are real and significant atti-
tudinal and value differences between these areas, however much the
people are intermarried and despite the fact that the plains had been settled
over the preceding fifty years by people from the mountain.

duced in Appendix E (chart 2). It will be seen from this chart
that a number of animals were divided by Kambuya between
Salimu and Andyema, but that the animals descended from two
heifers obtained in exchange for the remaining bull still belonged to the estate. After Salimu had given me the genealogy,
he said: "I told Andyema that our father gave each of us some
animals from Chepkware, but these that are left were bought
by my father. My father exchanged a bull for two heifers; so you
follow one heifer, and I will follow the other. That was agreed."
As we shall see in the following discussion, the matter was not
so easily resolved. Andyema became very angry over this discussion. He obviously questioned Salimu's right to any of the animals, though there was testimony from Fagio that Kambuya had
said three animals were to be given to Salimu.

The two lines were identified as "those in Sabila's kraal"
(descendants of Mokondo), and those in Kambuya's. As it happened, the two lines were very much alike in size and quality:
those with Sabila included five cows and seven calves, though
some of these must have been partly grown; those with Kambuya included three cows, seven calves, and one of the largest
bulls in the herd. When I asked Salimu which was preferable, he
said: "They are all the same, but the animals at Sabila's are more
mixed. I wasn't eager to take the cows in Sabila's kraal, and told
Andyema it was up to him; so he said he would take them."

This, however, takes us ahead of the story, for the decision
was not made at the kokwet. Not only did Andyema show anger
because Salimu was taking any of these animals; he appeared at
a disadvantage, as he did not control the relative merits of the
two groups of stock.

ANDYEMA: I mention this because there are some cows in Sabila's
   kraal which my father asked me to go and get. I went and got a
   bull, and my father said it would be mine. I would like to mention that, as my brother might claim that one.
SALIMU: This bull was taken to the auction, and we were offered 300
   shillings for it; but that was too little, and we brought it back.
   Since Andyema speaks about this, there are still some of this family at Sabila's kraal—he can take those at Sabila's, and I shall take
   those that are here.

NDIWA: Remember that our father said three cows should be given
to Salimu because the original ones all died. I am sorry, but I did
not ask the color. I think Fagio also understood this.

FAGIO: What Ndiwa said is true. The old man said that Salimu's
cows all died, and so he promised to give him some more. He
asked me to get Eryeza to come and write it down. He said three
cows must be given to Salimu. One of these three was killed as
kintet, and Andyema should not complain that Salimu has been
chased away. He should be given these three.[13]

SALIMU: One day when our kraal was raided by the Karamojong
many people answered the alarm, and they were fortunate to get
the cows back. So my father asked me for a bull to kill for these
people, and I gave it to him. He gave me the heifer that is in my
kraal. He said there was another bull in Sabila's kraal and asked
me to get it. At Sabila's kraal there were three more cows. One
became barren and was sold, and some of the money from that
cow is here [indicating the money at his feet]. The remaining
cows multiplied, but one calf died and there are now three.
Among the three was one nice big bullock, and my father asked
me to bring it to my herd to serve my cows. One of the heifers is
kamanaktay in Sabila's kraal. Sabila tried to make his own clan
marks on its ears, and I have been wondering why. Sabila was
given this cow only to get milk, as he was a friend of my father.
The old man ordered one of the bulls in Sabila's kraal to be sold,
and I took it to the market and got money, but the original cow
was exchanged for goats from my mother's house—and that cow
was called Tolyet.

ANDYEMA: What my brothers have said about giving Salimu three
cows—I also heard that from him. My brother Salimu has been
saying that I can take the cows from Sabila and that he will take
his from the herd. I am surprised about that.

SALIMU: I want to explain this clearly to you, my brother. The cows
that have been kamanaktay to Sabila were produced there, and I
have been describing them.

ERYEZA: Before Kambuya died he had borrowed a kanzu worth 10
shillings, which he has not paid.

SALIMU: You bought that for him, and we are not going to pay you
anything.

ERYEZA: All right—no matter. I will buy that for him.

[13] We recall that each son in turn was given his cattle, and had no
further claim on the tokapsoy. Both Salimu and Ndiwa had been given
their animals; Andyema had not. This is the central issue of the major
conflict that followed.

LABU: What happened to the money?

ANDYEMA: Sit down. We have not come to that yet. We want to settle which cows to give to Salimu.

STEPHANO: The cattle at Sabila's—they are known, and there is no argument.

SALIMU: It is not a difficult thing. If there are ten head here, but three outside, let me go and fight and get them back and they will be mine.

NDIWA: It was I who took the old man to my house, but he did not indicate the color of the cows to be given to Salimu. I thought Andyema knew that. But now Salimu says that there are more than ten for his younger brother.

FAGIO: Yes. It is a good thing that I know each of these cows. If Andyema wants to create difficulties, let Salimu here be kind enough to leave him that. If you think that Salimu takes too many cows, you should mention that right here.

LABU: How many are with Sabila?

FAGIO: Three.

ANDYEMA: If you think the cattle at Sabila's are more than ten, let us know. If there are three, then it is all right; Kambuya said that Salimu was to have three.

FAGIO: You old men, when Kambuya was sick he spoke like a man who was still quite well—very loudly. Nobody could expect that he was so sick he would die. Everybody in the house could hear him when he spoke. Even when Salimu went to look for treatment, he didn't think his father was sick. The day before he died, he sent me for paper; I went to Ndiwa's, and he asked about the old man, and I said he was sick and asked me to bring a paper. We met at the market. When Ndiwa came back from the market, he talked to the old man, who said that Salimu should be given three cows.

NDIWA V: There is one bull at Salimu's kraal which you should sell and share the money.

SALIMU: That bull was given me to serve my cows. There were two heifers from one cow, one of which is here and one is at Sabila's. The one here has five calves already, and the other one has only three. One of the bulls from the heifer that came here was very big, and was exchanged for two heifers; one of these has produced, and they are now nine in all. Why doesn't my brother think about this and not object?

ANDYEMA: What I mean to say is that Salimu has been given his cows and is gone, and that our father is kind enough to give him more cows. Do you mean to say that when our father is dead we divide out the cows as if none of us were married?

NDIWA: When the old man said three cattle, did he mean bulls or heifers? There aren't three animals at Sabila's—there are five. [I failed to get Salimu's response.]

—— [addressing Andyema]: When you got married, didn't your father give you cows of your own?

ANDYEMA: No. He gave me some for milking, but he did not give me any so that I could sell them.

NDIWA: He did the same with me. He was a very difficult man.

NDIWA V: When he said to give him three cows, you couldn't tell whether he meant to give him cows that each had calves.[14]

NDIWA: Andyema, you were misbehaving when our father was alive. You don't know about these debts. Salimu and I have been with my father; if you had talked to him and listened, you would be the one to know these things.

TESO: I am also the old man's son. When I came here I talked to him very much, and I know very much about the herd. You must know that Salimu is now your father. Andyema, I think that the way you attack your brother is stupid. I know your feelings; I know you think that Kambuya used to like Salimu very much. When I came here one day, I found that Andyema's wife was milking only two cows although there were many in the kraal, and I asked the old man why. He said: "This boy is cheeky, and misbehaves. I am just watching him. If he is short of milk, I can give him one more cow to milk." I asked him about Salimu, and he said, "Salimu respects me, but Andyema does not, and if he were not my real son from my own stomach I would send him away." So I wonder whether Andyema will prove right in his claim or not. Kambuya went on to say: "Salimu collects the debts, and this boy does nothing. If there is a law case, it is Salimu who takes it, and Andyema is only a witness." He said to me: "If I die, the only person who knows my cows, inside the kraal and outside, is Salimu. It is up to these boys to look to Salimu as their head, and Salimu should divide these cows." That is what I heard from Kambuya.

LABU: I have asked Ndiwa to describe the cows, but he has failed.

MWANGA: You have taken a long time to discuss this many.

STEPHANO: I am following the instructions given by the old man. He said—and meant—that Salimu should be given three cows, and that must be obeyed; it does not matter whether the cows have calves or not.

TESO [overriding]: What do you feel, Andyema? Do you think that

[14] This was partly our problem as well. A suckling calf is usually not counted as it is still likely to die; it goes with its dam.

if Salimu takes these cows he will never help you? Do you think
that if you want to take a second wife you cannot go to Salimu
for help?

ANDYEMA [petulantly]: No.

TESO: Are you jealous that Salimu is taking these three cows?

ANDYEMA [with mounting anger]: No, I am not.

SALIMU: Do you know that the cows at Sabila's are from a cow from
my own kraal?

NDIWA V: Salimu should take all the cows in Sabila's kraal. Also, he
has power over the cows here. Who is going to inherit from the
old man?

TESO: Everybody must look to Salimu.

SALIMU: I know that Andyema is going to sell all these cows. He
must never sell any; they must remain as when our father was
alive.

ANDYEMA [indignantly]: Do you mean that I am a cattle trader?

LABU: If you want to sell any cattle, don't do so without first con-
sulting Salimu. If you need clothes or want to marry again, you
must go to him.

During this discussion about the cows Salimu had in his own
kraal, the descendants of those given him by his father, and the
cows in Sabila's kraal, feelings and tensions rose. It would seem
that Salimu was engaging in some elaborate maneuver for his
own advantage, but he might in fact have had justice on his
side—clearly, he had the elders. Andyema grew increasingly
angry, and soon walked away from the group and went to his
house. He shortly returned, however, and sat at a distance of
perhaps 20 or 30 feet from the group, on the supports of a
granary. He tried to keep out of the discussion, but from time
to time he did enter into it. As we shall see, he ended by making
an elaborate accusation in a long harangue.

At this point, I shall stop to describe Andyema. He was overwhelmingly a younger brother in a household where the eldest
son was clearly the favorite. His efforts to assert himself had
always and repeatedly been thwarted by the manipulations of
his much cleverer brother, who always had control of the situation and the disputes that arose, just as he had in these hearings.
Further, Salimu's knowledge and his position combined to make
him the favorite of all the members of the council, thus putting

Andyema at even more of a disadvantage. As will emerge shortly, this interrelationship had a long history, and must have been the dominant motif in the formulation of Andyema's personality. Defeated in every situation, he endeavored to withdraw from conflict; but his passions could not always be contained, and he was given to outbursts of hostility and rage. His self-confidence was shattered by his relations with his older brothers. His handling of cattle seemed to have been faulty, though for this insight we are chiefly indebted to the statements of Salimu, whose testimony cannot be taken at face value. Andyema was an appealing, but weak, character.

SALIMU: All right. Let us forget that. We have mentioned the cows from our sisters and our aunts. Now about the tokapsoy belonging to my father—I want you to mention which is which.

NDIWA: I know that our father used to keep the cattle as his own, but I don't know them; perhaps Andyema knows them—but he has left us.

SALIMU: There were three cows that belonged to old ——: Kopsongora and two others.[15] Another bull, a very big one, belonged to my father; he exchanged it for three heifers, but one of them died. One of these produced, and those are now in the kraal. Kubrorwa produced a bull, which I killed. Arapsiya has one that is kamanaktay, and one of them is with me. There is a cow that was paid [namanya] to Araplewendi for a debt; it produced two bulls, and I brought it back and exchanged it for a heifer that is now here. Also here are a bull and a heifer. Another cow named Matrigut has two calves: Amerire and Merisyek. The second was given as namanya to Katage and then returned, and Father sold it and bought a heifer that produced a heifer and a bullock. Aloni asked for that bullock and hasn't paid for it. The heifer is in this kraal. The other is kamanaktay in ——'s kraal.

NDIWA: This is a new thing to me. I didn't know it.

SALIMU: Another cow, Kapsorigoria, produced a bull which I exchanged for a cow called Tolelyo, which produced three bullocks. One was exchanged for a spear. One bullock was given to Labu when his wife died. I have the third one, and Arapburich came and asked for it, as he had *chemerik*.[16] He has not yet paid

---

[15] Salimu was running rapidly through a group of his father's tokapsoy in the following two speeches.

[16] *Chemerik* are initiates. The animal was slaughtered for the feast at circumcision.

that cow back. The other cow was sick, and I sold it at the market for 30 shillings. I bought another heifer, which I paid on a debt; this one produced a heifer to release herself. I brought the mother back, and she produced another heifer. The original one died, leaving a heifer, who again produced a heifer; that one is in this kraal, and has a bull called Tolelyo. Another, called Aribui, is in this kraal here. [Salimu stands and thinks for a moment.] That is all the tokapsoy of my father.

MASAI: Those are the ones that belong to none of you?

SALIMU: Yes.

MASAI: Can you point them out if we go to the kraal?

SALIMU: Yes, I can do that.

TESO: Salimu has a very good memory. He can remember all the cows here and outside.[17]

MWANGA: Gentlemen, you have heard what Salimu has said—we did not ask for this information.

STEPHANO: Now the picture is clear. It is now up to Salimu to mention that such-and-such cow is given to each one. After that, those remaining here are kept as tokapsoy. If you don't mention this today, Salimu, it will be difficult for you later on.

SALIMU: There is another bull that——took to give to his oyik. He sold it for 360 shillings. There is a balance of 160 shillings; the old man received the rest. Amisi Mwanga has a bull he has never paid for.

KAMBUYA'S SISTER: Another ram was taken by Kambuya's daughter when her child was sick, and that has not been paid.

ANDYEMA [having returned, and sulking in the shade of a granary]: No, Kambuya gave that ram for nothing to treat his grandchild.

SISTER: It must be paid.

NDIWA V: Let us start dividing the cows that are from Kambuya's sisters and daughters.

TESO: One day these people [?] asked for three cows, and the old man said they belonged to my sisters and daughters. One cow from Sabila was taken by Ndiwa, and that is all right. Ndiwa claimed he took only one.

SALIMU: I told you that one was given to Chemisto and one to Andyema. We received a bull instead of goats or sheep, and that was exchanged for a heifer, which is here now.

STEPHANO: You say you exchanged this for a heifer and it is here— what about those small boys?

NDIWA: I don't understand what you are saying.

[17] By "outside," Teso meant those in other kraals, either as kamanaktay or owing in a namanya exchange.

STEPHANO: Salimu has said that one of the cows was given to Chemisto and one to Andyema and another to Ndiwa.

ANDYEMA: One of the cows is in this kraal, and it is Mangusyo's.

SALIMU: That's very good.

————: Maget and Mangusyo are brothers, and must share.

SALIMU: There are two animals paid in bride-price by Teso—a bull
and a heifer. Consider these, please, knowing that one is a bull.

ARAP B: Has Andyema received one?

SALIMU: No. He received one from our sisters, but this is from our
father's sister.

NDIWA V: It is difficult to divide. There must be three to share.

TESO: I give the bull to Salimu as though his father were alive; he
should sell it and get money and buy two calves and give one to
Andyema and the other to Chemisto.

SALIMU: There was a big bull that I exchanged for two heifers, and
one of these produced a bull, which was requested for exchange;
also, I have here a heifer that is not namanya; so there are now
three heifers.

NDIWA V: No, there are now only two. Even if Salimu has taken that
bull, these two heifers must be shared equally.

SALIMU: Andyema has sold one. May we know which cow you took?

ANDYEMA [rudely]: I think you do know.

SALIMU: It is up to you to know—you took the cow.

NDIWA: Be frank enough to tell us which you took.

SALIMU: From this aunt there is another cow, from which there are
four heifers and a bull. Ndiwa is to receive nothing, as he already
had one. A cow with its heifer goes to Andyema, another cow and
heifer to Mangusyo, and I take one. [There is general agreement
to this.] What do you think, my brothers?

FAGIO: I think Ndiwa is surprised at what Salimu told, because he
doesn't know these cows. But I want to say frankly that my
brother [Andyema] is sick about this and isn't satisfied.

NDIWA: I want to say that I am very happy about the way my brother
has been acting today. Andyema [turning to the brother still
sulking in the shade of a granary], if you feel you should get
some cows, you should speak out about it.

STEPHANO: Perhaps from among the cows that are being given out
there is one family that you prefer, and if so it can be given to
you. We are surprised at how you have been answering when
cows have been given to you.

KAPTYETELIN [a Sipi man, recapitulating how the division has been
made]: One heifer to Mangusyo, and one heifer to Maget, and
one bull kept by Salimu; and when it is big enough he must buy
three heifers, after which they should be shared by the three of

them. There are only three heifers that have not been divided. I
say that you, standing in the place of Kambuya, must retain the
cows and, when they produce calves, give one to Andyema and
one to Ndiwa—you retain the mother.

TESO: No, no. Andyema took a cow belonging to the first and cannot
be given one again. But Salimu must keep the cow and divide the
calves among brothers. Don't forget that you are four—Ndiwa,
Andyema, Mangusyo, and Salimu.

SALIMU: All right. I will keep the cows, as they are difficult to divide.
There is one more—another cow received from ———. There were
three, and Ndiwa and Andyema each took one. There is one left,
which I will keep and divide with Mangusyo.[18]

STEPHANO: What about these other cows? Andyema says some have
been given him but has not said which. Salimu has been dividing fairly, and most of the cows have gone to Andyema. The
trouble with Salimu is that when he is trying to divide the cows,
Andyema says he has received his; Salimu is stuck by that. He
doesn't know which have been given to him. Let the kokwet divide it to him [i.e., make the determination], since he has kept
quiet.

——— [to one of Kambuya's sisters]: How many calves does Aruso
[one of the cows] have?

AUNT: I don't know.

STEPHANO [teasing]: Why should we smear your cows with mud?[19]

NDIWA: There is one cow given to me—one died, and the other was
about to die but has recovered. When it was given to me, the husband [who paid the bride-price] saw that it might not survive,
but now I am happy.

SALIMU: If my brother doesn't mention the cow to be given to him, I
am not going to divide them. I must investigate further; there
may be more cows that they are trying to hide.

FAGIO: Perhaps Andyema is not satisfied because the cows are small
ones. He is the one who has been herding the cows, and he is the
one who can hide them. And when he receives some cows, he
should be happy.

[18] We must remember here that Mangusyo was still a minor and that it
was quite proper for the brother to hold the animals in trust for his minor
brothers, to be available when he was old enough to be independent. But
it should have been Andyema; we see Salimu sliding into the role of
guardian of the herd as well as of the boy.

[19] I do not know why the aunt refused to respond to his question; she
must certainly have known the answer. Stephano was being ironic—why
should cows be given a woman if she does not even know how many
calves it has?

KAPTYEPTELIN: Don't wait—divide right now, and make your investigation later. After you stop to investigate, who is going to help you [reach a decision]? There will be quarrels among yourselves.

The conflict that had characterized the kokwet throughout the day was now fully developed. Matters had nearly reached an impasse because of Andyema's truculence. Though he should have known the animals, he had refused to give adequate evidence. Salimu, who had always been in control of the situation, apparently established his authority when he rattled off the tokapsoy in a series of speeches (see pp. 130–133), notably at the time Andyema had absented himself, giving information that even Ndiwa did not know. The kokwet insisted on fulfilling its obligation, knowing the difficulty that a failure would bring.

STEPHANO: If there are quarrels, we are the people to be called upon to give evidence.

SALIMU: There is another cow with a small heifer that is tokapsoy.

KAPTYEPTELIN: We want you to divide the cows from the sisters and daughters, then go on to divide the tokapsoy, and then mention the color of the cows[20] to be given your relatives.

STEPHANO: What do you think? Shall we leave these undivided?
[A general response to divide now was made.]

FAGIO: These are already divided. We are stuck only because one was given to Andyema and because Salimu did not know which one it was.

SALIMU: All five are living, except the bull.

OLD MAN: Ndiwa complained about what you have divided. Some have already taken theirs.

NDIWA: No, those are different.

STEPHANO: Andyema, if you keep quiet without telling this kokwet, it will never be able to reach a decision.

ANDYEMA: I tell you, when I got married, one of the cows was smeared for my wife.

SALIMU: I know that one. It was given to me previously, but Father exchanged it for another one. What he says is quite true—it was given to him.

TESO: All right. He has been given a cow from this aunt, and so he is now finished.

ARAPBURICH: How many other people are there who have not received their share?

[20] Names of cattle usually refer to colors or to color combinations; this is a figure of speech.

ANDYEMA: That cow produced a bull, and that bull died.

NDIWA V: The original cow died, and he has remained without anything from this bride-price. If you divide the cow and one remains, he should be considered.

FAGIO: Salimu did this thoroughly well.

SALIMU: If he lost his first chance, let him take three of the cows. One is to be given to Mangusyo, and one is to be given to Noibei, the son of my father's brother. When he comes, let him take that cow. I will keep one.

NDIWA: I am still not satisfied with the division of the cows of our aunts. The cows paid by Kobolomon—what happened to them?

SALIMU: One is for our younger brothers.

ARAPBURICH: There were two cows, one of which is for the younger brothers, and there is still one more.

SALIMU: All right. Ndiwa takes one and one of the two that are yet to be paid; one goes to Andyema, and the other to the younger brothers; I will take the bull that was exchanged for goats. No [correcting himself], not that bull, but the white heifer. [He goes on to tell the color of the cows that each is to take.] There is only one bull remaining. I will keep that and sell it for heifers and decide how to divide it among my brothers.

ANDYEMA: Have you been giving cows to three of us?

SALIMU: Ndiwa has one, and you have also been given one heifer.

ANDYEMA: What about the bull that was exchanged for goats?

SALIMU: As I just said, I am going to keep that one.

NDIWA: What cow is being given to me?

SALIMU: One from Kobolomon.

NDIWA: I am satisfied.

SALIMU: No, that is not divided equally. Remember, there are one heifer and one bull, and we are four. The heifer is shared between Andyema and Mangusyo, and the bull is shared between me and Ndiwa.

NDIWA: Fair enough. You have divided the cows of three aunts; what about the fourth one?

SALIMU: What do you mean? Nothing was paid for that sister of Kambuya. There are a heifer and two bulls; Ndiwa is to be given a bull, Andyema is to be given the heifer with its calf, and I will be given the other bull.

OLD MAN: You must be happy, Andyema. Don't be gloomy like that.

SALIMU: Now let us divide the cows among the relatives [that is, determine which cow is to be given which of various persons who took certain official roles in the burial of Kambuya]. Andyema, you are given one bull.

ANDYEMA: Do you mean that very small one?

SALIMU: You cannot object—you must agree to whatever is given to you. One cow named Somu is given to Nablesa.

STEPHANO: No, you cannot give that color—it is bad.

FAGIO: Don't just agree with what Salimu says. If it is wrong, disagree with him.

TESO: Find a cow of the right color. Because if you give the wrong cow and other people hear about it, we will be insulted by people who say that we are stupid and that we don't know right from wrong.

SALIMU: We have to find two heifers to offer, one of which must be a brown one—one for Nablesa and one for Labu. [He pauses, thinking.] Let us postpone this until the cows return in the evening, and we will see which one.

OLD MAN: You people must take your cows to your own kraals right away.

MASAI: The cows have been given for this young woman [Kambuya's sister's daughter—the woman Salimu has been caring for], but the sticks have not yet been broken.[21]

SALIMU: Andyema, could you tell us if a young heifer which came from ——— has had a calf?

ANDYEMA: Yes, and it has just stopped sucking.

NDIWA V: That is fine. If it has stopped sucking, it can be given to one of the relatives.

FAGIO: Ndiwa, get your clerk to record the cows given to you by Salimu.

SALIMU: I think you are now playing. I think that because we are going to stay here, we should go back into the kraal with my brothers, and I will have to point out each of the cows given to my brothers.

At this time, there was some break in the discussions. Salimu came over to me and in answer to my queries said: "The three cows I mentioned just now are concerned particularly with the burial of the old man. Nablesa is the son of my father's brother, and Labu is the brother of Kambuya. Andyema is my younger brother. Now Labu is given a heifer because he speared the kintet that was slaughtered after Kambuya died. Nablesa is the

---

[21] "Breaking the sticks" is the phrase used for the bargaining session in which the bride-price is determined, in reference to the tallies used in the bargaining. Apparently, plains Sebei sometimes now give cattle and subsequently complete the arrangements. There was further discussion of this matter, but I was unable to record it.

one who buried the old man, and Andyema is entitled to a cow because he supported Labu by catching the cow when he speared it."

SALIMU: I should like to raise the matter of personal quarrels. Last night 1 said we had previously been enemies and had never shared a beer pot, but yesterday we did so. I should like my brothers to tell why we did not previously drink beer together and now we can share the pot.

SIPI: Ndiwa and Adyema, you have heard what Salimu said. Did Salimu hide any cows and fail to give you your share?

NDIWA: I once brewed beer here for my Pokot father-in-law. I invited Salimu. Kobolomon came and asked our father for a bull, and he came here and asked Salimu which bull it should be. I went home and gave beer to my father-in-law, expecting Salimu to join us. When Kobolomon came, he said Salimu went to another man who was also having beer. The two wives of Salimu came and joined us. When evening came, I asked those wives to return home. But one of his wives came back, and the *mutala* chief told her to go home as Salimu was not here; but she tried to insult the mutala chief. I also said she should go away. Salimu's daughter was asked to milk the cows, but Salimu's wife stopped her from doing so. That woman did not go home; she stayed the night with us. I killed a goat for my visitor and gave the thigh to my father-in-law [Masai Arapchungeywa], and he gave it to Salimu's wife and left to go to his house. Later I heard Salimu say that I was trying to have intercourse with his wife, and he became very much annoyed with me. There was beer at Salimu's house one day. Andyema and I were invited, but when we got there a big case was taken against us. Kobolomon gave evidence that the woman tried to go home. Salimu was very annoyed, and he cursed us and said that we should not live until we are old enough to have children who are circumcised. Even so, the old man asked us to be quiet and enjoy the beer. We never had any quarrel before. Salimu hasn't kept any cows hidden from us—this is the only trouble we have had. We have never had trouble over cows. From that time on, we never shared a beer pot together.

Several people asked for Salimu's point of view.

SALIMU: What he said is correct, but he has just started from the middle. There was a case I took against a man named Masai Arapchungeywa, Ndiwa's father-in-law. That man called my father as a witness, and I was happy because I was also going to ask

him to be *my* witness. In court my father gave evidence in my favor, saying Masai was wrong to live on my land, and that was the
end of that case. But later, Masai reopened the case and asked
Ndiwa to be his witness, and he gave evidence that that land was
mere bush and had been "captured" [taken up] by Masai in
1937. I gave my defense, saying I had come to this land in 1919.
[There was some joking about how he could remember so long
and whether he was born then. He would have been only about
five years old.] Ndiwa and I were asked by the court to show the
boundary markers, but we said that we could not. This case went
to the higher court, and was decided in my favor. After we broke
the case, we heard the news that Masai had said to Ndiwa that
he should invite his father and Salimu to beer, that he should
kill a hen for them and feed them both from one plate, after
which he should take the bones with which to bewitch them.
When my father heard this, he said, "Don't go to Ndiwa's house
—he is trying to kill us." That was the first thing. In 1960, I went
to the cattle market and sold cows and came back the following
day to the home of Salimu Kaptyemei, where we went to enjoy
his beer. We drank there through the night, and the next morning had another pot. Kobolomon came, and said that he had requested a bull from my father and asked that I come and talk to
my father. We came here and talked it over and gave him a bull.
Toboto came here, and said he had a bull at his house close by;
I went there and stayed until eleven o'clock in the evening. Then
I went home and found Chemisto and his friends dancing—they
were about to be circumcised. I asked for food, and was told
there was none because my wife was away enjoying her beer. I
was annoyed, and feared that I would seriously hurt her if I
waited for her; so I went to my next house [another wife]. The
following day I went home in the morning. When she returned,
—— met her and warned her that she would be beaten to death.
She met her son and said to him that she was going away; she
went, and never came back. Later I heard that my wife was going
to return, but that Ndiwa had stopped her on the way and kept
her in his house all night. Another point—there was beer at my
neighbor's house. Ndiwa and my wife slept together on one bed.
Even my father's sister there complained about this when she
saw it happening. And from that time, I said that I think that
man is really a sorcerer.

The transition may seem abrupt, but it is not. A man who sleeps
with his brother's wife is considered to be bewitching him, for
he wants to inherit that woman.

NDIWA: I never stopped my brother's wife from going home. I should have sent her away, but I was afraid to do so because then he would say that I was hating his family.

SALIMU: You are my young brother. I respect[22] your wives very much. I never stop them at all.

MWANGA: If this is the behavior you have been having, it is a bad thing. You are cursing each other if you sleep with your brother's wife. If you want a wife, go to your brother and ask for a cow and get a second wife. You boys are stupid—you should know that all fruits taste the same. [Laughter.]

SALIMU: Not long ago our father brewed beer. My father's wife had asked for beer to be taken in a calabash, and she took it to Ndiwa's wife, who had just delivered a child. Then Ndiwa and Fagio came back and said, "Here is Salimu, who has followed your wife." I became annoyed, and our father was also annoyed. I said to him that I had been here all the time and never went away at all. The next day they repeated the same thing, and so I got very annoyed and urinated in a gourd and asked my father to do the same, and he did so. My father cursed me so that all my children, except Chemisto, should die. Fortunately, the mutala chief investigated and found that they were telling lies. Fagio was forced to bring water all day long, and Ndiwa was made to give a sheep. Further, these boys were enjoying my father's young wife until she died. And I am still complaining that it is you [presumably Ndiwa] who killed my father—you planned to do magic on him, you had intercourse with his wife, and, finally, you took him to your house, where he died. At the time he was sick, you never supported him; and it was I who had to get the bull.

NDIWA: If you say it was I who killed him, let us go over there to the grave and jump over it. [There was no response to this threat of oathing.]

SALIMU: When I was sick and went away for treatment, you and your brother were saying that I was looking for magic to kill you. I was sick—look, here are my medical chits from the hospitals at Amudat and Kacheliba. [Takes chits out of his pocket and flings them on the ground.] Get your clerk to read these to you.

There followed statements by Mwanga and Labu which I did not get.

FAGIO: The last time Salimu came here he talked to the old man be-

---

[22] The same word is used for both "respect" and "fear"; a man should be circumspect in front of his brother's wife.

fore he went away. He went with his friend, and when we tried
to find out where he went we learned that they had gone to look
for gold and that Salimu had 700 shillings to buy the gold. Salimu's friend is trying to deceive Salimu and consume all his
money. Nobody said you were looking for magic to kill people—
just for the gold. When Kambuya died we sent people to look
for you, and we got many false rumors about where you were.

NDIWA: Neither I nor my brothers have ever said that you had gone
to look for magic to use against us. A man named Kamuza came
and found us drinking beer. Kambuya said to us that Salimu's
friend had asked him, "Who is the best man for magic in the
country of the Pokot?" mentioning the names of two different
persons. Kambuya said he had heard this from Simba. When we
heard that we were surprised.

MASAI: I heard about the magic from ———'s wife. She warned that
Salimu had said on his way back that people who hadn't been
friends of Salimu had better be careful. I was surprised that Salimu could say such a thing. If I were going to bewitch you, I
could have done that a long time ago if I had known how. When
I heard you mention witchcraft, I became very much annoyed.
So many things have been said here. We have done *mumek*[23]
many times. The cow was killed here, and we did mumek. All
this is mere lies.

FAGIO: Salimu, you have blamed your brother for killing your father.
I don't think you are right. Do you think that you went to get
magic to kill Ndiwa, and that as a result he did it? You are not
right.

It should be clear from the nature of the discussion that the
air was charged with emotion and that the speeches were rapidly
spoken in anger with much overriding. Chemtai had great difficulty in interpreting and I in recording at this most crucial
moment. Unfortunately, several speeches were lost.

SALIMU: I have explained how the hatred started.

CHEMISTO: One day there was beer at Ndiwa's, and we drank until
midnight. Ndiwa ordered me to go to the kraal and get a bull.
He sent one of his wives to show which one should be killed. I
brought it, and it was killed. Then Ndiwa asked his wife, "Who
told you to bring this sorcerer into the kraal?" When I heard this
I went home and ate none of the meat of that animal.

NDIWA: I never said that at all. Of course I sent him to get the bull.
When he went into the kraal he started laughing, and I asked,

23 *Mumek* is a form of oath.

"Why do you behave in this way?" I was amazed that he went and laughed in the kraal.[24]

CHEMISTO: I heard this from Arapburich, who told me the following day.

SALIMU: We drank beer at Kaptyemei's house, and Ndiwa and Andyema began to fight. I told the others that these were my brothers but that I was not going to separate them; I told Chemisto to do so. Later, Andyema blamed me for not stopping his brother from beating him.

ANDYEMA: We are just repeating these things that have already been said. Ndiwa was fighting a sick man, and I was trying to stop him.

At this point, there was much shouting by many people, which could not be recorded.

NDIWA V: These things that Salimu has mentioned happened many months ago, and we thank Salimu for mentioning them. Now Kambuya is dead, and Salimu has become your father. You must respect him and take your troubles to him. Never go out and listen to rumors. Now Kambuya is dead, and so from today you must forget all these things done previously. Throw this away and respect Salimu, and if he does something wrong, bring your matter before the kokwet. You must have respect. Ndiwa and Andyema, if you find your new father does something wrong, bring a case against him before the old men. You must forget your old quarrels.

ELDER: Going back to intercourse with the brother's wife—that is bad, indeed You also have a brother. If you do this with your brother's wife or your neighbor's wife, and your brother or neighbor gets sick, he will die right away because you have had intercourse with his wife. That is very, very bad.

SALIMU: You boys, if you hear complaints that I do anything against your wife, listen to me now. There was beer at Andyema's, and Ndiwa had stolen some cows from the Pokot and was grazing them on the hillside. This Pokot man kept looking at these cows, and Ndiwa sent him away, saying, "You are going to bewitch my cows."

NDIWA: I did that because I had stolen those cows and I didn't want him to recognize them.

LABU [repeating the note of moralization expressed by Ndiwa V]: You haven't heard my brothers complaining that I am having intercourse with their wives. You must stop that.

---

[24] Such laughter is considered evidence of witchcraft activity or intent.

NDIWA V: We have heard what Ndiwa has to complain about; what does Andyema have to say?

ANDYEMA: There are many troubles between me and my brother over many years, but let me forget some of them. In 1953, during the rainy season, we built our house near the foothills. In the following dry season, I went out early one morning to take the cows to the swamp and, after leaving them, I came back for food. When I returned I found that people were bringing the cows back and that Salimu had ordered them to take these cows. I stopped them. Those people called for Salimu, and when he came he called me a mere boy. He said he had given these people that bull and that they should take it. I refused them and tried to drive the cows back. We drove those cows back and forth; after a long time Salimu gave me a blow on the back, and all the people beat me and took my bows and arrows, until finally one of the men came and helped me.

Andyema continued this narrative for some time. Since early in the session when he had been attacked by the old men, he had been sitting on the supports of one of the granaries. Now he had come forth and was presenting his case with rapid, heated, dramatic oratory. It was impossible for me to get what he said— or Salimu's response—partly because of the rapid delivery, partly because I was exhausted from six hours of steady writing. A few days later, however, I asked Andyema to give me the substance of his narrative, which he did in a way that reflected what he had said but was moderated and lacking in the dramatic detail that had obviously characterized the presentation during the kokwet.

Andyema recapitulated:

My first reason for refusing to drink beer with Salimu was as follows. A man named Yunuso brought a heifer straight to Salimu's kraal when I was staying here with my father as herdsman. It happened that one day when I was taking our cows to graze I met two men coming toward me. They said they wanted to take one of the bulls in my herd. I asked who gave the bull to them, and they said that they had made an exchange with Salimu. I told them, "If Salimu exchanged a heifer with you, this is not Salimu's herd but the herd of our father Kambuya," and refused to let them take the bull. I drove them away. Not very long afterward, Salimu came and said that this bull had already been exchanged. I said to him, "I don't know who you are." I said this because it is our father's herd, and it is for him to tell me about the exchange of any bulls. Salimu didn't listen to me but went on driving the bull. I tried to return the animal to the herd, but Salimu just kept trying to chase it. When he saw that he had failed he called those two men, and they beat me very badly; if that man hadn't been nearby, I think I would have been killed. That was the first thing.

Second, Eryeza Sayekwo had brewed beer and engaged us to plow his field. Salimu had gone to Masop. The day he came back he found us still plowing for Eryeza. He went directly to the beer pot and started drinking.[25] I didn't blame him; he is our brother, and we should enjoy the beer together. Not long after, he asked Eryeza to stop us from talking because he had something to say. He had just come back from court, and we thought that he was going to explain the results of the case. He said, "I want to take a case against one of Kambuya's sons, who has neglected my land." Eryeza asked, "Who is that?" But Salimu kept quiet. So we continued drinking until about five in the afternoon, when he repeated the same thing. Again Eryeza asked him to mention the particular son of Kambuya who had neglected the land, but again Salimu remained silent. So at about the time it got dark, he said that he wanted to take a case against me because I had neglected the land. Eryeza told him: "You have been keeping quiet. Do you mean you want to attack this younger brother of yours?" I responded: "Please, what land have I neglected? If you mean about a man named Ngeynda who is living on the land, it was not I but our father who gave him permission. The land on which I live belongs to our father—it is not yours." Salimu said: "I don't know who you are. You are a very little thing to me. I don't think you are worth taking case against. Not even my son Chemisto can take a case against you. I think Chemtai [Salimu's prepubescent daughter] is the one to stand against you in court." When I heard this remark about Chemtai, who is my own daughter [by Sebei kinship terms], I felt much annoyed. This is the second thing Salimu did.

Here is the third thing. Arapsitaki had beer, and we all enjoyed it until late in the evening. Salimu was with his first wife. During the night his wife poured beer on my chest. I tried to ask her, "Sister-in-law, why have you poured this beer on me?" Salimu said, "I don't want you to talk to my wife." Our father said, "I think that you are troubling this young boy for nothing."

Remembering all these things, I felt very much annoyed. I think this man is trying to neglect me, and I don't trust him. I think that I should have my own food and he should have his own food.

With this summary, we can return to the kokwet discussion.

OLD MAN: I say Salimu was wrong to give the boy a blow.

[25] The compensation for the work is the beer provided by the owner; Salimu was taking a share of the beer without having worked.

NDIWA: I want to make this clear. Our father used to despise us young boys, and in everything we had to consult Salimu. We had to consult him about all the arrangements that were made. It is true that he was given authority to exchange that bull. The old man never told Andyema, who was his herdsman. That is why he stopped Salimu, for fear he was stealing that animal.

SALIMU: Yes, Kambuya was right not to consult these young boys. One day Andyema exchanged a bull for a heifer, which was barren. Later I had to exchange that barren cow for a heifer, which has since multiplied. That is why our father despised these young boys.

ANDYEMA: Our father was wrong. I didn't know he had given this bull. He should have sent word to his herdsman.

STEPHANO [to Salimu]: I think you misbehaved. After you saw that your brother had stopped these people, you should have brought your younger brother to your father so that he could be satisfied.

MWANGA: I support Andyema in this; he was right. You should catch and tie him but not beat him like that.

ANDYEMA: That is why I don't want to share the beer pot.

SIPI: I blame Salimu for beating the boy; another mistake is with Kambuya, who didn't tell his herdsman that he had given the bull.

ANDYEMA: How much money did the people give you to beat your own brother?

TESO: Salimu was wrong to beat the child. If you have your wife and she says, "No, don't give this cow," you should listen to what she says. So Andyema was in charge, and he should have been informed.

SIPI: You are now Kambuya, and you are chairman of the kokwet of your brothers. So forget this hatred, speak slowly, be friends with them, and treat them fairly.

SALIMU: Do you think that this rude boy will cool down?

SIPI: If he misbehaves, take a case against him. Your father has left all the cattle in your charge. He took nothing with him to the grave.

It was now about half-past three in the afternoon. There was a brief break in the meeting, and Chemtai and I left.

It was impossible for me to return to Andyema's house for further discussion that same evening or the next two days. I did, however, ask Chemtai to return and make notes on his observations. He went beyond my expectations, and presented me with a running account of some of the discussions.

Chemtai's record represents a somewhat different kind of detailing. I doubt that he could have kept up directly with a running conversation, and I suspect that he, less inhibited than I, might very well have slowed down the speakers to a pace he could record. He might also simply have eliminated what he thought irrelevant. I have no doubt whatsoever of the essential accuracy of his record, though I am sure that much side comment is lost.

Chemtai had returned that afternoon at about half-past five, and found that the men had been discussing the dispute between the brothers ever since we had left two hours earlier.

TESO: When we were discussing yesterday, we forgot about two grandsons of Kambuya—Chemisto and Cheptorus. Each of them should have one heifer.

STEPHANO: What you have said is true; it is very important.

LABU [to Salimu]: Can you do that? [Salimu does not answer.]

NDIWA V: How many grandsons are there?

LABU: Only two.

NDIWA V: Surely they are entitled to cattle; Kambuya has been trusting these two boys very much.

TESO: If Kambuya were still alive and one of these grandsons wished to marry, he could give them cows from his herd for bride-price.

The men went out to the kraal, where some of the animals, which by now had returned from grazing, were pointed out. Labu was given a heifer (Chebororon) "for crying for his brother." Ndiwa was given a black cow and a small bull; these two had been received in bride-price. Salimu was given one bull (Tolelyo) and one heifer (Sirwoi). Andyema was given three heifers (Aruso, Kebendo, and Tuya) and the suckling calf of one of these. Andyema was to share a black heifer (Tuya) with his young brother Mangusyo. Then Noibei was given two heifers (Aruso and Tyeptile). Mangusyo, the younger brother, was given three heifers and a calf (Sangiryeny, Legendo, and Aruso[1]). These are all cattle received as part of the bride-price from aunts and sisters.

SALIMU: Labu's sons, you'd better take your cattle right away; they cannot sleep in this kraal.[2]

TESO [addressing Andyema and Ndiwa]: Salimu has called you here to see the bull that should be killed for visitors.

[One of the tokapsoy bulls is pointed out by Andyema.]

SALIMU: The rest of the tokapsoy will be divided tomorrow. There is another cow, Chelemet, which is to be shared by Andyema and Mangusyo. This is also a bride-price cow. Though you have been given these cattle, you do not have to take them from this kraal. [Ndiwa and Andyema agreed.] I and Ndiwa will have to share the bullock Chemur.

By now darkness had fallen over the kraal, and the people returned to the house. According to Chemtai, "They had ordered too much waragi." There was a great deal of drinking throughout the evening. Chemtai therefore left, reasonably feeling that there was nothing more to be accomplished.

On the next day, Chemtai returned and found that everyone was asleep. Salimu told him that nothing was to be done that day. Further, maize beer was ready, and the people soon began to start drinking. On the preceding evening there had been some dispute over the land case, and it was brought out that none of the brothers would be allowed to sell any of the land. If they did so, Salimu would have the right to take a case against them in court. Andyema was not at all happy about this. He said:

[1] This is the third animal in this group named Aruso. Cattle names are usually descriptive; Aruso means a brown animal.

[2] It is considered bad for the cattle given to persons who officiated at the funeral to remain in the kraal. The animal given Labu was therefore taken away by Mangusyo. This rule does not apply to inherited animals, as indicated below.

"One day I was cultivating some land that Salimu had given his father-in-law; he had given me a very narrow piece of land to cultivate. Even the land I'm growing my crops on now, I got by force; so if you give him much more power, I think he will squeeze us by not giving us enough land." Salimu made no answer to this accusation.

There was also some discussion of the sisters' dowries and the division of the cows obtained from them, particularly two cows taken by Salimu. This matter came up again in the subsequent meeting.

On the next morning, a bull was slaughtered very early, before sunup. The meat was shared as follows: the ribs of one side were roasted for all the people to enjoy immediately; the short ribs and one foreleg were given to the sisters and daughters of Kambuya; the hump, both thighs, and the heart were shared by members of Kambuya's clan; part of a foreleg was given to the chief; the stomach and the intestines were shared among the sisters and daughters of Kambuya and other women of the clan; the remainder was eaten by the general gathering. Afterwards, the men returned to the house and divided the money. Salimu, Andyema, and Mangusyo were each given 150 shillings. Ndiwa was given 100 shillings. Kambuya's sister Kokopchyosye was given 50 shillings, because Kambuya had taken her he-goat and had promised to pay 50 shillings for it; she was also given another 50 shillings to replace what Maget had stolen. Each of Kambuya's two other sisters and each of his two daughters was given 10 shillings. These sisters and daughters complained bitterly that 10 shillings was too little. One of them cried; Andyema, meaning to give her an additional 20 shillings accidentally handed her a 100-shilling note, which he never did get back; Ndiwa also gave her 10 shillings more.

SALIMU: [to Kokopchyosye, Kambuya's sister]: Our aunt, you have now received the 50 shillings that Maget stole from you. Beer should be brewed, and Andyema should be the one to prepare it, so that you can spit on Maget, for surupik had been made.[3] My

[3] Maget, we will recall, who had stolen some of the old man's money, had been cursed through a ceremony of surupik when it was not known who had stolen the money. Salimu was calling for the ritual to remove this curse. Everyone agreed to this.

brothers, you have received all the money I had; none is left
with me. Therefore the money is now cleared. Let us go now
and divide the tokapsoy. [But by this time the cattle have left
the kraal to go out to graze, and the division is postponed until the morrow.]

Chemtai called Salimu outside to ask what was going to
Teso's wife, who was not included in the division of money or
asked what she should be given. Salimu said that Teso's wife was
to be treated differently. She would be given a heifer, because
she had been very kind to Kambuya; also, her bride-price had
been much higher than that of Kambuya's daughters. The rest
of the sisters and daughters did not know that she was to be given
a heifer. Chemtai did not find out whether the heifer was to
come from the cattle in Teso's kraal or from the herd in Kapsirika, or when this would be done. Chemtai was told that the
tokapsoy would be divided among the sons—Salimu, Ndiwa,
Andyema, and Mangusyo—and the two grandsons—Chemisto
and Cheptorus.

At one point in the discussion, Andyema made a complaint.

ANDYEMA: Salimu, if you say there are tokapsoy to be divided in this
    kraal, what about the cows that are in your kraal?
SALIMU: There are no tokapsoy in my kraal; the cattle in my kraal
    belong to Mangusyo; therefore, how can I give you Mangusyo's
    cattle?[4] Tomorrow, I should like one of you to point out any
    tokapsoy that are in my kraal.

This discussion of the division of the animals, only part of
which is here recorded, was between Andyema, Salimu, Ndiwa,
and the four elders, Teso, Mwanga, Labu, and Ndiwa V. The
group, having examined the cattle in the kraal, returned to the
house, where another matter was brought up.

MWANGA: Gentlemen, may I know whether my friendship is finished
    now that Kambuya is dead?
NDIWA V: Please, Mwanga, do not be roundabout—just speak frank-
    ly. I know that you are claiming for a cow for crying.
NDIWA: You have been saying that Mwanga should receive a cow.
NDIWA V [addressing Ndiwa]: Before Salimu was back, you said that
    Mwanga should be given a cow.

---

[4] Andyema should have been Mangusyo's guardian and held his cattle.

NDIWA: No, I did not say that; I said that we should wait till Salimu comes back.

SALIMU: It is very difficult to give this man a cow; if we do so, members of our clan who have been claiming the same and who have received no cow will hear about it, and we shall receive bitter complaints. Therefore I would suggest that Ndiwa and I each give him 50 shillings instead.

NDIWA: That is a very good suggestion.

[They each hand 50 shillings to Chemtai, who gives the money to Mwanga.]

SALIMU: We have now avoided future complaints from our relatives. The 100 shillings is equivalent to one heifer.

TESO: In our district, I could buy two heifers at the market with this money.

MWANGA: I shall try also to get two in my country. I thank these boys. I should like you to come and visit me so that we may know one another, that our sons may also become friends. The time will come when I will die without introducing you to them; you will not know one another, and this friendship will die completely. I have children who are about to be circumcised; you will be invited.

SALIMU: We shall be very much pleased.

Thus Salimu managed to compensate his father's close friend and fellow initiate without arousing the cupidity of Kambuya's many relatives. This was an example of a subtle difference between the use of money and the use of animals; the former could be handled surreptitiously, whereas the latter was a matter of public knowledge—though knowing the Sebei tendency to pass around rumor, I wondered if the difference would prove so clear as Salimu had hoped. At any rate, this closed the matter satisfactorily to all concerned. The whole party then went over to the house of Chemisto, Kambuya's grandson, where beer had been brewed for a work party for building Chemisto's new house.

On the following Monday, September 17, we returned to Andyema's house. This was the time for the actual pointing out of the cattle to be taken by each son, thus culminating and repeating most of what had occurred during the two intervening days. While waiting for the people to gather, I had an opportunity to speak briefly with Salimu about the intervening events. We discussed the matter of the two cousins who were his wards. Salimu told me that he had retained two cows when the second of these two girls was married, because he had received none from the marriage of the first. This had been challenged by Chemonges Labores, the brother of the two girls, and Salimu agreed that he would give one of the two cows from the second sister if Chemonges would give him a cow from the first sister. According to Salimu, the old men agreed with him, but Chemonges firmly refused. Chemonges was told that he might take a case in court. "It is up to him if he wants to take a case, but I doubt that he will."

I asked what had happened about the accusations between the brothers. Salimu said that Andyema and Ndiwa were considered guilty; Salimu was now head of the family, and they must cooperate and respect him. He went on to say that Andyema had stopped him from selling a cow, as his father had asked him to do; as a result, there had been a quarrel and they had fought. Finally, he said, they had all been told to shake hands and become friends again. This account was not exactly in accord with the spirit of the version given me by Andyema when he recapitulated his speech (as already quoted). Teso had also been present at that time, and both he and Andyema said that Salimu had not been asked to do anything; rather, he had been very much blamed for beating his younger brother. Teso said that everyone had been much annoyed that he had done such a thing. "One should not fight with a young boy; one should bring the matter to the father."

ANDYEMA: Salimu said that everything is now forgotten and that we are good friends. He is now our brother. Perhaps he will create new troubles, but for now we are friends.

In view of the acrimony expressed during these sessions, the long-standing antagonism if not downright hatred between the two brothers, and the fact that there were many remaining sources of conflict, we might reasonably wonder whether this "friendship" would last. But it was entirely in accord with Sebei attitudes that surface amity and verbalized sentiments should be taken for the real thing, and that the underlying emotions be suppressed.

While I was talking with Salimu, the mutala chief came up with a businesslike air. The mutala is the lowest-level chief in the hierarchy of Sebei official government. He is an unpaid local representative, often seeing this position as an opportunity for further bureaucratic advancement or for a measure of local prestige and advantage. The mutala chief of Kapsirika was Seperia, who made a big pretense of being busy and asserted an air of importance, which usually fell flat. He was being particularly important this morning. The government was about to inoculate the cattle in this area and had just started to build a "crush," a kind of corral with a narrow runway through which the animals were driven in order to restrain them during the moment of inoculation. Seperia was needed at the building of the crush; therefore, he asserted, he could not wait; the division of the tokapsoy should get on, and there was no use in waiting for Ndiwa—who again was missing. Nothing happened despite Seperia's insistence. I asked Salimu when the goats and sheep would be divided, but he said that this was a minor point and that the sons could divide these animals among themselves. Then the men gathered.

MWANGA: Ndiwa has created all these difficulties. I should have left this morning.

SALIMU: You must be present, or I will not divide the cows.

SEPERIA: I also have been asked to be present.

SALIMU: I have nothing more to say. I shall go and show you the cows.

[Salimu starts walking off to where the cows are waiting. Seperia, Andyema, Mwanga, Teso, a man from Sipi, and a couple of others follow him. Ndiwa V is ill. The cattle are moving around outside the kraal in the area where they are milked and where they rest.]

MWANGA: When Andyema and Ndiwa are together, they try to backbite Salimu.

[Salimu has started pointing out the cows that are tokapsoy, tapping them on the back with his stick. He points out eleven cows and also notes the ones already given to Labu and Andyema for crying.]

MWANGA: Are those all?

SALIMU: There is one at Sitaki's and one at his son's house. There is one at Eryeza's and one at Chesorei, and Ndiwa has taken one. Kamogan has taken one of the bulls, and he paid a heifer na-manya, but that is with Ndiwa.

[Salimu, still looking over the herd, then points out another to-kapsoy in the kraal.]

SIPI: Perhaps the old man kept tokapsoy with Ndiwa.

SALIMU: Yes. I mentioned that he has two.

SEPERIA [summarizing]: There are twelve in the kraal and two out-side and two with Ndiwa.

MWANGA: Yesterday you pointed to another cow—what has happened today?

SALIMU: No, that is the twelfth one I just pointed out. [Ndiwa ar-rives.] There is one more at Eryeza's. [Starts counting them.] There is one at Eryeza's, one at Sitaki's, one at Sitaki's son's, one in my kraal. Eryeza has a second one; Kamogan took a bull, and the heifer is with Ndiwa; another bull given Ndiwa by our fa-ther is part of the tokapsoy.

SEPERIA [to Ndiwa]: Could you confirm what Salimu says?

NDIWA: Yes. There is one in my kraal.

SALIMU: That is enough for you, and the one in my kraal is enough for me. Another cow that has not been paid is at Chesorei's, and one is at Eryeza's. One of these will be taken by Andyema; and one, by the young boy [Mangusyo]. The young boy will take the one from Chesorei's kraal.

NDIWA: You mean there is no heifer we could share?

SALIMU: There is no heifer. The one you should be asking for is the one that got barren. I took the heifer—that is the one I am keep-ing.

TESO: I want to say something about dividing the tokapsoy. If there were many tokapsoy, Andyema should be given the most. If there were many, Ndiwa would take four, and Salimu four, and An-dyema and Mangusyo six—but Andyema should be in charge of those of Mangusyo. If there are few, then it is all right if each takes one.

SIPI: How many cattle have been found in here?

SEPERIA: You have misunderstood how the cattle outside have been divided.

TESO: The cow with Chesorei is to go to Mangusyo; the one with Eryeza is given to Andyema; one is with Ndiwa, and one is with Salimu.

NDIWA: I am not at all satisfied; Andyema is given a heifer, but I am given only a bull.

TESO: Don't complain. If you are given a bull, it is all the same; you can exchange it for a heifer.

SALIMU: The bull given Ndiwa by our father, and the cow given me —let us forget those.

SEPERIA: Therefore, when counting the cows to be divided, forget those.

STEPHANO [reiterating]: When counting the cows to be divided, forget those.

MWANGA: Right! Divide the rest of the cows, and if there is an argument you can point out that you have already been given one and have it in your kraal.

TESO: What are you waiting for? Divide the cattle.

SEPERIA: We have thirteen head. Divide them as you like.

Salimu pointed to a cow and said it was for Ndiwa; he pointed to a second heifer, a small one, for Ndiwa; he pointed to two heifers and one bull for Andyema; he pointed to three heifers for himself. He said, "Ndiwa is to get a cow called Keiro from Sitaki's kraal." He then pointed to three more cows, and Sipi tried to determine whether some of these had calves. Salimu summarized: Ndiwa had received four heifers and a bull; Andyema, two cows, one of which had a suckling calf and a heifer; and Mangusyo, one brown cow and four heifers. He pointed to a bull and said, "I have to take that."

SALIMU: What is next? Have you seen what I have done?

SEPERIA [writing in a copybook]: Andyema, five head; Ndiwa, five; Mangusyo, five; Salimu, five.

SALIMU: It is up to you—you can take your cows to your kraal. Are you satisfied?

NDIWA: Yes, I am happy with what Salimu has done. But what about those outside?

SALIMU: Yes, I shall have to investigate; if there are others outside, I shall have to divide them. Any cow that has been namanya from each kota automatically goes to the person whose house it is. We are concerned only with the tokapsoy. There are some cattle with Teso; we must arrange to visit him so that he can show us how many animals he has. That ends that, but there are debts. We have divided the cattle equally; therefore we must share the debts equally.

NDIWA: We shall pay the debts according to our mothers' houses.

At this point, the calves were taken in one direction, and

there was talk about taking the cows in another; but I noticed that the cows went in the same direction as the calves.

SALIMU: Gentlemen, you know that this young boy here is under my control. His cows are here, and they must be looked after well. I don't want to be blamed in the future when young Mangusyo is grown up. Mutala Chief, if one of his cows is sold, report the man who sold it as a thief.

MWANGA: You are responsible for this young boy's cows. Ask the chief to count the cows and enter them in his notebook.

SALIMU: As you know, there are kamanaktay cows here which must be looked after as our father has done. [At this point, Mwanga advises Andyema to treat the bleeding rectum of a cow.] Yunusu Wandera has a debt that hasn't yet been paid. Aloni had another, and Lazima of Bukwa has one—these are all tokapsoy. I think each of you knows the debts you are to collect. If you fail, it is up to you. There will be another day when we sit together and count out all the debts. I shall ask the mutala chief to be present, and we shall divide them among ourselves. Returning to the debts of our mothers' houses—each of us knows the debts from his house. Andyema is to pay two of our debts, and I am to pay one.

SIPI: Nablesa has been given two heifers—one for dowry, and one for crying. Nablesa has been wasting his father's cows, and remains poor; we are just being kind to him.

SALIMU: There is another cow that father asked Nablesa to go to get; but he didn't want to go, and that cow got lost. That is why we are not in favor of giving him cows at all.

SEPERIA: He was a lazy boy. Had he gone there, that cow would have been here and might have multiplied already. I think he is not interested in keeping cows.

NDIWA: Yes. If Nablesa were interested, he would have already taken those that were given him.

SEPERIA: Anything more? I want to go on duty.

SALIMU: About paying debts—we will arrange that one day.

ERYEZA: The day you write down the debts is the day you will have to count the cows that belong to your little brother.

As the cows were moved out to graze, Salimu followed them, talking to one or two of the old men.

NDIWA: Chemisto should receive a cow with a suckling calf. My son should also receive one, but this has been forgotten.

MWANGA: Yes, we have been delaying. Had you come earlier, we would have done this. I think this should be taken up when we discuss the debts.

SEPERIA: This is very important. The grandsons of Kambuya should receive something.

On this minor note, the kokwet ended. Much had been accomplished. There had been a review of all debts owing and to be paid, with a resolution of most, if not all, of them. The basic division of the cattle had taken place.

Much remained to be done. There were the cattle at Teso's —perhaps as many as twenty—to be divided; then too, there were Teso's possible obligations to be resolved, and Teso's wife, Kambuya's favorite sister, to be rewarded. Apparently, neither of the grandsons had been given a cow, though it was generally agreed that they should have been. Nothing whatsoever had been said about the goats and sheep; although these were, as Salimu said, "a very minor point," they were nevertheless a potential source of dispute. But the most important uncertainty really lay in the distribution of the animals belonging to the kota of Salimu and Andyema. According to Sebei customary law, the cattle remaining in the house belonged to the youngest adult son of that house. The general consensus, supported by Salimu's strength and cleverness and by Andyema's weakness, indicated that this would not be true here. Kambuya's herd had grown from its pioneering beginnings in about 1914, and was viewed by all as a herd that should be kept intact. Apparently, all felt that Andyema would not keep it so but that Salimu would.

Not all the conflicts had been resolved; nor had all the loose ends been tied. One might confidently expect that the quarrels and bickering that had been aired in the course of this extended discussion would continue for years to come.

CHAPTER VIII *A Question of Witchcraft*

Perhaps the spirit of hearings had taken hold in Kambuya's household; perhaps it was the availability of elders; possibly it was mere coincidence. Whatever it was, another hearing took place in the familiar landscape around Andyema's house, involving many of the same participants but an entirely different issue. The issue was witchcraft. The accusation had been made by Tengedyes, the sister of Kambuya who had been brought back into the household when her husband died and no one wanted to inherit her. This situation has already been noted, but Teso gave me a rather full account.

The mother of this girl Sibora and of her sister is Kambuya's sister. She lives in this house. She had been the wife of Labores, who died when these two girls were still young. All Labores' brothers refused to inherit Tengedyes. She had only these two girls still alive—most of her children died. When Labores died she was neglected in an old house, where she lived until it collapsed. This poor old woman went to Chemonges Labores, who was a son of her husband by a different wife, but he refused to take care of her. Mwanga, Labores' brother, refused to inherit her. The time came when the young daughter got sick, and Chemonges was told about her sickness. He came, took her arm, pushed her away, and said, "Let her die!" When Kambuya learned that his sister was suffering, he went there and brought Tengedyes and her daughters to his home and took care of his sister and acted as guardian to her two daughters. When the first girl was old enough to be circumcised, Salimu sold a cow, bought beer, and arranged the circumcision; when she was healed, a man came and arranged a bride-price, after which the debt was paid. After the dowry was paid, Salimu asked Labores' sons to come; he showed them all the cattle from their sister, but asked that one cow be paid to him for caring for the girl. He was given one small bull—the bull that goes to the mother's brother. Salimu demanded that he should be given a heifer in addition to the bull, but he was refused. Salimu said: "All right. The young girl here—let me wait for her." When she was old enough for initiation, Salimu called her relatives and asked them to arrange it, but they said they weren't concerned. So Salimu had to make all the arrangements; three bulls were killed, and I was the one who killed them. The girl healed and she was ready; a man came, and the price was paid. Salimu and Kambuya called the relatives and said, "We want to take two cows"—one for guardianship, and one for kamama. Chemonges took away the cows, leaving only one heifer for her mother and one for her guardian, but nothing for kamama, because one had already been paid from the first girl.[1]

Then when Chemonges heard that Kambuya was dead, he came here and complained bitterly that he wanted to take these cows with him. But the old men of the kokwet said to him that this was quite impossible. He will receive no cows at all.

This situation was further complicated by the fact that the husband had paid cattle to Kambuya but had not formally reached a settlement in a ceremony of breaking the sticks. I do not know whether this reversal of procedure is old custom or not, but this is not a unique instance. It has, however, some bearing on the case.

At any rate, when Sibora, the young wife, came home to visit her mother, who was living with Kambuya at Andyema's compound, she was kept there at the insistence of the old woman. This happened while Salimu was away on his travels. He was annoyed, for reasons that will appear, and held this kokwet. Thus it was that we were back once more, listening to another drama of ordinary Sebei events.

Though obviously this hearing is not a part of the discussions that have already taken place, it is a piece of Kambuya's legacy in the broader sense of that term. Since this is so, since it involves much the same cast of characters, and, above all, since it adds to our understanding of the ongoing cultural events of Sebei, I have chosen to include it here.

We were invited into Andyema's house when we arrived, and

---

[1] This is not accurate. Ndiwa received the kamama, as is customary; successive mother's brothers receive animals from a series of sisters. I do not know about the animal for the mother, but Salimu earlier indicated (p. 55) that he had confiscated one of the animals; he was supported in this by the kokwet.

were served ears of steamed maize. Some of the people of Mokotu, the husband's village, were there; as we ate, there was talk
of many things having nothing to do with the case at hand. Some
of the discussion was relevant to the recent raid by Pokot on
Kilele's kraal and to the efforts that had been made to retrieve
the stolen animals. Seperia had organized a bivouac of all adult
males when rumor of raids became prevalent, and he was proud
of his efforts. He was chiding the people of Mokutu.

SEPERIA: I think you trust this hill [that lies between Mokutu and
  Pokot territory] and will just hide in it.
MOKUTU MAN: That is a good idea.
SEPERIA: You sit idle like women. In the old days there were few
  people, and they answered the alarm over a wide area.
OLD MAN: The warriors used to brag, "I would die before I would
  return without chasing the enemy away; I will never be speared
  in the back." Warriors, when they came back, were fed and had
  beer to drink, and the people would brag about them. Are the
  men who lead away these cows—the cows of Kilele, my pinta-
  mate—are they our people, or are they Pokot? I think they are
  our own people who live near Pokot country. One of the Sebei
  men living there, named ———, has a son who meets with people
  of Pokot. He started to brag that they would steal all the Sebei
  cattle; then the Sebei men shot at him three times, but they
  missed him and he ran away. I think he has got his meat. I think
  Sebei people are conducting the Pokot to our kraals. Consider
  that they passed all those kraals in between and went up the valley. They passed Megawit's kraal and went to Kilele's and swept
  all those cows away, leaving only one bull. Our cattle are stolen,
  and will never be traced.
SALIMU: Isn't Sitake encouraging his young men?
MWOGO: I think it is a good idea for Seperia to hold a meeting of
  our men.
SALIMU: Do you think that the enemies can always stop here and not
  go on to your part of the country?
MWOGO: If these people conquer this village, who is to be our shield?
  What will protect us? When I go to Kiguli [in the mountain
  area], I think that I will be killed like a goat right away. They
  don't call me Mwogo; they just call me Maluli, a child's nick-
  name given me by my mother. They don't respect me one bit;
  they just tease me. That is why I don't like to go there.
SEPERIA: They do the same to me when I go to Cheptui [another part
  of the mountain area].

The conversation drifted to other topics, including the weather, as an unexpected rain had forced us to meet indoors. Then followed by a discussion of the problem of getting people to cooperate and of the impossibility of finding somebody to serve as chief. Seperia said that Mokutu sangta should provide someone.

MWOGO: There was one good man, but he has been ruined by others.
SEPERIA: Who gets the chief's beer?

The general consensus was, nobody—everybody is his own chief. Then, complaining that laziness is contagious and striking the one-bad-apple theme, somebody said: "If you walk with a thief, you must always be thieving."

Finally, the threat of rain at an end, we all picked up our stools or chairs and went outside under the familiar thorn tree, Salimu, as head of the kota and out of natural leadership, took charge. Sitting around in a rough circle were Andyema (our host, Kambuya's son); Chebok (Salimu's neighbor, who had lived for a long time among the Pokot but was a Sebei); Seperia (the mutala chief who was there in his official capacity); Mwogo and his son Arapmwogo (neighbors of the girl's husband, from Mokutu); the husband (also called Andyema; so I shall identify him simply as husband); Yapchepkoti (the first wife—the accused); Sibora (the young wife, Kambuya's niece); my wife and I, our respective interpreters, and other hangers-on.

SALIMU: I am not satisfied how our daughter came here. I asked her why she stayed here, and she says that she is being kept here by her mother and Ndiwa.
HUSBAND: Ndiwa said it was he who had asked her to stay here after receiving a request from this house.
ANDYEMA: The husband came here after going to Ndiwa's house, and tried to find out why his wife was being kept here. My aunt said: "I asked Ndiwa to keep her because ever since my daughter has been married, the first wife has been running away. I think she is doing that to look for medicine to bewitch my daughter, and I wanted this to be discussed before the public."

At this point Salimu left the conference and went into the aunt's house to talk with Tengedyes. While he was gone, Andyema teased about Tengedyes' wanting to keep this young daughter with her.

SALIMU [returning]: Our brother-in-law, let us hear your troubles.

HUSBAND: I thought she came here to help her mother, who was sick; later, I was told she was stopped by this house.

SALIMU: What do you mean, "by this house"? There must be somebody.

HUSBAND: Yes. It was my mother-in-law and my brothers-in-law Ndiwa and Salimu. And when I inquired why, I was told something about my first wife.

SALIMU: Who told you it was I, your mother-in-law, and Ndiwa?

HUSBAND: I was told by my mother-in-law.

SALIMU: As for me, I am not concerned with stopping her. I have just come home to hear her trouble. I would have prevented her from staying here if the sticks had been broken.

HUSBAND: Ndiwa said that he had just been asked to stop her.

SEPERIA: Who asked him to do that?

HUSBAND: My mother-in-law.

SALIMU: If Ndiwa did not ask the girl to stay at home, would there be any trouble?

HUSBAND: There would be no trouble.

SALIMU: I have nothing to say, but let us hear about your family's troubles.

SEPERIA: Who is to start?

SALIMU: The husband is to start. I don't know what happened at our home.

SEPERIA: Our sister-in-law complained.

SALIMU: Ask your sister-in-law. If she says there is no trouble, that is all there is to say. [To Sibora:] Will you please let us know if there is trouble in your home?

SIBORA: No trouble. I have just heard things.

SALIMU: Mention what you have heard.

SEPERIA: What did you hear?

SIBORA: I heard only that Ndiwa had sent for me to come home, saying that the other wife is running around and perhaps looking for medicine.

ANDYEMA: Salimu, you have just seen our aunt. What does she say?

SALIMU: She is coming out now.

HUSBAND: Ndiwa has mentioned this to me, that you have kept her here because my wife is looking for medicine to bewitch this second wife.

SALIMU: I am telling the truth. I have just been hearing rumors. I know nothing. Therefore today I want somebody to give the proof. If he can prove it here, we will do something.

SEPERIA: Did you hear this?

SIBORA: Yes.

SEPERIA: Brother-in-law, you say it was Ndiwa who told you. Did he tell you when he heard it?

HUSBAND: He said, "I myself am saying it because your first wife is running away." But he didn't say to me that we would gather together so that we could find out about this matter.

SEPERIA: Does your first wife run away from time to time?

HUSBAND: Yes. She ran away once since I came to arrange the bride-price and once long ago.

SEPERIA: Did your wife stab herself? Had you fought with her?

HUSBAND: Yes, we had a quarrel. We were about to fight but were separated.

SALIMU: What was the basis of this quarrel—was it just concerning the two of you, or was it concerning the whole family?

HUSBAND: No, it was our own fight. There was nothing concerning this home. Before she stabbed herself she said, "People are accusing me of trying to find medicine to kill my young co-wife; so I had best kill myself."

SALIMU: From whom did she learn this?

HUSBAND: She learned this from the neighbors when they said she had been looking for medicine.

SEPERIA: Did she return on her own, or did you follow her?

HUSBAND: I followed her.

SALIMU: What did she say to you when you found her?

HUSBAND: She said she had gone to her parents to ask them to buy cloth for her.

SEPERIA: The second time, where did you find her?

HUSBAND: At her parents'. She said she had just gone to pay a visit, but I said, "I think you are running away."

SALIMU: Had she run away before you married the daughter of this house?

HUSBAND: No, except once long ago.

SALIMU: I mean, since we started arrangements.

HUSBAND: No. She did run away when I started making arrangements for my second wife.

SALIMU: That is why people suspect her.

SEPERIA: When you have a quarrel with your wife, do you ever hear her mention the name of the second wife?

HUSBAND: No.

SEPERIA: When you go off to the beer parties and return, do you find them happily at home? [The answer to this question was not recorded.]

How did these rumors happen if your wife is just staying at home happily?

SALIMU [disregarding Seperia's leading question]: Whenever your wife runs away and you find her, what does she say to you?

HUSBAND: She says this and that.

SALIMU: What do you mean by "this and that"?

HUSBAND: She says that she runs away because people say I am trying to bewitch the second wife. When I ask her who says that, she just keeps quiet.

SALIMU: Did you try to settle this in front of your neighbors there?

HUSBAND: Yes. After inquiring, she did mention Kaptera's wife as one who told her. She said, "That old woman says that I am trying to refuse to stay with my junior wife." I went to the old woman, who denied saying such things to my wife. This old woman stayed with me, but when she denied this I decided she was going to spread false rumors. I sent her away, and she is now staying with Mwogo's neighbors. By the time I took my second wife home, she had been running away from time to time, and she was always giving an excuse that people were blaming her for looking for medicine.

SALIMU: Has she run away since our girl came back here?

HUSBAND: No.

SEPERIA: I think this matter requires Ndiwa's presence because he is the one who told the sister-in-law. So it is up to Ndiwa to tell us from whom he learned this.

HUSBAND: When Ndiwa comes here, he will say the same thing—that he heard it from somebody else. Again, Ndiwa said he wanted our daughter here so he could find out what makes the first wife run away.

SALIMU: I think our aunt should be here. The reason I agreed that this girl should remain with us is that when I returned home I was told the following. My aunt went to Mbai and met Aramalinga, father of your first wife. This man asked my aunt if her daughter was married, and he asked her whose daughter the co-wife was; but my aunt did not tell Aramalinga. He went on to say, "I don't know if her husband has another wife." Then Aramalinga said to my aunt that our daughter had been looking for medicine to kill somebody; when asked if she was going to kill her husband, she said: "No, he is a polite man. I am going to kill the second wife." That is why my aunt should come here.

SEPERIA [to Yapchepkoti, the first wife]: Have you ever been to Aramalinga's?

YAPCHEPKOTI: Yes, I have been there.

At this point, an old woman came out of one of the houses and sat at the edge of the group. She was scowling and unpleasant. She was Tengedyes, Kambuya's sister, the mother of Sibora.

SALIMU: Our aunt, we have asked you to come out because we have failed to find the truth.

TENGEDYES: There are people who can tell the truth.

SALIMU: Why didn't you come out here sooner?

TENGEDYES: I didn't know there was going to be a meeting. One day I paid a visit to my grandfather and was given some maize. They said they weren't ready to prepare porridge but that I could take some maize home with me. I started to walk, and went to the house of Mwogo's daughter to grind my maize. When I was about finished, she said people were using the mill without paying. I said I was just a visitor there begging this maize. When I left, she was wondering, saying, "Hoo, hoo." I met another woman, and told her I wondered about that woman. I said nothing and didn't ask why she was wondering. I kept quiet. I thought: "Do the people think I am going to bewitch them?" Then I remembered that one of these daughters was bewitched and that they claimed it was I who was responsible. From that time they thought I was a good bewitcher. This maize was taken to the husband's home, and it was the first wife who said that I should not use this mill. The first wife said that perhaps I had gone into the house and cut pieces of cloth from the child [in order to do witchcraft], and she went on wondering, saying, "Hoo, hoo." I asked her what she was wondering about, and she said, "I am wondering about the old women who may have cut pieces of the children's clothes."

SALIMU [impatiently]: This happened before the marriage arrangements had been made. We want fresh ones.

TENGEDYES: One day when your niece [Sibora] was chemerik, this man's first wife said, "Here is a girl with scars on her head, and she has so many fleas." By this time her husband had already reported here to speak about our daughter. By that time his first wife was pregnant. The first wife said; "I had best remove the womb, because I will have no milk when you pay for the second wife—this girl with the scar. Before the cows are paid there, if the husband pays the bride-price, I will have to fight hard with my husband." I told them that that is their affair. Another thing— Yapchepkoti went to Mbai. When she was asked if she had come for a visit, she said, "No, I have come because my husband has bought a second wife; if he brings her home, I am not going to stay at all." At that time, the local chief was present. Yapchepkoti told her father that she was looking for medicine, and her father asked, "Are you looking for medicine to kill your husband?" She said, "No, I am going to kill my husband's second wife." At the same time, I went to Mbai and I saw Aramalinga. I said I would visit him on market day, and he said he could kill a hen for me to enjoy; but I asked if it was all right for me just to carry it home. I went to his house and found he had gone to the market. I went on and found him at the market, and after a long talk he asked me whose daughter is going to be married by the man that married Yapchepkoti. I just said I didn't know. He went on to say that the daughter of —— [Yapchepkoti] was asked for medicine and that she was looking for Arapsali, but I didn't tell him whose daughter was going to be married as a second wife to her husband. On that very day the chief came and asked the same questions; but as he is my mama [mother's brother], I had to be frank and say it was my own daughter. My mama advised me that I shouldn't give this daughter to him but should keep her home, but when I returned I found she had already been given. So I was conquered, and kept quiet after I had found the girl had been given away.

SALIMU: No use waiting to ask Ndiwa about these matters. He learned everything from our aunt.

TENGEDYES: That's why I thought I should ask my daughter to stay here. How could I go to my son-in-law and enjoy beer if this is the kind of behavior they have? A long time ago some of the people warned me about bewitching in this family.

SALIMU: That was a long time ago. Who asked the daughter to stay home?

TENGEDYES: It was I. People say things jokingly, and later you learn it is true. I decided to bring this out before it got worse. Before our daughter went to her husband's home, he had bought a mat for her. This mat was bought after her husband sold a cow, but when the mother of the first wife learned that her husband had bought a mat and a vest for the second wife, she complained about this as a waste of money; and they used up the rest of the money from that cow.

SALIMU: Did you buy these things?

HUSBAND: Yes.

SEPERIA: I don't like to go further. I think all is understood. I think the mother of the woman wanted these things explained.

SALIMU: Have you more to say?

TENGEDYES: Yes. The matter of my *kalaya* [a kind of iron basin]. I went to the river with the wife of Kambuya's son, and I asked her to hide my kalaya. At the same time Yapchepkoti came by from the market with another woman and saw the kalaya and took it to her home. When I returned I could not find it. Later, when Kambuya's son asked for it, I said it was taken by two women of Kobotu. The next morning he went to her house, but they had hidden it in the millet granary. I told him to return and ask them if they did pick it up, but they denied having seen it. I came to identify the kalaya and asked that other woman why she stole my kalaya. She denied having stolen it, but said it was Yapchepkoti who had stolen it. [Sepcria and Chebok indicate that they remember this case.]

SALIMU: Do you have any more to say?

TENGEDYES: Perhaps when I go back I shall think of more.

ANDYEMA: I think you want this kalaya to be paid.

TENGEDYES: The father of Andyema [the husband] said that Kambuya was a very bad man, for he was causing trouble between my sons and they were about to fight. The husband and his second wife, Sibora, went to the market. His brother went there also and offered Sibora a ride back home. Instead, he took her by lorry to Mbale, where he kept her a long time. Her husband got very mad. At Mbale, Sibora didn't know where to go; and she planned to kill herself and found a tree.[2] Her husband's father came home and found Sibora in the tree and was very annoyed with his son; he came here and reported to us that Sibora was at Mbale. Eryeza had to go to Mbale and bring her back. Therefore I am very annoyed with the husband's brother for taking our daughter to the town of Mbale.

MWOGO: I want to say one thing. What do you think about the information given this old woman by Aramalinga and the chief regarding the medicine?

YAPCHEPKOTI: Is it time to defend myself now?

SALIMU: No, let the old woman finish first. Do you have more to say?

TENGEDYES: No, that is all. Wait for something to happen in the future.

SALIMU: The old woman has said all she can. It is your turn.

YAPCHEPKOTI: I did not know that my husband was arranging to marry the daughter of this house until one day he went to buy tobacco. He brought tobacco in the wrapping paper for sugar and asked me to bring those things here, but I said that he should take such tobacco in gourds. Then I put the tobacco in a gourd and brought a packet of sugar. The total was 2 shillings. I came here and found our mother-in-law happy to take this. She fed me and gave me milk to take home. Later, I heard people saying that I was seriously beaten by my husband because I refused to bring it here and was forced to do so; but these were false statements. At that time we were living in Kaparik, but we

---

[2] Sebei suicide is characteristically by jumping from a particular species of tree. It seems to be a rather frequent occurrence; it is certainly a frequent threat.

moved to Mokotu. I heard rumors that I had stood at the kraal
gate when the cows were brought to our new house and refused
to let the cows be taken. They also said that I had said the second
wife had never had cows with calves old enough to be paid for
our own bride-price [?]. Those people told my husband that he
should bring the cows by force and should see that I did so. Later,
I went to the Ngenge market and met Ndiwa, son of Kambuya.
He took me aside and accused me of not wanting my husband to
marry a second wife and of trying to bewitch her. I came home.
One day I fought with my husband, after which I ran away to
Mbai. After two days my husband came, but I had gone on to my
father, Aramalinga, and he killed a hen for me and another visitor. Then it was dark, and so I found some place to sleep.[3] The
next morning when I got back, I found that my father had gone
to the market. My father returned very late, after I had again
gone to find a place to sleep. The following day I again found
my father gone—I was told he was looking for waragi. He did not
return. That was the day my husband arrived. The next day I
came back with my husband. I never had a chance to talk to my
father. That was the last time I went to see him.

CHEBOK: You didn't talk with your father?

YAPCHEPKOTI: No. But from what my mother-in-law says, my father
should be asked to come here and explain this. Coming to the
second point, the time I was wondering if my mother-in-law had
gone into my house for some clothes [to use in witchcraft]. I
strongly deny that—I have not said anything at all. Whenever
the old woman comes over, she stops at a big tree and shouts to
ask for fire from my daughter,[4] and then goes to Mwogo's home
and never comes near my home at all. Recently, Sibora came to
our house at the time of weeding. She asked that we share the
work by going to one shamba one day and the other the next.
One day when it was my turn, my mother-in-law passed by here
and asked what happened to Sibora. I said that Sibora was working my shamba because we were doing the work by turns. The
old woman asked: "Who asked Sibora to do that? She should
have left the shamba unweeded." My mother-in-law said this to
Sibora, but Sibora said, "Forget what my mother said." Then
one day Sibora came back here to this house. She has been
stopped by her mother-in-law's and has never come back home.
I was surprised. How could her mother-in-law stop her from
working? I was the one to teach her. Does our mother say that
she should teach her the homework?

---

[3] A woman cannot sleep in her father's house.
[4] A junior wife is sometimes referred to as daughter.

TENGEDYES: Yes, I said that because if I didn't teach her, her shamba would go to bush.

SIBORA [interposing against her mother]: If it goes to bush, it's my shamba, not yours.

YAPCHEPKOTI: Recently, my father took away his cows that he kept with us as kamanaktay. This old woman said perhaps it was I who asked him to take my father's cows in order to prevent their being milked by the woman with a scar.

TENGEDYES: Do you deny now that you have said this?

SALIMU: Keep quiet!

YAPCHEPKOTI: You people say I am running away looking for medicine. I am running away because I am tired of hearing rumors. My neighbors know how I behave. This old woman who was staying with us should be invited to be here. She has been spreading rumors. What was mentioned about the mat and vest? I deny having said anything about that.

MWOGO: I think that things should be pending, waiting for witnesses.

SALIMU: I don't think we need witnesses; we must finish this today.

MWOGO: This is all from Mbai—I do not believe it.

SALIMU: Before I give my decision, I think I'll bring this matter out indirectly. I think you, mother of Sibora, want to be given something, and that is why you are bringing these false views.

YAPCHEPKOTI: Concerning the kalaya: we were three women; they were saying it was I; if we were thieves, we were all three thieves —we were all carrying the kalaya. I have nothing to say about the kalaya. I admit that.

SEPERIA: We have been talking, and our throats are dry.

SALIMU: I think my aunt and Yapchepkoti are the ones who caused the trouble, and I think they are the ones who should be buying beer. [Laughter.] I find this is open, easy, and understood by all. When I first heard this, I expected somebody to say I heard this for myself. I do not see that this is anything to delay our decision.

SEPERIA: What I think may be true is the information said to have been received in Kaptcrit. The old man said she had been there, and she admitted having been there. Before we decide, I want to know how often you have visited your father.

YAPCHEPKOTI: Only once.

SEPERIA: The old woman said you went looking for medicine that Arapsali had.

YAPCHEPKOTI: I don't know about Arapsali.

SEPERIA: Since my sister-in-law was married, have you run away?

YAPCHEPKOTI: Yes, I have run away. People have nicknamed me Teraka [a person who runs away].

SEPERIA: Have you run away to Mbai?

YAPCHEPKOTI: No.

SEPERIA: Were you able to stab yourself?

YAPCHEPKOTI: I stabbed myself when I returned from Mbai.

SEPERIA: You fought your husband from time to time. Have you ever brought this before your neighbors, claiming that he mistreats you?

YAPCHEPKOTI: No. If I brought this before the neighbors, he would give as his defense that I had been trying to stop his second marriage.

SEPERIA: Has your husband not mentioned to you that you were trying to stop him from getting a second wife? If your husband has mistreated you for this reason, did you ever come to me [as chief]?

YAPCHEPKOTI: No. Because the people said I was trying to stop his marriage.

At this juncture, Salimu summarized the case, but unfortunately I could not record his summary.

SEPERIA: Yapchepkoti, since you have been married, has your husband tried to speak about his second wife?

YAPCHEPKOTI: No. The only woman I remember is a Pokot girl he was trying to marry. I did stop him from marrying the Pokot woman—I didn't like that at all. People say I am already a witch doctor. I have nothing to say.

SEPERIA: He had also gone to Psiwa to arrange for a wife, but I stopped him.

HUSBAND: Let us not bring jokes into this situation.

There was laughter here, but I do not understand the reference.

SEPERIA [addressing the husband]: Andyema have you heard about anything wrong done by your wife?

HUSBAND: Since we married, we have been in peace. What she says about Masop—I did speak of it, but I never went to arrange the bride-price. Concerning the Pokot woman—I did go to pet with her. Later there was a fight between me and my wife; people said it was because I went to that Pokot woman. My first wife has been happy since we started to arrange the bride-price with this home. If she has learned new things, it is recently, for she has been a very good woman. When I heard that she was trying to behave this way, I was surprised, thinking that perhaps she had found somebody to teach her.

SALIMU: We have been asking our brother-in-law about his wife's behavior. I don't think he would tell anything wrong, because he wants to keep his first wife and to have his second wife too.

HUSBAND: Only one thing that I cannot hide—she has been running away from time to time.

SEPERIA [turning to the aunt]: This news from Mbai—is that anything that can stop your daughter?

TENGEDYES: No. Only I was surprised at what I heard at Mbai. I wouldn't mind if that was the only trouble in the house.

SEPERIA: We are important people here—we cannot wait for witnesses—we must finish this matter today.

SALIMU: Gentlemen, we have heard all this story. I think we must decide the matter today. As I am in charge here, I shall reserve my judgment until I have heard from you.

SEPERIA: Chebok, give your views.

CHEBOK: From what was said about this woman's running away, she did so after hearing rumors around the village. She was followed by her husband and brought back; her husband has been patient, but she did not improve. According to what I have heard, perhaps she has plans to do something against her friend, but still we are not certain. Therefore I say to her that she must stop this behavior immediately.

SALIMU: Decide this as a court case. Decide who is right and who is wrong.

SEPERIA: If this were a simple matter—the people to be made friends —I do not think we would be asked here. I think this is a case because it concerns bewitching, and there is no joke about that. If this were a simple matter, do you think these people could have held this daughter? If something had gone wrong, this would have been more serious. We must decide the case and not just make friends.

SALIMU: If this woman had killed herself, people would have blamed our daughter.

Chebok started to ask more questions, but was stopped on the grounds that enough material had been brought before the kokwet.

SEPERIA: Before we go on, I would like to ask Mwogo, their neighbor, to give us valuable news he may have heard.

MWOGO: I say that of course the first wife is just roaming about and it is because of the second wife. Also that she did stab herself. I think she is wrong about that. But coming back to the medicine —I don't believe that. I think it is mere rumor. By stabbing herself she indicated that she would not block her husband's marrying the second wife.

SEPERIA: Yapchepkoti, your husband brought you here after hearing this important complaint, knowing that if his second wife marries somebody else, you will have an unhappy home, as Andyema will blame you for sending away his second wife. It was not we but your husband who asked you to come here. We want you here so we can tell you that you are wrong. He wants to settle this so that his home will remain in peace. I am the chief of your santga. You will remember that I did blame you one day at Kambuya's home when there was beer. Your matter started a long time ago, when your husband first came here. We thought it was up to your husband to try hard, but later we learned that your brother-in-law took this girl to Mbale. This girl [Sibora] was brought back to Andyema. Soon after, I was told you had run away. I thought you had run away because you didn't like the second wife. I learned again, when I was at Ngenge market, that you had stabbed yourself. The gombolola chief told me. Your husband said you had stabbed yourself but not seriously. You have lived here many years, and though you have fought with your husband you have never stabbed yourself. The parents of your junior wife have become afraid. Again, regarding the matter of medicine, if you had not been in Mbai, I would say that what she has been saying is mere lies. If the old woman said she heard it here, I would not believe it; but she said she heard it from your father, and you had been in that particular home. Another small matter, regarding the kalaya—you have admitted that. You know that people of this sangta heard that you had been behaving differently, and could not help thinking it was because of the second wife. The people outside the sangta blame you. If you hadn't stabbed yourself, this matter wouldn't be serious. If somebody dies, it is very important. This is not to state that you are guilty. I don't want you to do this any more, but to be friends. If you have been persuaded by somebody to stop your husband from marrying a second wife, stop that. The Sebei's life is to have many children. The second wife is to help you so that you can have visitors and plenty of food. Go home and act as mother of this girl and ask her to respect you as a mother, for she found you there in her husband's home. I suspect that you have already done so. I don't want to go to the councils and hear this again. Go home and act as a mother to your friend, and she should respect you as your daughter. I think you are acting differently because people have been mistreating you. You should treat these people as being very stupid. Don't mind about not having enough milk because of paying out cows for bride-price. It is better to eat greens and have two women in the home. Down here women always stop the husband from having a second wife because of milk. To you, Andyema [addressing the husband], please forget the rumors from the outside. Never come back rude and fight your wives when you return from a beer party. If you hear rumors, come back here and sleep and ask the next morning if they are true. By then you will be sober enough to understand which wife likes you. You will never believe a wife if she is speaking when you are drunk. When you hear rumors, go to the source; after learning the facts, you can explain to your wife what was told you. I think this first wife is bewitched. I advise you to build a second house for your second wife.

SALIMU: He has built one for her.

SEPERIA: You should treat your wives like a man. My sister-in-law [addressing Sibora], don't believe in rumors. You tell your mother, and she runs mad.

SIBORA: Have you heard anything from me?

SEPERIA: When you hear anything at all, please tell your husband, who should make inquiries about it.

SALIMU [addressing me]: Labu, what is your opinion on this matter?

The request came as a shock, though as I look back at it now, I realize that I had had a queasy feeling from the moment Salimu requested of the elders their opinion about my being included among them. I was so used to being noninvolved that I was totally unprepared, and my concentration on recording had made me less aware of the dominant attitude than I might otherwise have been. Naturally, I would have preferred not to render a judgment, for both personal and ethnographic reasons. But to have refused would have been no less than insulting. With no little misgivings, and in as tentative a way as possible, I decided to ask for mumek—that is, an oathing ceremony. In a sense, the situation called for this, as there had been accusation and denials of a most important delict. Yet it is clear from context (clearer when I went over the record than when I was recording it) that none of the principals in the case, least of all Salimu, bore any genuine hard feelings, and that the enmity implied by any strong oath would be destructive rather than constructive. My ethnographic curiosity was, I admit, my motive. I felt that the reactions to such a suggestion would be interesting and useful, and that I could do no damage by such a suggestion. I was further emboldened by the fact that Kilele was threatening a similar action against one of his neighbors, and that oathing had been a part of the internal fights among Kambuya's relations.

After I had unwillingly become an actor on the stage, I could not of course record my own remarks or those that immediately followed. But the reaction was immediate. Politely, firmly, and with some consternation it was made clear that an oathing ceremony would be quite out of the question; that it would bring harm to their own family, wherever the guilt may have lain. Later Chemtai, who had been shocked at my suggestion, said that this was a "fat" marriage, a desirable one from the standpoint of the guardians. I of course immediately withdrew my suggestion and then Salimu presented his conclusions.

SALIMU: For what the chief and Labu [i.e., I] have said, I thank you. As this was an emergency, I asked my daughter to remain at this house. I was pleased by that. Concerning giving the woman away—it was not I but others who did that. When I returned from my trip, I did not blame them for doing it. If she can stay in peace in her house, I would say that it is all right for her to be married to this man. But as they were unhappy, and this woman was brought back, I think I must say something. I was the one who brought up this girl. She was a small girl at the time she came to stay with us. All the circumcision costs were mine. After circumcision, somebody eloped with this girl. My brothers asked Andyema to take this girl who had eloped with a man who was too poor, and they knew I would not blame them for doing so. So I am very annoyed to learn that witchcraft is going on. That is why I wanted my neighbors to help me to decide this. This should have been settled by the husband before his own neighbors and stopped at his house. This has come to me, and I agreed as father-in-law[5] to hear the matter. It is a shame. So what my aunt has said she learned in Mbai when this woman went there—to Kiguli, to the country from which they come—I believe what she said is true even if there is no truth in what she said.[6] Our aunt asked for witnesses to be called, and I am sure

[5] Salimu is of course not father-in-law. I believe this and earlier references to sisters and to brother-in-law are correct renditions of the words used; they make the analogy to the social relation that has resulted from this unusual guardianship.

[6] I take this to mean that Tengedyes had truthfully said that she had heard the rumors even though the rumors were false.

they would have proved this. He is the mama of my aunt and could not falsify. Therefore I say I don't want to hear this matter at all. [Addressing Andyema, the husband:] When you took this girl, you never broke the sticks. Go prepare yourself to break the sticks. Go back with your wife happily. You must go home alone now. I will talk to the girl and to my aunt, and she will be returning one day.

It was explained to me that it was now up to Andyema to prepare beer. He had paid cows, but he didn't know how much he was to be charged; he had not broken the sticks, nor had he had beer for a ceremony.

With this, the hearing formally closed. It was explained that Andyema was to brew beer and arrange for the formal bargaining for his bride, with the expectation that life would resume in Andyema's dual household as if nothing had happened.

But Yapchepkoti was aware that this would not be so. She had sat through the hearings angry and resentful. She had made her own case with dignity, barely veiling her resentment. Now she got up, slung her child on her back, and stalked off. Before her departure she said that she was dissatisfied with this whole matter, that now she would be falsely accused and condemned of witchcraft in the eyes of all, and that indeed she felt that mumek should be done to make it clear by oath whether she was a witch or whether the mother of her co-wife had falsely accused her.

This infuriated Salimu, who was a man of short temper. He said that now it would be up to Andyema to brew beer and to settle this matter properly, that it could no longer be passed over lightly, for his wife had insulted this family. Then we all departed.

The kokwet to hear the case against Yapchepkoti was an example of Sebei legal action at the local and informal level. It was a family kokwet rather than one sanctioned by the general community, even though Seperia lent it added importance by virtue of his official position. An issue of potentially great importance had been raised; the matter was thus brought into the open; both sides had had an opportunity to state their case; the evidence was examined, and opinions were rendered. A sense of fairness pervaded the hearings, perhaps because Salimu neither credited the charge nor wanted the breach. Salimu's feeling was expressed in denying Tengedyes the recital of ancient troubles, even more clearly when he overrode Seperia's minatory question, and finally when he asked the elders present to express their views first. We were also impressed by the separation of rumor or hearsay from evidence of a substantial nature, and by Salimu's protection of Tengedyes' veracity while effectively denying the reality behind her accusation by suggesting that others were gossiping idly. Although Yapchepkoti had not behaved beyond the shadow of suspicion, it was clear that her behavior could be explained by a lesser fault than that of which she was accused. Sebei men see it as a breach of conduct for a woman to oppose her husband's subsequent marriage; Yapchepkoti's distaste in sharing her husband was the basis for the moralizing of Seperia and the other elders. But nobody felt the evidence adequate to suggest that she was seeking the wherewithal to engage in witchcraft. It should perhaps be made clear that this was the extent of Tengedyes' accusation: not that she had engaged in sorcery, but only that it was her intent to do so.

We might examine this session in another way, for clearly we entered into the portals of domestic life through this discussion. We saw relations between co-wives, both their cooperation and their antagonisms. We saw the acceptance of quarreling between husband and wife, and were told a great deal about how such quarrels were handled. And finally, we had a brief and inadequate glimpse into the wife's ties with her family of origin, and how these might be used for her personal protection, even though in this instance we were aware that Sibora had no desire for such protection. In all these matters, Seperia's sententious moralizing, for all its self-righteousness, gave us the standards against which people were to guide their actions.

Why was the accusation made in the first place? It was clearly established at the very beginning that the matter stemmed entirely from Tengedyes, who seemed to have had a long-standing dislike for the family of Yapchepkoti. We first met this woman under an aura of sympathy—she was widowed and had no sons, and was therefore rejected by the family of her husband and left to eke out a living for herself and her two children, until she was pitied by her blind brother. Yet it was she who had made the accusation, had kept her daughter away from her husband, and had forced the matter into the open. My wife, who had more opportunities for this kind of observation, said that she was a woman of little understanding, very demanding of attention, and much given to creating difficulties. It is not irrelevant here that, as a still fecund woman, she was rejected by those who might have inherited her. One cannot help but feel that she had found an opportunity to make herself felt, that she was seeking public attention and perhaps, at the same time, evening a score or two.

But the motivation of Tengedyes had an even more serious element. Salimu gave us the clue when he said, "I think you want to be given something, and that is why you are bringing these false views" [p. 167]. To appreciate this statement, we must remember that Andyema had not yet arranged the bride-price and must also be informed on a special aspect of such bargaining. The girl's mother was present, but did not participate in the negotiations; she might, however, raise objection to the suitor or demand a special compensation on the basis of some ancient wrong his family had done. Salimu had apparently assumed that this was her hidden purpose, that Tengedyes was laying the basis for a special demand against Sibora's husband when they broke the sticks—a kalaya, certainly, and perhaps an extra cow. Salimu would assuredly not object to such a demand, but, more than that, he wanted to preserve the liaison, which was advantageous in comparison with the man with whom she had first eloped.

CHAPTER IX *Kambuya's Legacy and the Character of Social Interaction*

This study has reversed the usual pattern of ethnographic reporting. The usual method is to proffer a description of the behavior, whether in cultural or in structural terms, and, among the better modern ethnographers, to give meaning and depth to these descriptions by brief illustrative use of actual events. Here, the events have been at the center of the narrative, and cultural norms have been supplied when necessary for understanding. I cannot argue that this is a more efficient mode of describing the generalities of the culture and social behavior, but it has other advantages which suggest that such a mode of reporting should be added to the ethnographic repertoire. I want here to explore this use in relation to ethnological theory.

The primary advantage lies in the fact that it takes us deep into the attitudes and sentiments of the people. We not only understand what cattle, kin relationships, witchcraft beliefs signify among the Sebei, but we see these sentiments infusing everyday behavior. For this reason, we get a better sense of how the Sebei live than we do from the ordinary analytic and descriptive reports. Because ethnology is concerned with the understanding of behavior, this advantage is extremely important.

The desire to reach into and understand exotic cultures has been a recurrent theme in ethnology, and most scholars have made it at least one of their primary aims. Paul Radin was one of the first to express this concern when he wrote in 1920:

One of the greatest drawbacks in the study of primitive peoples is the difficulty, one might almost say the impossibility, of obtaining an inside view of their culture. . . . For a long time most ethnologists have realized that the lack of "atmosphere" in their descriptions is a very serious and fundamental defect. . . .[1]

This was Radin's rationale for publishing an autobiography of a native. Since that time there have been dozens of detailed accounts of individual lives of native peoples, either biographical or autobiographical, and these have helped us appreciate the character and complexities of primitive life. But, as Langness'[2] recent survey makes clear, these life histories have never been put to truly comparative use; they have added to our insight but not to our scientific knowledge. The same, it seems to me, can be said of other means of attaining an inside view of culture.

The history of anthropological theory can be seen as a series of orthodoxies and discontents: the first generation of field ethnographers found early evolutionary theory remote from the realities of cultures as seen in the field, whereas the second generation found the cultural-historical explanation too simple to serve the complexities of social life and psychological reality. Today, the deterministic qualities of cultural causation, structural theory, and Freudian imprinting are being rejected by scholars otherwise as diverse as, for instance, Morris Opler, Lévi-Strauss, and A. F. C. Wallace.

Among the widely held theoretical presuppositions that seem suspect and at least worthy of closer examination are the notion of human malleability and its obverse, the denial of behavioral universals; the essential homogeneity of behavior on the primitive level, except among "plural societies," with their divergent subcultures; the assumption that intracultural variation of behavior is a product of diverse role demand with the sometimes overt, more often tacit, implication that human beings in primitive societies are not motivated except insofar as they have been enculturated to act in conformity with cultural dictates; and

---

[1] Paul Radin, *The Autobiography of a Winnebago Indian*, University of California Publications in American Archaeology and Ethnology, vol. 16, no. 7 (1920); reprinted by Dover Publications, New York (n.d.). See Dover edition, p. 1.

[2] L. L. Langness, *The Life History in Anthropological Science* (New York: Holt, Rinehart and Winston, 1965).

the idea that social systems are in equilibrium and that therefore social change is rare rather than the rule.

Since the theoretical outlook of the scholar establishes both the kinds of information he records and the framework in which he presents it, the corpus of ethnographic data reflects the prevailing modes of thought, and it is difficult to confront the orthodoxies of the past. It becomes necessary to break into the narrow circle between structured data and structural theory, between normative descriptions and the comparative study of norms. We need new kinds of data not hampered by the preconceptions of established theory. It is this need that motivates the so-called new ethnography, which is devoted to finding the reality categories, as these are understood by the subject people, just as it motivated Radin.

But it is not enough to be taken inside another culture. To be useful scientifically, the data must be amenable to comparative analysis. In order that these data may be used to confront established theoretical conceptions, they must be free of the structured-in preconceptions of existing theory. It seems to me that the factor that has prevented the scientific usefulness of life histories is precisely that they were precoded, either by the ethnographer-biographer or by the natives themselves. In other words, the categories of meaning were established by the preconceptions of the authors of the works, and only by inference and indirection can one break through to other meaningful parameters of the data. The same kind of stricture applies to other forms of inside-the-culture reporting. The events described in the present study, however, have suffered a minimum of precoding.[3]

The advantage of unstructured data is that they can be used in any structural framework that one wishes to employ, and to which they are relevant. In the remainder of this chapter, I want, first, to show how the discussions in Kapsirika shed con-

[3] For this reason, among others, I have been at pains to include everything I recorded. The exercise would admittedly have been better if it had been recorded in Sebei and if I had had a more complete record of nonverbal behavior.

siderable doubt on some of the cherished tenets of anthropological thought, and, second, to suggest a framework of comparison
which is significantly at odds with such established theory but
which I believe has general cross-cultural relevance.[4] I cannot
of course engage in a truly cross-cultural analysis, since this is a
pioneering kind of reportage, but I can bring in relevant descriptive material to show the potentialities of this approach.
Nor do I think it irrelevant that there are clear counterparts to
our own behavior in what occurred at Kambuya's kokwet. I was
impressed by the fact that when we learn a few cultural rules
and presuppositions, when we learn how cattle are manipulated,
what the inheritance patterns are, some attitudes and beliefs
about witchcraft—then we realize that the social encounters of
Kapsirika are not so very different from those much closer to
home.

This exercise immediately presents a dilemma that must first
be resolved. We are faced with the paradox created by the assertion that though the events here recorded are unique they are
also typical. If they were atypical, then we merely stumbled on
a bizarre occurrence, and the actions would have little or no
significance; if they are not unique, then this is simply a set of
structured events prescribed by Sebei culture. Certainly no
Sebei had ever witnessed precisely this set of events, this pattern
of interaction; yet nothing that took place was viewed by the
participants as shocking or out of the ordinary—except, perhaps,
the presence of an ethnographer.

The kokwet was a standard set of events in that it fitted within
the structured framework of Sebei society and operated, with
a few notable exceptions, within the legal and moral norms of
the community. In this sense it was a patterned activity that
must have taken place hundreds of times in past centuries in
Sebeiland. But the assertion of typicality cannot rest there; we
must also presume that the behavior was typical in that clashes
of interest, accusations, manipulations, and the diverse mani-

---

[4] This is admittedly *my* cross-cultural use of the data; it represents the
structure of my own theoretical preconceptions. The data remain for other
uses to which they are amenable.

festations of interpersonal relationships were within the range
of the culturally permissible, in the context of such a standard
social situation.

But they were not *culturally* standardized—and that fact is the
solution of our paradox. The culture did not assert, nor did the
rules imply, that Salimu should behave as Salimu did, that a
younger brother is less capable than the older, that some men
are avaricious for cattle whereas others are indifferent. The
actors in this drama were not merely playing roles in the socio-
logical meaning of that term. A Sebei fully at home in his culture could have predicted that a rich cattleman's death would be
followed by a kokwet, over which some elders would preside and
in which issues regarding debts and inheritance would be raised.
He could probably have predicted that there would be conflicts
and impasses, raised voices and heated argument; and he might
have correctly said that matters would close with an outward
show of harmony. Unless he knew the particular individuals involved, however, he could not have predicted the nature of the
conflict, the kinds of argument induced, or the outcome, precisely because these depend on the particular character of the
actors.

I want next to show the degree to which flexibility and diversity are structured into the situation. The first point is that Sebei
rules lack specificity in many particulars. The Sebei recognize
both flexibility and uncertainty, and discuss these matters among
themselves as well as with the ethnographer. This flexibility is
not merely a matter of local differentiation or subculture; rather,
it is found within a single location. It allows for the fact that
both behavior and procedures may be other than standard. Second, the actors may, and often do, bring divergent personalities,
talents, definitions of the situation, and private aims to social
encounters. In fact, as the matter of sibling rivalry within agnatic
ties makes clear, not only is there diversity of aims among individuals, but individual persons may bring to social situations
an internal conflict of values, an internal disharmony (evidence
for this fact does not find much overt expression in the present
record). Third, the actors redefine rules and procedures, abro-

gate them occasionally, perhaps make up new ones, and, above all, manipulate the situation both in discourse and in action so as to come out advantaged by the encounter. Although such activities are illustrated for present purposes in the discussion surrounding Kambuya's legacy, there is evidence in the text that these activities are recurrent in Sebei social encounters generally and that such manipulation plays an important role in the position and circumstances that the individual enjoys.

The Sebei themselves argue as to what the proper rules are, even in matters of importance, such as the limitation on the incest regulation applicable to the daughters of one's age-set. This marriage tabu was one of the first and most forceful that I heard expressed; yet there was considerable diversity of opinion as to how, in fact, it was applied and as to the nature of the sanctions operating against it. Again, it was considered "dirty" for a woman to have intercourse with an uncircumcised boy, and the matter was reiterated and reenforced by examples of evil consequences; yet instances where such consequences did not follow were blandly discussed, and much of the detail was left in doubt. There was considerable dispute over whether the bull should have been slaughtered before Salimu returned; the matter was resolved not by appeal to rule or by discovering an acceptable circumstance but by Salimu's very common-sense observation that the bull could not be brought back to life.

In the face of such flexibility and uncertainty, there were other instances in which the rules were expressed with such rigidity as to make one start: the possessions of the deceased could not possibly be anointed with moykutwet root—it must be ram's fat; a funeral ram that had no horns could not be slaughtered. On such small matters—and, I daresay, on great ones too—there was no room for maneuver. I do not think that the events gave us a basis for formulating any generalizations as to when to expect flexibility and when rigidity; both circumstances existed side by side.

There are many instances of a kind of pragmatic and objective attitude toward the regulations under which the Sebei operate. In another context, I shall discuss an important instance in which a rule was restated in response to felt pressure; here, we may exemplify with trivial but telling examples. In one instance, Kapsilut asserted that he was of the wrong age-set to take on the ceremonial role he wanted to avoid. I suspect he did so quite conscious of the fact that he was using this (perhaps even making it up) as an excuse. At least he made his refusal stick, even though the rule was ultimately not followed and despite some banter about the problem of burying the last survivor of an age-set. A second instance was some of the colloquy over the ram, particularly the matter of whether descendants of the deceased should or should not furnish the animal.

Something like the reverse of this process is involved when the Sebei seek "explanations" for something that has happened. Sebei will explore one "cause" until it proves fruitless, then explore another—like some members of our culture who go from doctor to chiropractor to herbalist and back to doctor in seeking a cure. This attitude was expressed by Kapsilut's summary of the situation, described by Fagio, of an uncircumcised man's visiting his wife before his ritual was completed: "All right then, if he dies, never say he was bewitched." It seems that custom stands ready to "explain" an event that has not yet happened. This is far removed from the idea that people operate under the dictates of customary procedure.

Sebei objectivity toward their culture was expressed in another way—a kind of teasing about customs and their consequences. There were remarks made about the restrictions on the use of cattle for performance of certain funerary rites, concerning which Ndiwa said, "The Karamojong used to rush over here when there was a burial; they got rich from that." There was also a great deal of banter surrounding marital customs; for instance, a sister's son would have provided beer if he had been married or a cow if he had been a girl.

All this does not mean that custom was disregarded as of no consequence, or that the individual was never concerned with proprieties. As Teso remarked, if they make a mistake "other people hear about it; we will be insulted by people who say that we are stupid and that we don't know right from wrong."

The cultural uncertainty and flexibility that we found within the local community were manifestly greater when we went be-

yond Kapsirika to Sebeiland as a whole or to the closely interre-
lated tribes of the Sabaot group. We heard much gossip in
Kapsirika about the way things were done differently in other
parts of Sebeiland, particularly in handling matters of circum-
cisions and deaths. That these should have been expressed in
prejudicial terms did not surprise us; the fact that, despite such
prejudice, there was an overtone of envy indicated that Kapsirika
might soon emulate its mountain-dwelling neighbors. Our interest here lies, however, in seeing this cultural flexibility not
only as observed fact but as one that the Sebei themselves are
fully aware of and regularly express. Such expressions of cultural
variation were heard in all parts of Sebeiland about other parts;
these expressions dealt with various aspects of culture but tended
to dwell particularly upon behavior and temperament. But such
spatial variance is more often recognized and dealt with in anthropological discourse.

This pattern of cultural flexibility and uncertainty was demonstrated in the kokwet itself. Sebei rules provide that at such
a family kokwet the senior member of the clan or kota should
preside. The senior man in this instance was Labu. No stranger
coming upon this group would have had any basis for suspecting
the fact. He was present but largely silent. He neither opened
nor closed discussion, neither led nor summarized; nor was he
physically placed so as to dominate the proceedings. That he
did not do so seemed to disturb no one present. Instead, the
hearings were dominated from beginning to end by Salimu. To
be sure, he was head of the "house" of Kambuya now that the
old man was dead, but he was also an interested party to the outcome, a party to the disputes, to the controversy that underlay
the whole affair. Yet it was taken for granted that he would play
this role, and no overt action or statement came to my attention
suggesting any protest or demurrer. That this role reversal took
place was an expression of the personalities of the two individuals: Labu was an ineffectual person; Salimu was a man of strong
character despite his small size and poor health. That is to say,
in view of the personalities of the two men, the reversal is not
surprising; but it is not, so to speak, in the Sebei script.

Even more dramatic was the difference between the two full

brothers Salimu and Andyema. Salimu was not merely a strong character; he was a person with a great devotion to cattle and a knowledge of their husbandry. His success was a product of this ability. Andyema, on the other hand, had little ability to retain the details of matters pertaining to cattle. Then too, he was chided for remaining with but one wife, but I suspect he preferred it this way. In short, he tended to withdraw from the battle rather than to enter the lists.

It does not take deep psychological insight to see why, with Salimu as an older brother, Andyema should have been what he was. There is plenty of evidence that Andyema was in many ways a product of his older brother, of the constant references to this "mere boy," of Salimu's exercise of the prerogatives of being the older and, as the record indicates, his abuse of these as well. But this is beside the point. We are not concerned here with how Andyema came to be Andyema or how Salimu came to be what he was; we are concerned with what happens when two such personalities find themselves in a particular social encounter. It is of interest, however, to note that this particular pattern—of the older bullying the younger—was not a universal and regular expression of Sebei culture. It was not a part of some standard expression of social roles, but the particular working out of their personal interrelationships within the context of the permissible, as this is defined in Sebeiland, and occasionally slightly beyond the permissible, as the verbal chastisement of Salimu by the elders suggests.

This sibling relationship points up an aspect of Sebei cultural orientations which is not directly manifested in these events but which is nevertheless of first-order importance: the fact that each man is a member of an agnatic kin group—a clan—and that this tie is inescapable and perduring.[5] He owes to his clan a high measure of loyalty; he must pay cattle for the wergild resulting

[5] An examination of Sebei economic transactions, marital attitudes, legal actions, and, especially, supernatural beliefs leads to a common assumption that agnatic ties are deep and significant at the nonexpressive level of Sebei culture, despite the fact that the clan itself is not very evident in social life. I discuss this point at some length in *Sebei Law* (Berkeley and Los Angeles: University of California Press, 1967).

from a murder committed by one of his brothers, or be the potential object of the retaliatory action of an avenging clansman of the victim. Behind this lies the threat of sorcery, which works on the clan, not on the individual. It will be remembered that Kambuya's family made a surupik oath against the person who stole Kambuya's money, not knowing the guilty party. When they learned that it was Maget, the stepson and clansman, they became most concerned that this action be speedily removed, for it endangered the whole clan.

It follows from this that Salimu, Ndiwa, and Andyema are not merely brothers but fellow clansmen, drawn together as a unit in this spiritual and temporal world, destined to protect and uphold one another. Yet their interactions here may hardly be described as centripetal: the major theme is certainly the rivalry and hostility between the three, at all times latent and not infrequently overt. Nor, as the accusations of fornication with their father's young wife and Andyema's recounting of the fight between him and Salimu indicate, may these be seen as a product of the immediate situation. It was endemic in Kambuya's kota; it is endemic throughout Sebeiland. Fratricide is a frequent occurrence; brothers repeatedly quarrel over land and cattle. The point is that the cultural dictates of clan solidarity, sanctioned by the deep fear of spiritual powers, does not override the actuality of rivalries and hostilities that exist among siblings. Nor—it should be quickly stated—do these rivalries and hostilities deny the reality of clan solidarity. If there were a Sebei novelist, certainly this theme of conflict between fraternal hostility and clan solidarity would afford the most obvious plot. It is also a matter that deserves consideration when we speak of the corporate character of clans.

The record indicates that the kokwet occasionally abrogated established rules, disregarding to some degree the mandate under which it was operating, as, for instance, in the example of the ram belonging to Megawit (claim 5). It is a clear and recognized rule that evidence of the destruction of an animal must be preserved. Yet Andyema merely said, "There was no skin—I just threw it away." Though Eryeza moralized at him, Salimu summed up the situation by saying the debt was clear: "His sheep died here, and nobody ate it. We are the ones who lost. We will not ask anything, and he is not to ask anything." (Elsewhere, however, the actions were dictated by the rules. In claim 30 a poorly informed man was given short shrift, but his rights were protected by the kokwet. Kapsilut said: "This man isn't satisfied. I ask you to consider the claim when his mother comes"; and this was done.) The hearings brought out many other instances that were not directly a part of the controversy: uncollectable debts; the impossibility of getting bride-price from a recalcitrant husband; the failure of Labores to share his bride-price with Salimu, which required Kobolomon to give an extra cow; the treatment of Tengedyes.

There is another kind of flexibility which the record brings out. Dominant in the value system of Sebei men are two things: cattle and wives. The two are inextricably intertwined, for wives are acquired through cattle; but each is itself important. This focus upon cattle and the purchase of wives is an ancient tradition, shared by all the cultures belonging to the language family and many others in Africa as well. Most Sebei respond to a question of preferences with either wives, cattle, or children. Yet, significantly, Nablesa did not share these values at all. He simply could not be motivated to care for cattle, and he did not even feel the need to maintain face regarding the matter. He was chided about his attitude toward animals, but when his father tried to claim a cow from the herd, he was the first to deny the right. There was nothing particularly acculturated about Nablesa. Whatever motivated him, it was not a denial of native life. Nor was he a mountain dweller newly come to the plains. He was simply a young Sebei man who otherwise fitted well into his community but who had not internalized the values toward cattle and wives.

Contrast him with Salimu, in whose veins the blood of cattle seemed to flow. Clearly, his mind tended to dwell on cattle as a stockbroker's does on the market or a novelist's on his characters. And Salimu too was unusual: the Sebei around him recognized his special knack of memory in cattle matters. Salimu and Nablesa were poles apart in the very attributes that are the quin-

tessence of Sebei culture on the plains—the high psychic involvement with cattle.

Let us next consider the major focus of contention between
Andyema and Salimu, for it illustrates the capacity for gross
disregard of custom, and lies at the heart of the matter with
which I am concerned here. It has to do with the division of the
tokapsoy.

According to Sebei customary law, the father is expected to
provide for each son; he provides for the initiation, the cattle
for his first wife, and a few head of stock with which the young
man feeds his family and builds his herd. Neither the timing
nor the number of cattle is specified; it is up to the father as
pressed by his sons. When these cattle are given to the son, he
is "chased away," and has no further claim on his father's herd,
though he may "beg" one cow from his younger brothers at the
time of his father's death. Thus we get a form of ultimogeniture:
the last adult son becomes responsible for his father's herd, takes
care of his father, and is the residual legatee of the estate. These
are the rules. They apply to the tokapsoy for all the sons together
and to the cows for each kota for sons of one wife. Salimu and
Ndiwa had long since been chased away. Andyema, according to
his own undisputed testimony, had not. Mangusyo was far from
ready.

Two items in the hearings are of direct interest here. On the
day that the tokapsoy were divided (chap. vi), there was a lengthy
discussion concerning the cows in Sabila's kraal: Should they
be taken by Andyema or Salimu? It was the issue that most an-
gered Andyema, so that he absented himself from the kokwet and
was consumed with rage for the rest of the day. The key speech
here is: "What I mean to say is that Salimu has been given his
cows and is gone [chased from the house], and that our father
is kind enough to give him more cows. Do you mean to say that
when our father is dead we divide out the cows as if none of us
were married?" Here is the basic legal question, which was not
answered; the men talked about details while Andyema made
it clear that he had not been chased away: "He gave me some
[cows] for milking, but he did not give me any so that I could
sell them." Andyema seemed to be quarreling over which cows

he was to get; in fact, he was furious that Salimu was given tokapsoy at all, perhaps as much because it reiterated Kambuya's favoritism (as one of the elders hinted) as because it deprived him of cattle.

The theme returned in the last session when the cows were being pointed out in the kraal. Teso, who was a close relative and almost an elder, suggested the basic division of the tokapsoy. He was explicit in laying down a rule from the very opening of the speech: "I want to say something about dividing the tokapsoy. If there were many tokapsoy, Andyema should be given the most. If there were many, Ndiwa would take four, and Salimu four, and Andyema and Mangusyo six—but Andyema should be in charge of those of Mangusyo. If there are few, then it is all right if each takes one."

As already noted, this is not quite the rule; as a matter of fact, it is already tempered in favor of Salimu. According to the rule I was explicitly given in abstract discussions, the sons who have been sent away have no right to any tokapsoy, though in this instance Kambuya had made some not very specific allocation just before he died. But even Teso's modified version was overlooked, and the actual division of cows was very nearly even, so far as the record goes. In the end, Salimu got nine of the tokapsoy, Andyema eight, Ndiwa six, and five were held for Mangusyo, with sixteen remaining undivided (see Appendix E, table 4).

Certainly, these Sebei knew these rules. At one point, Salimu told me privately that he was going to give all the tokapsoy to Andyema but was not going to tell him so, as he would merely squander them. I judge this to be an expression of recognition of what he really ought to do. I have no reason to believe he intended it or that he subsequently did so; the allocation we witnessed had the sanction of a court order. Here then we see ongoing events taking place which are contradictory to established procedure but which gain at least the tacit approval of those present.

It may be that the Sebei are unique, or at least unusual, in the degree of their cultural flexibility. Indeed, there are reasons

for believing that this is true: the Sebei live in diverse environments, and have adapted themselves to very different life modes;
in the period just before Europeanization, they were undergoing
a major shift in their economic life from one primarily (but not
exclusively) devoted to pastoralism to one in which farming
played an increasingly and in some areas overwhelmingly important role; they rapidly shed a number of traits as a result of
only modest pressure from the Baganda and Europeans, despite
the rather remote position they occupied until a generation ago;
and our study data in the Culture and Ecology project indicate
that they showed the least sense of cultural commitment of any
of the four tribes we investigated. There are thus reasons to believe the Sebei *are* less firmly entrenched in cultural demands
than is often true, and it is conceivable that in this they are absolutely abnormal.

However, when one looks for diversity and adaptability in
culture, one seems to find a great deal of it. This was repeatedly
uncovered in our examination of the four East African tribes
that were the subject of our Culture and Ecology project, and
was repeatedly expressed in the symposium presented by the
research team.[6] It was the central theme of Oliver's analysis of
the Wakamba lack of cultural commitment. Winans demonstrated a series of adaptation of economic and social features
over an extensive protohistoric and historic period. Conant
showed how one concept regarding an aspect of the physical and
social landscape differed between two closely related Pokot communities. Such adaptability would not be possible without cultural flexibility, and suggests at least that individuals operate to
meet their personal needs in a given situation.

[6] Walter Goldschmidt *et al.*, "Variation and Adaptability of Culture: A
Symposium," *American Anthropologist*, 67 (April, 1965), 400–447. This
group of essays presents the central issue of the project; particularly rele-
vant to the present discussion are Francis P. Conant, "*Korok*: A Variable
Unit of Physical and Social Space among the Pokot of East Africa," pp.
429–434; Symmes C. Oliver, "Individuality, Freedom of Choice, and
Cultural Flexibility of the Kamba," pp. 421–428; Edgar V. Winans, "The
Political Context of Economic Adaptation in the Southern Highlands of
Tanganyika," pp. 435–441.

There always remains the suspicion that this phenomenon occurs only under conditions of acculturation, that the native in his normal circumstances retains a strong commitment to cultural norms and adheres to the rules and therefore cannot engage in such manipulation. Aside from the fact that this idea of an unsullied native has lost its charm and force as a result of increased ethnographic sophistication, the problem is insoluble. It is insoluble because no anthropologist was there that century earlier, at that time when there was no contact with Western civilization. On the other hand, not only did the events take place in Kapsirika under relatively unacculturated circumstances, but the other instances, both in East Africa and elsewhere, involve situations that are relatively little affected by the European presence. I think it is worth making the assumption that the characteristic of behavior which was evident in Kapsirika in 1962 is an essential quality of normal Sebei behavior and is not merely an expression of cultural breakdown, if only because to do otherwise would be to abandon all hope of getting answers to many significant problems.

I have been at pains to show that the kokwet demonstrated cultural diversity and flexibility, despite the fact that this was a presumably homogeneous tribal society. The internal diversity was evident not only in the rules under which the people operated but also in the capacities, interests, and values that the several individuals brought to social encounters. We must not forget that this was a funeral kokwet for a very important man, and therefore presumably operated under a more than usually heavy burden of traditionalist sanctions. The existence of such diversity is important to the major theme I want to develop—that individuals enter into such encounters with a basic orientation toward the maintenance and furtherance of their own self-interest. It should not be necessary to repeat here that how they define that self-interest emerges from their indoctrination, their within-culture experiences, which, as we have seen, is not itself uniform among the actors. In brief, I want to show that the Sebei enter into social encounters with the intent to manipulate events to the extent possible so as to come out personally advantaged by the encounter.

If we look for such manipulation, we naturally focus on Salimu, for he more than anybody else was in control of the situation. His seniority contributed to this, but it was certainly his superior knowledge of the herd which made it possible. As soon as Salimu appeared, he wasted no time in validating his behavior and taking charge of matters. He established the legitimacy of his trip; he let Siret play up to him; he denigrated "these young boys" and their knowledge of the herd (p. 45); and he set up his cases against Ndiwa (p. 57) and against Andyema (p. 56). We must remember that we have recorded only a small part of Salimu's social contacts; it is reasonable to presume that similar conversations took place around every beer pot that Salimu enjoyed between his return and the final hearings. He appealed to the need to preserve the unity of Kambuya's herd, and publicly doubted that Andyema would do so (p. 58) or was able to do so (p. 59). Very early, Salimu had captured the most important of the old men, Mwanga, who said: "We have been living here a long time [waiting for Salimu's return], and what I have been hearing is that Salimu is a bad man and that he can't take care of his brothers; but from what I have heard from his own tongue, I think these are mere lies."

As already noted, Salimu took full charge of the situation. Though I had been told that the kokwet would be conducted by Labu, it was Salimu who ran the show throughout. Even the session that Salimu avoided was dominated by him; when he finally showed up that day, he completely took charge of matters.

In all these actions, Salimu used his superior knowledge of the herd as a positive weapon, threatening to expose the ignorance of his brothers from time to time (e.g., pp. 64, 107, 113). He almost always had an answer to every question, and dramatized his few lapses with elaborate pondering. Sometimes he seemed to be bluffing, filling in data that nobody had the power to contradict. Like any good bluff, this emanated from an underlying strength; though Salimu's knowledge might not have been so nearly perfect as the record suggests, it was impressive by

Sebei standards. From time to time, Salimu overwhelmed the
group with his detailed knowledge, as when he enumerated the
cows from Kambuya's sister (p. 112) or responded to a question
raised by Ndiwa (p. 117). He seemed to be quite clear about
what he was doing; he later recapitulated a dispute for me, and
said, "By this, Ndiwa was defeated." In the process, he seemed
to take every opportunity to undermine confidence in his brothers—"these mere boys"—and to assert their incompetence.

Salimu had one other trick that he used effectively. He knew
when to give in gracefully—to take his losers, in the terminology
of bridge. He did not question real and clear debts; he conceded
matters in such a way as to reassure us of his integrity and generosity.

The contrast with Andyema was striking. Observing the
events, we were likely to think, without knowing the culture,
that all the advantages were with the older brother, the senior
man of the kota. This was not true. Though Salimu had certain
positional advantages because of his seniority, Andyema had the
advantage of being his father's most recent herdsman, as the
elders repeatedly pointed out, the person who should by law
have had the bulk of the tokapsoy and the cows of his mother's
kota, as well as current knowledge of the herd. But a lifetime of
being the younger brother to an able and aggressive older one
had deprived him of his confidence and his capacity to act. All
Andyema's efforts to question his brother's operations seemed
ill-conceived. Finally, in his anger over the matter of the cows
at Sabila's kraal, his behavior was so inadequate that he alienated
even his natural ally Ndiwa, who summed up Andyema's problem when he said: "Andyema, you were misbehaving when our
father was alive. You don't know about these debts. Salimu and
I have been with my father; if you had talked to him and listened, you would be the one to know these things." And the
whole kokwet—spearheaded by Teso, who gave us the background—turned against Andyema, who stalked off, petulant and
ineffective. In short, when by dint of personality, Salimu seemed
to manage matters, Andyema, for the same reason, was unable
to take advantage of his opportunities. As his heated speech
made clear, it was not from want of trying.

The encounter between Salimu and Andyema offered an opportunity to separate what might be called the cultural definition of the situation from what must be seen as the interplay between two individuals of differing capacities, needs, and aims; we must be as clear as possible about what is and what is not "cultural" in the situation. The central event of the encounter between Salimu and Andyema was the conflict over the tokapsoy, and this was handled by legal (culturally approved) means but arrived at an extralegal (culturally unsubstantiable) conclusion. Salimu's behavior in the matters outlined above was not customary, in the sense either that a sophisticated informant could tell you that that was the way older brothers behaved or that, if one had a large number of instances, older brothers would be found statistically to behave thus. Nevertheless, this behavior was carried on within a particularly Sebei cultural frame of reference, of which two elements were especially significant. First, Sebei culture supports the psychological advantages of the older person over the younger. For instance, any adult may chastise any child who is doing wrong, and all initiated persons have, by virtue of their secret knowledge, a hold over all uninitiated, which they are free to use in order to demand compliance—even sexual compliance when the younger person is a woman. Second, Sebei culture defines as appropriate the idea that each individual should seek personal advantage or, on the other hand, should not subordinate his own interests to the dictates of community welfare or of deference to others. This quality is expressed in diverse ways in regularized social interaction. A clever bride refuses to go through certain ceremonies unless she is given a cow, and may—as some wives in our own society are said to do—withhold her sexual favors until the husband meets such a demand. Similarly, Sebei boys will refuse to undergo certain ceremonial acts until their parents have promised to reward them with an animal. We saw, in fact, that this was precisely the manner in which Chemisto, Kambuya's grandson, began to build up his herd. Thus the Sebei define not only legal rights and obligations but also subtle attitudes and orientations. These elements are a part of Sebei culture.

It would have been equally within the rules of Sebei culture for Andyema to have scored heavily in the encounter. Had he been his father's favorite, and had thus brought confidence into social encounters, had he had the superior knowledge of his father's contractual arrangements, he could have turned Salimu's disquieting absence to advantage and, using manipulative techniques of the kind Salimu employed (though here with a proper show of deference), he could have had the bulk of Kambuya's cattle. We can say that the stratagems employed are a part of the culture in the sense that they would not be possible except as notions of this kind are inculcated; but how they are used, who uses them, and the success they enjoy—these are matters of personal motivation, self-control, and talent.

It would be a gross error to focus too sharply on Salimu in discussing the manipulation of events for private gain; he was in no sense the villain of the piece, but merely the most successful practitioner of the art. We might note, for example, the efforts made by Labu, who tried to insert his son Nablesa into the group sharing the heritage (p. 108) and who tried to claim a cow for his son (p. 120). He was thwarted more by his son than by Salimu—not because he could not play the game but because he did not care what the score was. But what about Nablesa? Was he not giving up cattle in a spirit of generosity that would leave more for his brothers? There is nothing in the record to substantiate the view that he was motivated by altruism, either in act or in speech. What seems the more likely, from my admittedly inadequate knowledge of Nablesa and the situation in general, is that he knew he would suffer more from the criticism for squandering another cow than he would enjoy the proceeds of his profligacy.

We may also note that Eryeza seemed to have been capable of no little manipulation of events to his own advantage; certainly, he benefited from Kambuya's abundance more than any man not an actual descendant, to judge by evidence brought forward during the kokwet.

Lest we tend to think of these manipulative activities as an unusual occurrence that took place only in the special circumstances provided by the funeral of a rich man, it is perhaps well

to digress a moment and show that they had more mundane—
and, by the same token, more important—implications. I want,
therefore, to interrupt this discussion to examine some of the
data on, and the significance of, economic transactions in which
Kambuya engaged.

The following is based on the material presented in Appendix
E, where information on the nature of the data and other details
may be found, particularly in tables 5 and 6. These data demonstrate that on the basis of 559 animals subject to analysis, Kambuya and his sons engaged in 327 exchanges (namanya, outright,
and cash transactions) involving 296 animals, or more than half
the total herd. Significantly, this latter figure compares with a
total of about 119 social uses of animals (prestations, bride-price,
ceremonial slaughter, and anointing for wives). The distinction
between "economic" and "social" uses of animals is not an absolute one, but these two kinds of uses differ fundamentally
relevant to this discussion: in the one, there is a clear expectation
of quid pro quo, carefully analyzed and bargained by the principals involved; in the other, any return will be in the form of
a moral or social obligation. Kambuya clearly involved himself
in numerous instances where direct manipulation of events for
personal gain was the express aim of the social encounter.

It is reasonable to assume that Kambuya was a rich man by
Sebei standards because he manipulated these transactions to his
own advantage; he was, in a real sense, a capitalist. His use of
the namanya exchange custom was such that on balance he
acquired heifers (i.e., animals with the potential of increasing
his capital value) twice as frequently as he gave up such animals
in favor of "consuming" a bullock. In the category of outright
exchanges, his performance is even clearer; indeed, it would
seem that he almost never made an outright exchange that was
a detriment to the furtherance of his cattle holdings. In sales
and purchases, his conduct also displayed his economic acumen;
by reasonable extrapolation of our base data, he can be said to
have made a net profit of more than 5,000 shillings in the cash
transactions recorded.

These transactions were social encounters in the everyday life of the Sebei, social encounters in which the individual had the opportunity to manipulate events in such a manner as to further his self-interest if he was so motivated and if he had the ability to do so. I have no doubt that Kambuya saw these events in this light, that he was conscious of his own desire to preserve and further his livestock holdings, and that he was shrewd enough to do so effectively. I had no expression on this from Kambuya, but it was clearly stated several times by Salimu, as, for instance, in the exchange between him and Siret about the preservation of the herd in relation to such transactions (p. 45). This analysis shows that the kinds of manipulation that took place in Kapsirika played an important role in the activities of Sebei in everyday life and that they offered rewards, in terms of the shared values, to those who manipulated their encounters advantageously.

An interesting manipulative device in the repertoire is the accusations of one against another, accusations of sexual transgressions and of witchcraft. In this context these are almost the same thing, for adultery between a man and a woman he may inherit if the husband dies is tantamount to an act of witchcraft against the cuckolded husband. Such accusations are repeatedly made by brothers against one another. It is not possible to know whether each believes this particular evil of the other or whether it is merely an effort to undermine confidence and then to press personal advantages; but I suspect it is largely the latter, for though the accusations are readily voiced, there is no effort to follow with oaths or any other culturally approved device for apprehending the witch. Indeed, I feel that the function of witchcraft on the Sebei plains lies largely in its use as a form of calumny in such social interaction.

From this standpoint, the action of Tengedyes in the dispute between co-wives (chap. viii) was particularly revealing. Here was the second major instance of the manipulation of events for personal reasons. So far as we could tell, Sibora and her co-wife had no quarrel. Apparently, Yapchepkoti did not want to share her husband with another woman, and she, like Salimu, took advantage of her seniority in handling her husband's young wife. But the two women worked together, and no instance of

direct hostility was brought forward. The most that can be said
of these facts is that there was evidence of motivation to engage
in witchcraft. It is not so much that the evidence that Yapchepkoti sought medicines to engage in witchcraft was merely circumstantial; it is, rather, that the whole treatment of it seemed
to indicate that those at the kokwet either gave it no credence
whatsoever or considered it of no consequence. Certainly, it
was of less consequence to Salimu and his brothers than the per-
petuation of what Chemtai described to me as a "fat"—which is
to say, a "good"—marriage.

It is impossible to know whether Tengedyes believed her own
accusations. We can, however, explain her actions in terms of
pure self-interest. She opened her account with matters of the
distant past, which Salimu cut off. Yet she had made a point
about the family on which she would later score heavily. In
order to see how this worked, we must remember that the husband had not yet arranged the bride-price, though he had given
some cattle. When the sticks were broken for Sibora, her mother
would have no direct part in the bargaining but would sit in
the background and, at the proper moment, would raise the
issue that she had been accused of witchcraft and would demand
an extra animal. This was a standard procedure which I first
learned of when a group of men enacted for me a bargaining
session in which one man played the part of a grandmother who
had brought up an imaginary ancient family quarrel. Furthermore, Tengedyes would no doubt demand a kalaya and other
items based upon these presumed wrongs. Because the husband
seemed anxious to preserve his marriage and because he was
either unusually wealthy or exceptionally generous, we might
presume that Tengedyes would profit.

Meanwhile she was undoubtedly satisfying an urge for a role
of importance. She was an old woman and, as the Sebei would
say, "useless." When her husband died in 1947, she had two
young daughters and was still fecund; yet nobody wanted to
inherit her. I therefore suspect that she was not personally desirable. By making trouble in this instance, she was gaining
attention from those around her, whether or not she gained any
material benefit. In the process, she had done a great deal of

damage, particularly to Yapchepkoti—but Tengedyes was not one to worry about that.

Tengedyes' actions were certainly legal and not to be condemned by Sebei standards of conduct. I had the clear feeling that Salimu would have preferred that the issue had not been raised at all, or not at this time, and he might have prevented it if he had not been away; but he made no public condemnation of her, nor did he display any disapproval. We saw enough evidence of witchcraft accusations in the kokwet over Kambuya's legacy to know that this was a standard tool in Sebei manipulations. At the same time, it hardly lies within the realm of cultural directive; it cannot be said to be a part of normal procedure. A concatenation of events made Tengedyes' actions possible: a rich husband, delay in breaking the sticks, a senior wife who demonstrated in actions that she did not want her husband to take a second wife, and an accusation against her for which she could retaliate. She was using available cultural tools for the manipulation of events in a manner to satisfy personal goals stemming from her own psychological needs.

Accusations of witchcraft ran throughout the discussions regarding Kambuya's legacy as well. They were inherent in the situation from the outset, for they became attached to Salimu's mysterious absence. Of this he seemed aware; he went to great pains to tell me and the other listeners just what he had been doing—or what he wanted us to believe he had been doing—and he reiterated his story, flinging down his medical receipts, during one of the hearings. Suspicions were attached to his association with his enigmatic friend, an association that was not built upon the normal ties of Sebei life—kinship, pororyet affiliation, or age-set membership—and which was therefore suspect. These suspicions did not go unnoted by those who wanted to undermine Salimu's influence and power; they were even repeated as suspicions by one of the elders. Witchcraft accusations took on a more specific form in the discussions involving Kambuya's young wife and the reference to Salimu's urinating in a gourd, an allusion that would need no glossary for Sebei listeners. There was good reason to believe that we heard only the occasional rumblings of sentiment more firmly expressed in our absence; at any rate, these rumblings were sufficient to enable us to see this use of witchcraft as a threat rather than as a psychological conviction. The accusation of communism as a means of character assassination has been likened to witch-hunting; I am here suggesting that, when applied to the Sebei, the analogy can be reversed and that at least one of the important aspects of their belief in witchcraft is the provision of a means of character assassination in the course of everyday encounters.

The manipulation of events seems perfectly understandable to us. Not only do we know of such events in the marketplace and in the political capitals, but we see similar ones daily in the faculty club, taking them for granted as a natural part of our social system. But attention to such activity is remarkably absent from the theoretical writings of students of primitive society, who have been indoctrinated with cultural determinism, social homogeneity, and the fixity of systems among tribal peoples. Such absence prevails despite the fact that, as we will presently demonstrate, evidence for such social manipulation is far from absent in the ethnographic literature.

We must take explicit cognizance of the fact that this pattern of behavior is not adequately accounted for by role theory. As developed by Linton, Parsons, and Nadel, the concept of social role has reference to the socially expected behavior of persons in specified social positions. In such theory, role is a part of the system, an aspect of social structure; it is not an attribute of individuals. As Erving Goffman points out, "*Role* consists of the activities the incumbent would engage in were he to act solely in terms of the normative demands upon someone in his position," and cites Linton in substantiation.[7] S. F. Nadel, whose early training in psychology leads him to discuss "Motives behind Behaviour,"[8] rapidly backs away from a concern with individuals when he writes:

[7] *Encounters: Two Studies in the Sociology of Interaction* (Indianapolis: Bobbs-Merrill, 1961), pp. 85–86.

[8] *The Foundations of Social Anthropology* (London: Cohen and West, 1951), pp. 68–72.

We must clearly not overstate the case for consciousness behind regulated action. In many respects social conduct runs a smooth, given course, and its phases need not be carried by fully conscious aims. At any moment of acting the individual may have no real choice, in the sense that he is simply carried forward by a habitual and unanalysed impulse without asking himself what satisfaction this will gain him, or whether this is the "normal" and "proper" way to act.[9]

With Nadel's shift to the passive voice, the individual as actor has been lost to the discussion and reappears in his later work[10] as a person merely deviating from his role. Interaction and conflict do not enter; personal motivation plays no dynamic part.

I am here asserting precisely the opposite: that societies— primitive or otherwise—are peopled with human beings who are consciously (and unconsciously) motivated; that social encounters regularly take place; and that in these encounters individuals operate so as, to the best of their ability and within the limits of the permissible, to advantage themselves. What they consider advantage is always culturally induced, and the fact that the means they employ are usually in accordance with culturally established rules neither contradicts this thesis nor reduces its significance. People do enact the roles that their status endows them with, but they do something else that must be put into our theories of social behavior.

Lest some feel that this is self-evident, and that all anthropologists really presume this to be true (and I admit that such presupposition is frequently hidden in theoretical writings), I cite the discussions of economic behavior in tribal societies. Certainly, the dominant mode of thought has been best exemplified by Karl Polanyi, who asserts the absence of a "market mentality" in primitive economic behavior.[11] It can be taken for granted that markets may not exist; and it is self-evident that, in the absence of money, people cannot translate their acts into pecu-

[9] *Ibid.*, p. 70.
[10] *The Theory of Social Structure* (Glencoe, Ill.: Free Press, 1957).
[11] "Our Obsolete Market Mentality," *Commentary*, 3 (Feb., 1947). For a summary of this position and some important counterarguments, see Scott Cook, "The Obsolete 'Anti-Market' Mentality: A Critique of the Substantive Approach to Economic Anthropology," *American Anthropologist*, 68 (1966), 323–345.

niary terms. But if a concept like market mentality is to have any meaning in cross-cultural usage, it must have reference to underlying attitudes of the kind described here. It must mean the efforts at self-gratification through social encounters, not merely the exchange of goods for a price.

Such social encounters may be of diverse sorts; they may or may not involve goods or even economic well-being. In order to establish a frame of reference that is amenable to the diverse conditions of man, we must retain the concept at its broadest level. When we do so, we find that the ethnographic data are not without reference to this quality in primitive social life. This is not the place for a detailed survey of materials showing this phenomenon in action, but a few references will suffice to indicate what I mean.

C. W. M. Hart and Arnold R. Pilling showed in detail how the Tiwi of Australia utilize marriage arrangements in an elaborate status game, apparently difficult to play, but with the highest possible stakes (women, services, children, and social standing) in this society poor in material goods.[12] Richard Thurnwald showed how the people of Buin manipulated their exchanges to further their social position through alliances and obligations.[13] Similar observations have been made by Raymond Firth[14] and Leopold Pospisil.[15] A recent analysis of the Northwest Coast potlatch by Philip Drucker and Robert F. Heizer shows how these social encounters are used as a means of personal advancement.[16] I have shown that, farther south, the Hupa and Yurok use legal cases for the same purpose,[17] and that in central Cali-

[12] C. W. M. Hart and Arnold R. Pilling, *The Tiwi of North Australia*, Case Studies in Anthropology (New York: Holt, 1959).

[13] "Pigs and Currency in Buin," *Oceania*, 5 (1934), 119–141.

[14] *Primitive Polynesian Economy* (London: George Routledge and Sons, 1939), esp. chap. ix.

[15] *Kapauku Papuan Economy*, Yale University Publications in Anthropology, no. 67 (New Haven, 1963).

[16] Philip Drucker and Robert F. Heizer, *To Make My Name Good: A Reexamination of the Southern Kwakiutl Potlatch* (Berkeley and Los Angeles: University of California Press, 1967).

[17] Walter Goldschmidt, "Ethics and the Structure of Society: An Ethnological Contribution to the Sociology of Knowledge," *American Anthropologist*, 53 (1951), 506–524.

fornia there were actually traders who operated directly on a profit motive, taking advantage of the value differential in goods along the trade route across which Nomlaki territory extended.[18] Fredrik Barth has shown the pattern of interaction among the Pathans in his game-theory analysis of their behavior.[19] If we examine M. N. Srinivas' writings on legal conflicts in an Indian village, we find a similar pattern of behavior.[20] When An-Che Li reexamined Zuni behavior, which, since Benedict's classic work, has been viewed as the quintessence of community solidarity, he found elaborate manipulations for personal advantage.[21]

Thus we find the recurrence of a theme in tribal societies— that individuals utilize social encounters as a means of advancing their position in society. Whether it is true of *all societies*, or of *all persons* within each society, is a question that requires more conscientiously assembled evidence. Those few anthropologists who are trying to use game theory in the analysis of primitive behavior, as Barth has done, are involved with this theoretical presupposition, whether consciously or not. Among others, even in economic anthropology or in legal anthropology, where it is perhaps even more relevant, this has not generally been the practice.

The very concept of culture has come to be questioned by many modern students of society. I think this is an error. Group actions and shared attitudes form the essential matrix to which each individual must adjust and within which his social encounters take place. Each individual gains a measure of himself through such social encounters, and particularly from the out-

[18] Walter Goldschmidt, *Nomlaki Ethnography*, University of California Publications in American Archaeology and Ethnology, vol. 42, no. 4 (1951).

[19] "Segmentary Opposition and the Theory of Games: A Study of Pathan Organization," *Journal of the Royal Anthropological Society*, 89 (1959).

[20] "A Joint Family Dispute in a Mysore Village," in "A Study of Disputes" (mimeo.), Department of Sociology, Delhi School of Economics, University of Delhi (n.d.), pp. 1–36; "The Study of Disputes in an Indian Village," *ibid.*, pp. 37–47; The Case of the Potter and the Priest," *ibid.*, pp. 48–74; "A Caste Dispute among Washermen of Mysore," *ibid.*, pp. 75–111.

[21] "Zuni: Some Observations and Inquiries," *American Anthropologist*, 39 (1937), 62–76.

come for him as measured against the community standards. Therefore, this external definition of the situation is of the highest importance. But if the activities surrounding Kambuya's legacy have any meaning whatsoever, certainly they tell us that culture is not a blueprint for action, but only a context for action, and that individuals operate in accordance with their own tastes and capacities. The implication is that there is an inner dynamic of motivation which inspires the acts of individuals in any social encounter. If this is true, then it follows that any model of society must take cognizance of the factors that determine such motivation. We are caught, whether we like it or not, in the necessity of facing our preconceptions regarding individual psychodynamics.

In *Man's Way*,[22] I suggested that central to a model for society was the individual hunger for acceptance and esteem, which I have called the "need for positive affect." The essence of this need lies in the fact that self-seeking individuals can meet their personal needs only through taking cognizance of the needs and expectations of those around them. In *Comparative Functionalism*,[23] I tried to develop this theme in more detail, noting especially some of the contextual factors that must be recognized in the formulation of social models, particularly the fact of individual diversity in taste and talent. In the present work, I have had an opportunity to show that social life is made up of such diversity, and that encounters can be understood in terms of individual self-help, variantly conceived and variantly managed, within the context of culturally established rules and expectations.

This line of discourse has taken us a long way from the thin shade of the thorn trees in Kapsirika, from the old men listening to the encounters between the sons of Kambuya, from our original intent merely to record for posterity a sector of ordinary

[22] Walter Goldschmidt, *Man's Way: An Introduction to the Understanding of Human Society* (New York: Holt, Rinehart and Winston, 1959).

[23] Walter Goldschmidt, *Comparative Functionalism: An Essay in Anthropological Theory* (Berkeley and Los Angeles: University of California Press, 1967).

Sebei life. Yet perhaps it is not so far as it seems. That original intent was justified by the belief that this record would convey to the reader—better than the disquisition on Sebei law I have written or the general ethnography I am still writing—the real character of life as it is lived on the plains below Mount Elgon. This is a human document, a document in an idiom that *we* can understand. The strange customs of exotic places, which tend to be the fare of anthropological writing, become merely the props and stage setting for a human drama that, for all the foreign idiom we must master, becomes fully understandable. If we can understand, if we can bridge the physical and cultural distance between ourselves and Kapsirika, is it not reasonable to ask whether we are not also reaching into universal human attributes?

APPENDIXES

Sebei life is not lived in closed communities; each Sebei has a wide range of personal interactions. Many people are mentioned casually in the text. This list of persons includes only those who played a significant role, who reappear or are discussed in various parts of the text. They are listed by the first name as used in the text. Principals in the action are printed in italic type. The Sebei, particularly the women, have diverse names used according to context; most men use a first name only, and some regularly use nicknames. The prefix *Arap-* means "son of," and helps to identify the individual. The relationship among Kambuya's lineal relatives is given in Appendixes B and C.

Amisi Mwanga	A pioneer in the plains area and a wealthy contemporary.
Andyema (Arapkambuya)	Second son of Kambuya by his first wife.
Aramalinga	Father of Yapchepkoti; involved in the accusation of seeking to do witchcraft.
Chemisto (Arapsalimu)	Son of Salimu Arapkambuya, the favored oldest grandson of Kambuya, the only one circumcised and married. His wife was carrying her first child at the time of the hearings.
Chemtai	Granddaughter of Kambuya, second-oldest child of Salimu by his first wife. This girl of about thirteen had been gored in the vagina while milking.
Chemtai, Yovan	My interpreter.
Cheptorus	Second-oldest grandson of Kambuya, a boy of about twelve. He is the son of Ndiwa.

Eryeza	Eldest son of Labu; a man whom Kambuya would also call son. He had been a minor chief, owned a small duka in nearby Ngenge, and was literate.
Fagio	Son of one of Kambuya's sisters; he is young, unmarried.
Kambuya	Old man who died.
Kapsilut	One of the elders, a leading older citizen of the area. He belonged to the same clan as Kambuya's father's mother. The relationship is not unimportant to the Sebei, though I think it had no particular influence on the role Kapsilut played.
Kilele	Man of Kapsirika whose kraal was raided just before the witchcraft hearing. He was not present at the kokwet.
Kobolomon	An important man in the neighboring village. Married to Kapkeben, one of Kambuya's sisters (actually she was the daughter by a former marriage to a woman whom Kambuya's father later inherited).
Labores Kamwasir	The deceased husband of Tengedyes, one of Kambuya's sisters.
Labu	A "brother" of Kambuya, now the senior man of the kota.
Maget	Son of Kambuya's fifth wife by Kambuya's brother Musani. Kambuya had inherited this wife after Musani died. It was Maget who had stolen the money.
Mangusyo	Fourth son of Kambuya by his fifth wife; a boy of about six.
Mangusyo	Deceased younger brother of Kambuya.
Masai Arapchungeywa	Man of Kapsirika, nicknamed Ishirini, originally from Bok. His daughter was married to Ndiwa.
Musani	Deceased older brother of Kambuya.
Mwanga Kapkapajum	Age-set mate, close friend, and former neighbor of Kambuya, when they both lived in Kapcheptemkoiñ; the most important of the elders.
Nablesa	Son of Labu; a man who cares nothing for cattle.
Ndiwa (Arapkambuya)	Son of Kambuya by his second wife,

	halfway between Salimu and Andyema in age.
Ndiwa V (Ndiwa Kapchepkwony)	One of the more important elders. I was told that he was married to one of Kambuya's sisters, but I do not have it thus in my genealogical information.
Noibei Arapmusani	Kambuya's brother's son; young, unmarried, and unmotivated to seek cattle.
Sabila Araplabu	Neighbor who had a number of Kambuya's animals under contract. His daughter was married to Salimu.
Salimu (Arapkambuya)	Oldest son of Kambuya, a child of his first wife.
Salimu Kapchemei	Neighbor, married to Pitya, daughter of Kambuya's sister Tengedyes, who had been raised in the household of Kambuya.
Seperia (Kapchemei)	Local (mutala) chief; older brother of Salimu Kapchemei.
Senguru	Kambuya's favorite sister, married to Sumotwa ("Teso"); present at the hearings.
Sibora	Daughter of Kambuya's sister, Tengedyes; raised in Kambuya's household.
Siret Chemaswet	Wealthy neighbor; planning a circumcision at the time.
Tengedyes	One of Kambuya's sisters. Because her husband's sons would not take care of her, she and her two daughters were taken in by Kambuya and Salimu. It was Tengedyes who made accusations against the co-wife of her daughter Sibora.
Teso (Sumotwa Kambalyany)	Married to Senguru, Kambuya's favorite sister; had a number of Kambuya's cattle at his home in Teso tribal territory.
Yapchepkoti	Co-wife of Sibora, accused of planning to do witchcraft against her.

APPENDIX B *Genealogy of Kapmundarit Clan*

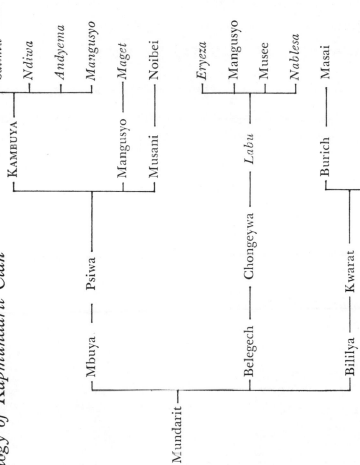

NOTE: Stefano Kamwasir and Bartega Kambuya were listed as clan members but their relationship is not indicated. Personnel whose names are italicized played an important part in the hearings.

APPENDIX C *Genealogy of Kambuya's Close Kin*

KEY: Roman numerals: wife, in order of marriage. Arabic numerals: age (shown for minors only). Asterisk: by previous marriage. Double asterisk: uncertain which sister is mother. Dagger: deceased.

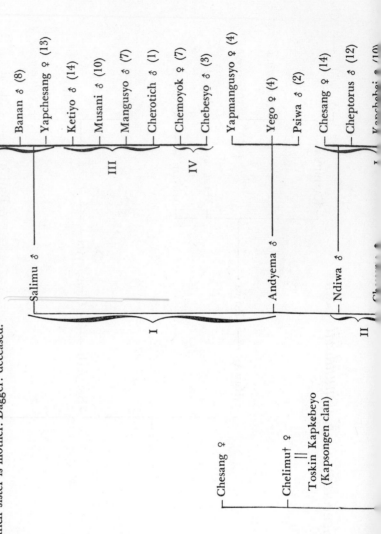

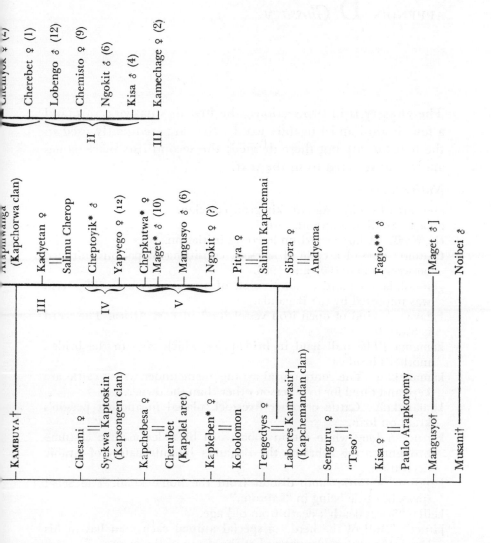

The glossary is in two sections: the first lists native terms (and a few Swahili and Luganda words) that are frequently used in the text but are not there defined; the second lists place-names and tribes referred to in the text.

Native Terms

aret (arosyek, pl.)   Agnatic kin group or clan.

askari   Soldier; a Swahili term.

chemerik   A boy or girl undergoing initiation.

Chumo   One of a cycle of age-sets, consisting of persons initiated between about 1907 and 1920.

gombolola   A political subdivision of a county or saza. The term was imported by the Baganda.

kalaya   A kind of open iron vessel used in East Africa. The word is Swahili.

kamama   The bull paid in bride-price which goes to the bride's mother's brother.

kamanakan   The contractural arrangement under which cattle are kept and cared for by a person other than the owner.

kamanaktay   Cattle or other livestock placed in another person's kraal on loan.

kanzu   A long white cotton robe worn by older men; a costume brought to the Sebei by the Baganda but ultimately of Arabic derivation.

kaptum   A cattle camp distant from the home kraal. The Sebei speak of cattle being in "kaptum."

kelil   "Sweet death"; death from old age.

kintet   "Bull of the herd," a special animal each man has in his kraal; the animal slaughtered at the death of the owner.

kirwokintet (kirwokik, pl.)   An elder whose judgment in council is respected; loosely, a judge.

kokwet   A council.

kota (korik, pl.)   The primary meaning is house; it is used to mean lineage or any lesser agnatic kin group. Applied also to a line of cattle.

Maina   One of the cycle of age-sets. It includes the oldest living men, initiated just before European contact early in the twentieth century.

mama   Kin term for mother's brother.

manyatta   A fenced area, including houses and cattle byres.

metsu   The location in the house to the left of the entrance, sitting place for visitors.

miruka   A minor civil division in modern government, roughly equivalent to the native sangta.

moykutwet   A plant whose roots are chewed and spit upon objects as a blessing.

mumek   A public curse against an offender, whose identity is not necessarily known.

mutala   A subdivision of a gombolola.

namanya   A contractual arrangement involving the exchange of a bullock for a future cow; by extension, other exchange contracts. In accordance with interpreters' habit, I have used the thematic or short form of the word as both adjective and noun.

oyik   Spirits of the dead.

pinta   An age-set; that is, a group of men initiated over a fixed period of time. Each major age-set has three subdivisions, also referred to as pinta. Originally, the larger unit covered a span of about twenty years, but initiations are now held at two-year intervals; thus a pinta covers six years.

pororyet (pororisyek, pl.)   Basic territorial unit; subdivision of tribe.

sangta (songmwek, pl.)   Minor delimited territorial unit; village.

saza   The Luganda term for a major administrative district; county.

shamba   Swahili word for a cultivated plot of ground.

sokoran   Sinful. A cow that sucks itself is regarded as sokoran.

surupik   A form of oath against an unknown person.

tetapsoy   See tokapsoy.

tilyeñu   Term of address for person with whom one holds namanya contract; "my kin of the cow."

tilyet   A person who has a namanya cattle contract.

tokapsoy (tetapsoy, sing.)   Cattle retained by father and not allocated to a wife.

were   Boy.

Places and Peoples

Amudat   A town in Kenya (Pokot territory), about 75 miles north of Sebei.

Ankole   A pastoral tribe of western Uganda. Many Ankole men have sought employment as herders throughout Uganda.

Atari   A village on the escarpment, just above Kapsirika.

Baganda   The people of the kingdom of Buganda, in central Uganda. The Baganda conquered eastern Uganda tribes, including the Sebei, at the turn of the century.

Bagisu   The Bantu-speaking people living southwest of the Sebei; they were traditional enemies, but may live in Sebeiland.

Bok   One of several Sebei-speaking tribes living on the south slope of Mount Elgon, in Kenya.

Bugisu District   The territorial division of modern Uganda southwest of Mount Elgon. Sebei was a part of Bugisu District until 1962.

Bukwa   The easternmost area of Sebeiland.

Bumet   A Bantu-speaking people who moved into Sebei territory about a hundred years ago and have amalgamated with the Sebei; also the part of Sebeiland where they are concentrated.

Cheptui   A Sebei town on the escarpment, in the Sipi region.

Gisu   Shortened form of Bagisu, a Bantu-speaking tribe living on the southwestern slope of Mount Elgon.

Greek River   The river that forms the northern boundary of Sebeiland, and a settlement on that river.

Kabruron   A Sebei village on the escarpment, just above Kapsirika.

Kacheliba   A town in Kenya, about 50 miles northeast of Kapsirika.

Kapambam   A village or minor territory on the Sebei plains.

Kaparik   A village on the Sebei plains.

Kapcheptemkoiñ   A pororyet or native territorial division on the escarpment, above Kipsirika.

Kapenguria   A village on the escarpment.

Kapsirika   The plains village in which the hearings took place. It is a delimited area and a social unit, but the Sebei houses are scattered over the land, like American farmsteads.

Kapterit   A plains village.

Karamojong   A pastoral tribe living on the plains just north of the Sebei. They are distantly related in language.

Kiguli   A village in the territory of the Bagisu.

Koin   One of several Sebei-speaking tribes of Kenya, living just southeast of the Sebei.

Lake Kyogo   A large swampy lake northwest of Sebeiland.

Masai   A large pastoral tribe of Kenya, speaking a distantly related language.

Masop   Upland. Not really a place-name, but used as such. People on the plains refer to the escarpment as Masop; people on the escarpment refer to the highlands as Masop. Yet people in the latter area are called Masopyek, people of the uplands.

Mbai   Originally one of the "tribes" that made up the Sebei; now refers to the region they occupied, the western, plantain-growing end of the escarpment.

Mbale   A city located southeast of Mount Elgon, headquarters of the Eastern Province.

Mount Elgon   An extinct volcano, 14,000 feet high, on the Uganda-Kenya border, occupied by Sebei-speaking tribes and, in the southwest, by the Bagisu.

Nabokutu   A village on the plains. Kambuya lived there twenty or thirty years ago.

Nandi   A large tribe, largely pastoral, of Kenya speaking a language closely related to Sebei.

Ngenge   A town, and gombolola headquarters of the plains area, which has given its name to the whole Sebei plains.

Pokot   A largely pastoral tribe of Kenya, living to the northeast of Sebei, and speaking a closely related language. Also known as Suk.

Riwa   An outlying foothill lying to the northeast of Mount Elgon, and the region it comprises.

Sipi   The western area of the escarpment, and the settlement that is headquarters for Sipi gombolola.

Siroko   A town in present-day Bagisu territory, west of Sebeiland.

Suk   See Pokot.

Sundet River   The stream that runs through Kapsirika.

Teso   A Nilo-Hamitic people living in the lowlands of Uganda, west of Sebeiland.

Kambuya's Herd and Cattle Transactions

The Nature of the Data

It was my intent to obtain from Salimu a list of the animals held by Kambuya, by various relevant categories, but Salimu was unable to provide that kind of tally. The only way he could indicate the content of the herd was to run down the "genealogy" of each "family" of animals, a method that proved to be of even greater interest than my proposed method. It is my purpose in this appendix to examine aspects of the herd and of the cattle transactions engaged in by Kambuya.

The Sebei speak of a "family" (kota) of cattle. A family line is established when an animal is first brought into a herd; it follows the line of descent (disregarding the sire, which in Sebei animal husbandry is often unknown); it includes also all the animals that have been acquired by exchanges, whether these are namanya exchanges, outright exchanges, cattle won in a legal case involving an animal in this line of descent, or even cattle purchased with money obtained for the sale of an animal that is the offspring of the original acquisition. These family lines may therefore be thought of as "social" rather than genetic. Salimu gave me the kota of each of seven animals obtained as bride-price for the sisters of Kambuya, of two families obtained from Kambuya's daughters, of six families that remained tokapsoy, of fourteen families anointed for Salimu's mother, and of two families anointed for the mother of Mangusyo. He refused to give me the kota of cattle descended from the animals anointed for the mother of Ndiwa, either because, as he claimed, he did not know them well enough or because he felt it would be inappropriate for him to do so. Nor did he give the geneal-

ogies of cattle anointed for Mangusyo's mother and held by
Ndiwa. He did not give me the history of any animals whose
line had completely died out. He also occasionally followed
through the history of lines of cattle descended from animals
that Kambuya had given him.

Before examining this material, the reader should understand
the limitation imposed upon the data by the mode in which
they were obtained. The animals recorded here must be considered a sample of all the cattle owned by Kambuya in the
course of his adult life. Certain classes of animals are unrepre-
sented: those descended from cows that were anointed for the
mother of Ndiwa and perhaps the mother of Mangusyo; those
families of animals which were once a part of the herd but
which had completely died out by the time of Kambuya's death;
and those families of animals (or individual animals) which
Salimu may have failed to mention. The first two categories were
explicitly excluded; we can only surmise the existence of the
third. We have no measure of the size of any of the categories.

Let us examine the manner in which these circumstances skew
the data and limit our analysis. First, we know that Ndiwa's
heritage is underrepresented because his mother's animals, all
of which would go to him, are not included. Mangusyo's inheritance may also be underrepresented. When we deal with either
the bride-payment cattle or the tokapsoy, however, this limitation does not apply, and we can therefore make some compari-
sons. Second, as we know that the animals are not evenly distributed through time, we cannot make temporal distinctions
based upon numbers. It would have been impossible to do so
in any event, because Salimu did not regularly give dates for the
acquisition of animals. Occasionally he did indicate when a particular exchange was made, and it would be possible to determine the variance in exchange rates. Salimu took note of the
fact that the price of cattle was very low during the 1930's—a
point of some interest because the low price seems to have been
a response to the worldwide depression of that time, despite the
remoteness of Sebeiland from the centers of commerce. We
must assume that there were many animals in Kambuya's possession at one time or another which did not find their way

into this record, for neither the number of animals received in bride-price nor the number of those paid in bride-price is adequate to meet the expectation, which generally runs to about seven animals (it was a lesser amount in early years). I assume that this underenumeration derives from families not reported because they were no longer represented in the herd.

We cannot so readily determine the effect of Salimu's selective memory. Indeed, we cannot be certain of the magnitude or even the existence of error through this source. We can only surmise that if there is error it would tend to be an emphasis on detailing of animals with which Salimu himself was concerned. An error of this kind would further emphasize other errors—increased attention to those animals later in time and those allocated to, or used by, his own mother as against Ndiwa's or Mangusyo's.

It is important to appreciate that any error in Salimu's detailing was entirely unintentional. Salimu had a prodigious memory for matters pertaining to cattle; he was recognized widely by other Sebei for this knowledge, and he took pride in it. I have confidence in his accuracy, having observed how Salimu presented the material to me. In following the history of an animal, he would indicate, for instance, that Mataret had six heifer calves and would list their names. He would then follow through the progeny of the first one and return after perhaps two pages of my notes to a consideration of the second, and so forth. He never had to be reminded of any that he missed, but would unfailingly go through the list. Furthermore, he provided a great deal of circumstantial detail about the nature of the exchanges, the person with whom an exchange was made, sometimes the date when an action took place, and so on. I believe that he found the exercise a challenge and took pride in endeavoring to make the record as accurate and as complete as he could. I should add that the details in these genealogies were all spontaneously given by Salimu; when he indicated a date, a price, or a person with whom the exchange was made, the information was always unprompted. In only a few instances did Salimu fail to give me the ultimate disposition of the animal, and then I could usually infer it from the context. On the other hand, it was impossible to establish any satisfactory internal checks. I could not get comparable data from Ndiwa, either for the herd as a whole or for the cattle anointed for his mother. It is not always possible to determine precisely which animals in the genealogies are being talked about in the body of the text, possibly because the animals in the text are not in fact involved in the genealogies. Frequently, however, an appropriate reference can be made. It is my judgment that the record given by Salimu is substantially correct, and that it represents some 90 percent of the animals that Salimu purported to be discussing, though these are an undeterminable fraction of the total animals that passed through Kambuya's hands in the course of his lifetime. I believe also that the transactions described are accurate in all the details made explicit in each instance. It seems to me, therefore, we can use this sample of material for certain analyses if we keep in mind the initial limitations that characterize the data.

A further point must be made about the character of the data. Occasionally, Salimu would follow through the genealogy of an animal that Kambuya had given to, or exchanged with, him— animals in Salimu's herd which had never belonged to his father. There were fifty-one animals so distinguished; there were a few others that I believe Salimu considered his. Most of these animals derive from one genealogy. For certain purposes, they must be kept distinct; for other purposes, it does not matter. Of course Salimu did not follow the histories of animals given to his brothers.

I have reproduced three of the thirty-one genealogies according to the notation system I developed for the analysis of these data. The "descent line" is shown in the center; the source, the transactions, and the ultimate fate of the animals are indicated by lines leading into and out of this central column. I have given the name of the animal when Salimu gave it to me, and have indicated "heifer" or "bull" when he designated only the sex of the offspring. Animals still living at the time the genealogies were given are represented in italics. Sometimes an animal is represented by a debt; obviously, this refers to a demand on the estate for an animal that has been exchanged. For convenience, I have sequentially numbered the items in the genealogy. It should be noted that the numbers do not correspond to the total number of animals, inasmuch as Salimu would occasionally indicate that "several calves" were born of one cow. Salimu usually gave the exact number of offspring born to a cow that had died— numbers running from one to as high as seventeen. Sometimes, however, he merely said that "many calves died" or "several calves died," in which instance I arbitrarily assigned the number as three (assuming he would not indicate fewer than that by such adjectives). In obtaining the total of 704 animals recorded in these genealogies, I have included these estimates. I judge the result to be a slight underenumeration, but it affects only the rate of "infant mortality."

The first genealogical chart here was the second I recorded from Salimu. It represents the family of a heifer given to Kambuya (or his father) as bride-price for Tengedyes, the third sister of Kambuya. The two animals indicated here represented the total of the bride-price, according to Salimu. When they were paid is not indicated; but inasmuch as only three generations of descendants from the original animal (Shemá), are recorded, I am led to believe either that Salimu collapsed this genealogy (which I doubt) or that the payment was much delayed (which is not unlikely). It is possible that this animal was the last one received, or the only one from Tengedyes' bride-price which was given to Kambuya by his father. Bride-price was low at the time; the payment for the first of Kambuya's sisters was a spear.

The second genealogy lists the descendants of a cow named Chepkware, which Kambuya had anointed for Salimu's mother. I have selected this genealogy for inclusion because the animals descended from Chepkware were involved in the major dispute between Salimu and Andyema. The offspring of Chepkware, indicated in the first part of this genealogy, were previously distributed to Salimu and Andyema. The animals over which there was dispute were those indicated as kamanaktay to Sabila Arap-labu and those listed as being in Kambuya's kraal; more accurately, these are the descendants, respectively, of two cows, numbers 16 and 26 in the chart.

The third genealogy gives the descendants of Chepteger, a descendant of Chemereo, which had belonged to Kambuya's father. Kambuya's father had smeared Chemereo for Kambuya's mother, but subsequently the cow and its heifer were returned to Kambuya's father for reasons not indicated. One of Chemereo's granddaughters formed its own line of descent, which is recorded in another genealogy not reproduced here. I have included the genealogy of Chepteger not only because it is the longest of those received but also because the individual transactions reveal a great deal about the nature of the relationships maintained and the patterns of action that had taken place in the course of the history of Kambuya's herd. It will repay glancing through the transactions to discover how a Sebei herdsman handles his livestock and their exchanges.

CHART 1
GENEALOGY OF SHEMÁ

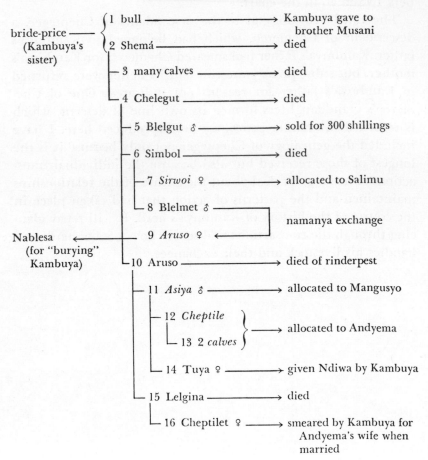

bride-price ——
(Kambuya's
sister)

{
1 bull ————————————→ Kambuya gave to
                                           brother Musani
2 Shemá ————————————→ died

3 many calves ————————→ died

4 Chelegut ————————————→ died

5 Blelgut ♂ ————————————→ sold for 300 shillings

6 Simbol ————————————→ died

7 *Sirwoi* ♀ ————————————→ allocated to Salimu

8 Blelmet ♂
                           namanya exchange
9 *Aruso* ♀ ←————————

Nablesa ←
(for "burying"
Kambuya)

10 Aruso ————————————→ died of rinderpest

11 *Asiya* ♂ ————————————→ allocated to Mangusyo

12 *Cheptile* ⎫
                   ⎬ ————→ allocated to Andyema
13 2 *calves* ⎭

14 Tuya ♀ ————————————→ given Ndiwa by Kambuya

15 Lelgina ————————————→ died

16 Cheptilet ♀ ————→ smeared by Kambuya for
                                         Andyema's wife when
                                         married

CHART 2
GENEALOGY OF CHEPKWARE

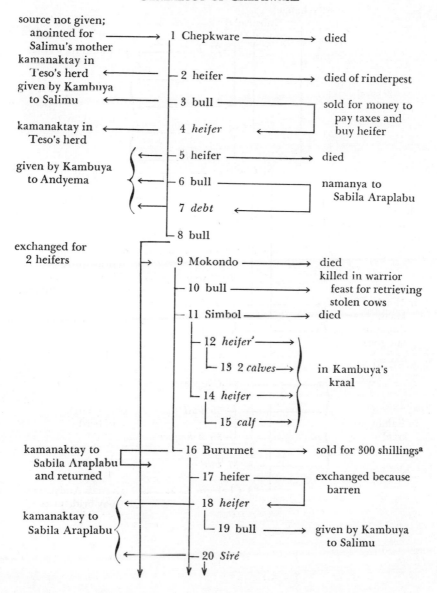

source not given;
    anointed for ——————→ 1 Chepkware ——————→ died
    Salimu's mother
kamanaktay in
    Teso's herd   ←—————— 2 heifer ——————→ died of rinderpest
given by Kambuya
    to Salimu   ←—————— 3 bull ——————→ sold for money to
                                                    pay taxes and
kamanaktay in   ←—————— 4 *heifer* ←——————   buy heifer
    Teso's herd

given by Kambuya   ←—————— 5 heifer ——————→ died
    to Andyema   ←—————— 6 bull ——————→ namanya to
                                                    Sabila Araplabu
                       ←—————— 7 *debt* ←——————

                       ——————— 8 bull

exchanged for
    2 heifers   ——————→ 9 Mokondo ——————→ died
                                                killed in warrior
                       —————— 10 bull ——————→   feast for retrieving
                                                stolen cows
                       —————— 11 Simbol ——————→ died

                       —————— 12 *heifer'* ——→

                            —— 13 2 *calves* ——→
                                                    in Kambuya's
                                                    kraal
                       —————— 14 *heifer* ——→

                            —— 15 *calf* ——→

kamanaktay to   —————— 16 Bururmet ——————→ sold for 300 shillings[a]
    Sabila Araplabu
    and returned   —————— 17 heifer ——————→ exchanged because
                                                    barren
kamanaktay to   ←—————— 18 *heifer* ←——————
    Sabila Araplabu
                            —— 19 bull ——————→ given by Kambuya
                                                    to Salimu
                       ←—————— 20 *Siré*

Chart 2—*Continued*

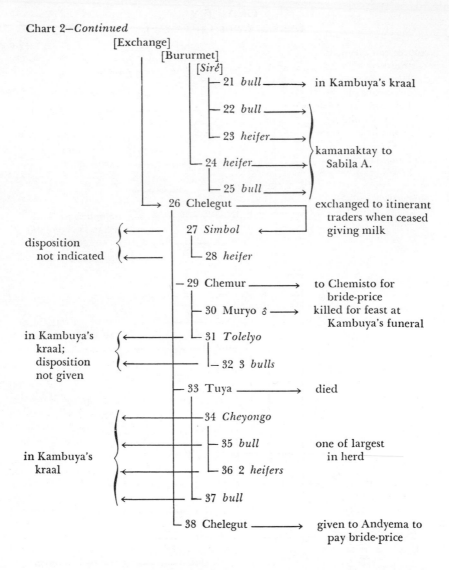

[Exchange]
   [Bururmet]
     [*Siré*]

— 21 *bull* ⟶ in Kambuya's kraal

— 22 *bull* ⟶

— 23 *heifer* ⟶

— 24 *heifer* ⟶ } kamanaktay to Sabila A.

— 25 *bull* ⟶

⟶ 26 Chelegut ⟶ exchanged to itinerant traders when ceased giving milk

disposition not indicated { ← 27 *Simbol* ←

{ ← 28 *heifer*

— 29 Chemur ⟶ to Chemisto for bride-price

— 30 Muryo ♂ ⟶ killed for feast at Kambuya's funeral

in Kambuya's kraal; disposition not given { ← 31 *Tolelyo*

{ ← 32 3 *bulls*

— 33 Tuya ⟶ died

in Kambuya's kraal { ← 34 *Cheyongo*

{ ← 35 *bull* one of largest in herd

{ ← 36 2 *heifers*

{ ← 37 *bull*

— 38 Chelegut ⟶ given to Andyema to pay bride-price

ᵃ Money obtained from this animal entered into sum discussed at length in kokwet (see page 76).

CHART 3
GENEALOGY OF CHEPTEGER

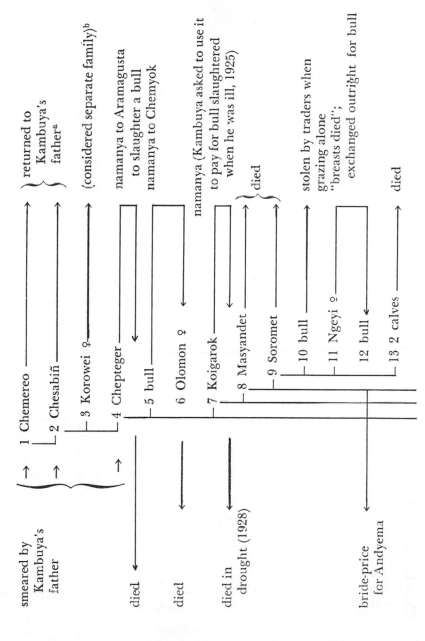

Chart 3—Continued

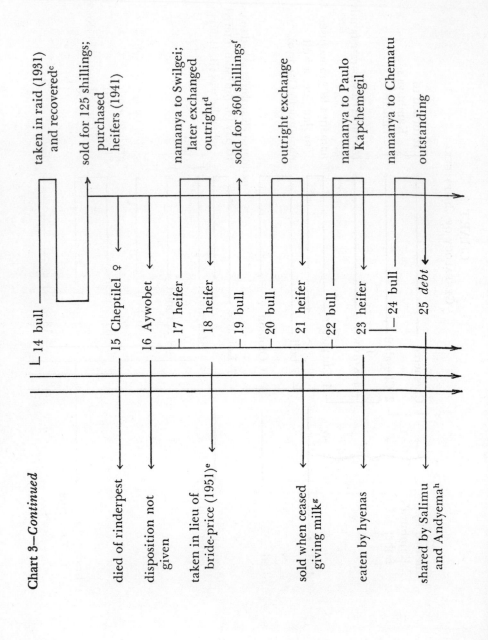

ᵃ The genealogy here is somewhat confused. Salimu first said that Kambuya's father had smeared Chemereo for Salimu's mother (which is frequently done by a father for his daughter-in-law), but later he said both Chemereo and Chesabiñ were returned by Kambuya to his father. It seems likely that these were treated as namanya, successively allowing a heifer to replace its dam, though Salimu did not so state. At any rate, this genealogy is for Chepteger, one of the calves of Chemereo's calf.

ᵇ This family was reported in a separate genealogy.

ᶜ Salimu said: "In 1931 the bull was stolen. One night a lion came and frightened the cows in the kraal, after which the cows broke the kraal and went out in the bush. One of the cows was eaten by the lion; the rest ran, crossed the river, and the following day were found by the Karamojong, who drove them away with their own. We followed the tracks east of Nomalo and got to a certain kraal, but the owner had already moved away. We returned, and soon afterward our neighbor's cattle were stolen. We followed the tracks to Nomalo, and again the tracks were lost. By now we were accompanied by three constables. We were roaming about the swamp when I saw the cattle grazing on the hill and I identified our bull and three other animals. It was about 300 yards away. I told the police, but they said I was telling lies. After some argument the police said, 'Let's go and see—it is too far to identify a cow.' We were accompanied by an old man named Sitaki. When we got there we saw the bull, but they said it was too big and not ours. As I stood there, I was lucky and the bull came and licked my hands. I saw all four cows, and the police proved they were mine; so we brought them back. There were two bulls and two heifers. One bull was eaten by Sabila, and that is the debt I asked Ndiwa to collect. It was given to Ndiwa. That bull belonged to another cow that belonged to my father. [Salimu did not indicate here the disposition of the two heifers that were recovered. These three animals do not belong to this genealogy.] In 1941 I took Masyandet's bullock and sold it for 125 shillings (when prices were very low). I went to Mbale and Kamuge market and bought three heifers with this 125 shillings."

ᵈ This heifer became barren when held as namanya by Swilgei, and so he exchanged it for two heifers, one of which was claimed by Salimu as return of the original heifer in an outright exchange.

ᵉ Frequently, after an elopement, a bride's father or brothers raid the cattle from the kraal of the son-in-law in lieu of the bargained bride-price. This cow was subsequently stolen by the Pokot (1957) and later retrieved by Salimu and returned to the father-in-law (1961).

ᶠ Father used 60 shillings for clothes; Salimu kept 300 shillings, as was discussed at the hearings, but he claimed this sum as his own because it came from his mother's cow.

ᵍ This is part of the money that was divided at the hearings; it was given to Andyema.

ʰ This is an irregular exchange. The heifer given as namanya by Paulo Kapchemagil was killed by a hyena, which did not eat the carcass; Paulo asked to have the meat. Kambuya asked for a namanya replacement, but Paulo refused; Kambuya therefore kept the bull as an outright replacement for the bull Paulo had taken.

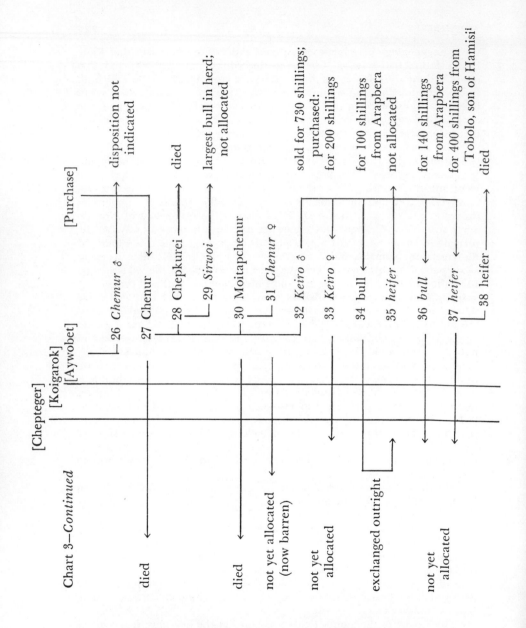

Chart 3—*Continued*

[Chepteger]
[Koigarok]
[Aywobet]
[Purchase]

26 *Chemur* ♂ — disposition not indicated

27 Chenur → died

28 Chepkurei — died

29 *Sirwoi* → largest bull in herd; not allocated

30 Moitapchenur → died

31 *Chenur* ♀ — not yet allocated (now barren)

32 *Keiro* ♂ — sold for 730 shillings; purchased: for 200 shillings

33 *Keiro* ♀ — not yet allocated

34 bull — for 100 shillings from Arapbera not allocated

35 *heifer* — exchanged outright

36 *bull* — for 140 shillings from Arapbera

37 *heifer* — not yet allocated

38 heifer → for 400 shillings from Tobolo, son of Hamisi[i] died

[i] Three hundred shillings came from the sale of Keiro; 100 shillings was added from another source.

[j] The disposition of the animals was to be made at a later date. Only

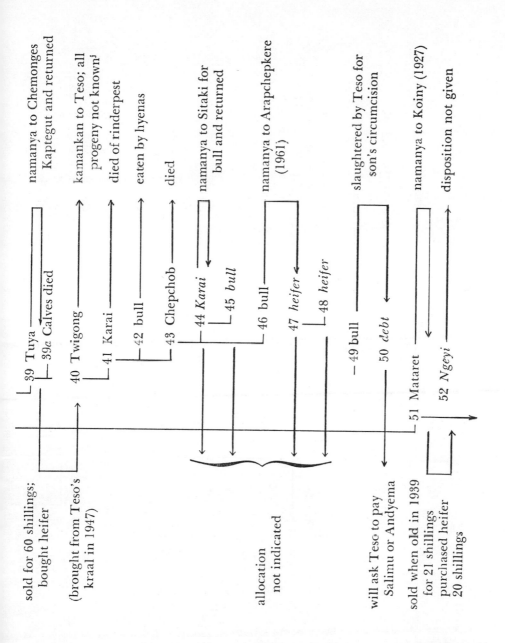

Teso could give further details of the animals held by him. I had no opportunity to ask him, and could not make arrangements to see the cattle there. This one heifer was brought back in 1947.

Chart 3—Continued   [Mataret]

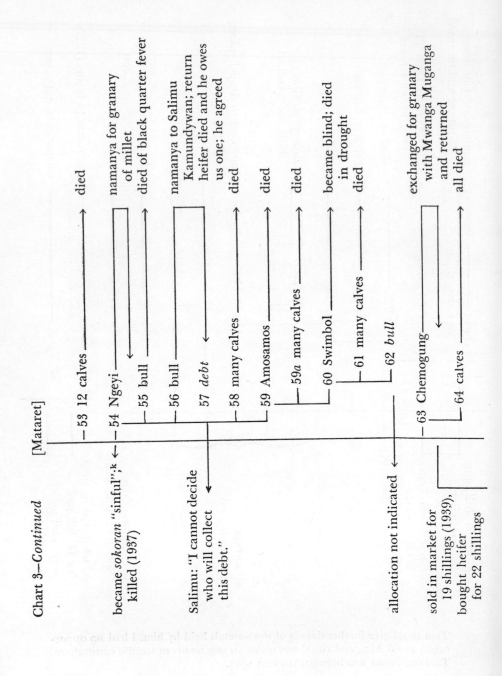

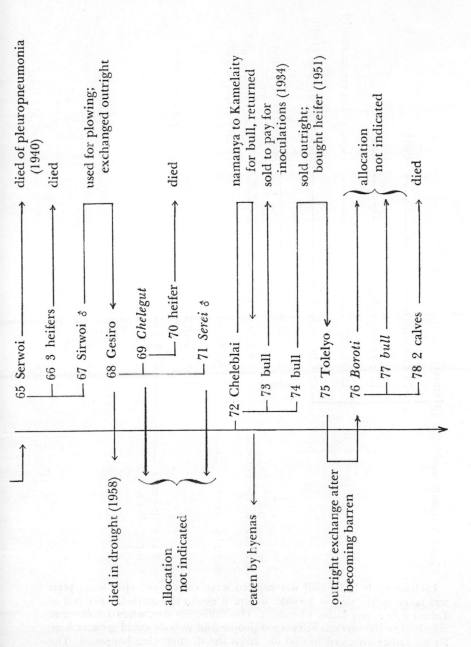

65 Serwoi — died of pleuropneumonia (1940)

66 3 heifers — died

67 Sirwoi ♂ — used for plowing; exchanged outright

68 Gesiro — died in drought (1958)

69 *Chelegut* ⎫
70 heifer — died ⎬ allocation not indicated
71 *Serei* ♂ ⎭

72 Cheleblai — namanya to Kamelaity for bull, returned

73 bull — sold to pay for inoculations (1934)

74 bull — eaten by hyenas

75 Tolelyo — sold outright; bought heifer (1951)

76 *Boroti* — outright exchange after becoming barren

77 *bull* ⎱ allocation not indicated

78 2 calves — died

^k *Sokoran* is used especially for sexual misconduct. She sucked herself. "In 1937 I got sick and the people thought this sokoran cow was causing my illness and might cause my death; so she was killed."

Chart 3—*Continued*

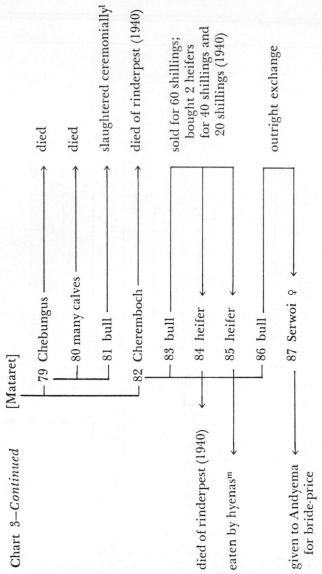

[Mataret]

- 79 Chebungus ——→ died
- 80 many calves ——→ died
- 81 bull ——→ slaughtered ceremonially[1]
- 82 Cheremboch ——→ died of rinderpest (1940)
- 83 bull ——→ sold for 60 shillings; bought 2 heifers for 40 shillings and 20 shillings (1940)
- 84 heifer ——→ died of rinderpest (1940)
- 85 heifer ——→ eaten by hyenas[m]
- 86 bull
- 87 Serwoi ♀ ——→ given to Andyema for bride-price, outright exchange

[1] Salimu said: "The bull was kept to serve calves, but after some years was taken to the market for sale. Before it got to the market, I stopped at Labu's house (my father's brother). The following day, when I wanted to take him to the market, he charged people and nobody could go near him. So my father arranged to find out from the diviner what happened. The diviner said my father's oyik were stopping this sale because they didn't want this cow to be killed; it should remain in the kraal until it was old. So it was left at Labu's kraal and they performed a ceremony when it died."

[m] Given by Kambuya to Salimu when he married. Later became blind and lost her way and was eaten by hyenas.

Analysis

The following tabulations have been made on the basis of the total corpus of data given me by Salimu in these cattle genealogies. Table 1 gives the number of genealogies according to the major categories and the number of cattle in each category. It is perhaps important to remember that the animals belonging to the kota of Ndiwa's mother are not included.

TABLE 1

GENEALOGIES OF KAMBUYA'S CATTLE ACCORDING
TO MAJOR ALLOCATION

Category	Number of genealogies	Cattle Number	Percent
Bride-price of Kambuya's sisters	7	82	11.7
Bride-price of Kambuya's daughters	2	22	3.1
Tokapsoy	6	119	16.9
Kota of Salimu's mother	14	390	55.4
Kota of Mangusyo's mother	2	91	12.9
Total	31	704	100.0

Table 2 shows the source of each animal by genealogical category. A family of animals may be initiated by a gift, by a bride-price payment, or by an exchange. For instance, "Chepkware" (chart 2) means "daughter of goats" (*warek*). But subsequent animals may be born in the kraal or may be obtained through exchange or purchase and yet be a continuation of that family by Sebei reckoning. Table 2 shows that of the 704 animals in the sample, 514—or nearly three-quarters—were born in Kambuya's kraal. It shows also the various major sources of acquisition; columns 2 and 3 indicate what we may call prestations, whereas columns 4, 5, and 6 include exchanges. The latter exceed the former in a ratio of four to one.

TABLE 2

SOURCE OF LIVESTOCK IN GENEALOGIES BY CATEGORY

Category of genealogy	(1) Birth[a]	(2) Bride-price	(3) Gift[b]	(4) Purchase	(5) Outright exchange	(6) Namanya exchange	(7) Misc. or not known	(8) Total
Bride-price of Kambuya's sisters	47	17	0	0	5	13	0	82
Bride-price of Kambuya's daughters	4	11	0	0	0	7	0	22
Tokapsoy	95	0	3	4	12	4	1	119
Kota of Salimu	303 (35)[c]	0	4	19 (1)	25 (7)	31 (8)	8	390 (51)
Kota of Mangusyo	65	0	0	2	19	4	1	91
Total	514	28	7	25	61	59	10	704
Percent	72.9	3.9	1.0	3.4	8.7	8.3	1.5	100.0
Percent acquired from outside[d]	—	14.7	3.7	13.2	32.1	31.0	5.3	100.0

a Column 1 includes the 145 calves that were born in kraal and died as calves.
b Chiefly from Kambuya's father.
c Parenthetical figures in this row indicate animals that belonged to Salimu. The animal he was given initially in each instance is included as part of Kambuya's herd because it had once belonged to Kambuya.
d This row shows the distribution of the 186 animals acquired by means other than birth to cows already in kraal.

TABLE 3

DISPOSITION OF KAMBUYA'S ANIMALS

Mode of disposition	Number	Subtotal	Percent
Death			
As calf	145 (6)ᵃ		
Ceremonially slaughtered	7		
All other	127 (6)	279 (12)	40.3
Given away or paid in bride-priceᵇ	70 (5)	70 (5)	10.1
Exchange			
Namanyaᶜ	58 (6)		
Outright exchange	47 (3)		
Sale	31 (1)	136 (10)	19.6
Remaining in herd	208 (24)	208 (24)	30.0
Total	693ᵈ	693	100.0

ᵃ Figures in parentheses indicate number belonging to Salimu.

ᵇ These categories have had to be lumped together; as Salimu might say, for instance, "This animal was given to Andyema, who paid it for his wife," thus leaving it unclear whether it was a gift to Andyema or a payment of bride-price.

ᶜ About half of these were bulls paid in exchange for heifers, but Salimu would sometimes give the name of the heifer received, which would then be returned when she produced the heifer "that released her."

ᵈ The disposition of eleven animals, mostly those acquired early in Kambuya's career, is unknown.

Table 3 shows the disposition of the herd by general categories. Of these animals, 145 were born in the kraal and died as calves (calf mortality rivals infant mortality). Another 127 died of disease, predators, and drought. I have included also in this category all animals stolen and not returned.[1] I have again distinguished between prestations, of which there were 70, and exchanges, of which there were 136. The latter exceed the former in a ratio of about two to one.

It must not be assumed that the seven animals slaughtered represent the only beef consumed. It is unusual for a man to slaughter his own animals. Most of the bullocks obtained by namanya exchange were slaughtered, for that is the usual purpose of such exchanges. Sometimes, at least, animals that die or are killed by predators are eaten.

[1] Salimu gave the cause of death in about half the instances; the figures are: disease, 31; drought, 9; killed by predators, 10; accident, 3; stolen, 15.

Table 4 shows the allocation of Kambuya's animals. Inasmuch as allocations of animals in the herd are related to prestations made earlier by Kambuya to his sons, we must examine this group as well. These prestations and allocations are meaningfully related to categories of genealogy, and I have shown them in these terms. Consider first the bride-price columns. The nine animals given by Kambuya to his brothers represent something of a falsification, for some of these were doubtless merely being held by Kambuya for his younger brother. Next, note that Ndiwa obtained five animals from his sisters' bride-price. One of these sisters was by the same mother, and he received four animals from her. Sebei law does not hold that full brothers have special rights to a sister's bride-price, but this instance (as well as other data) shows that in practice the full brother receives most of the cattle. A similar consideration accounts for the large number that went to the stepson Maget, for these were from a sister who was of the same mother as Maget's father.

If we lump together the bride-price cattle given to the sons (and include Chemisto's with those of his father Salimu[2]), we find the following allocations: Salimu and Chemisto, 7.5; Ndiwa, 8.5; Andyema, 9.5; Mangusyo, 7.5. This is close calculation of equivalence, probably understated, as I have included sucking calves, which the Sebei do not regard as independent animals.

Column 3, dealing with the animals that had been smeared for the mother of Salimu and Andyema, also reveals important facts. First, it is clear that although Salimu received more animals than his brothers (fifteen as against eleven, if we consider those given to Chemisto), the difference is not of such magnitude as to support Andyema's claim about differential treatment. Second, it is clear that the division here continues to be troublesome. It would seem that the kokwet did not consider the allocation of animals in this category as part of its mandate. The disputed animals of Chepkware fall in this category.

It is clear from table 4 (column 4) that Kambuya tended not

---

[2] In one instance, Salimu said that he was satisfied because Chemisto had a cow from that sister.

to make prestations from among his tokapsoy. Two-thirds of the animals of this category in the herd were allocated by the kokwet, the allocation being reasonably equitable, assuming that each son retains a right to them. The allocations in column 5 are of less interest; in fact, I have inferred that the cattle were assigned to Mangusyo—Salimu made no mention of these allocations—but Sebei law would so hold. I believe, in fact, that the genealogy from which most of these animals came was of a fam-

TABLE 4

GIFTS BY KAMBUYA AND ALLOCATION OF CATTLE IN HERD

Disposition	(1) Sisters' bride-price[a]	(2) Daughters' bride-price	(3) Kota of Salimu	(4) Tokapsoy	(5) Kota of Mangusyo	(6) Total
Gift to:						
Kambuya's brothers	9	0	0	2	0	11
Salimu	1	1	13	0	1	16
Ndiwa	1	5	0	0	0	6
Andyema	1	1	11	0	0	13
Mangusyo	1	1	0	0	0	2
Maget	4	0	0	0	0	4
Chemisto	2	0	2	0	0	4
Other	0	1	4	2	2	9
Total	19	9	30	4	3	65
Allocation to:						
Salimu	2.5[b]	1	2	9	0	14.5
Ndiwa	2.5	0	0	6	0	8.5
Andyema	6.5	1	5	8	0	20.5
Mangusyo	4.5	1	0	5	36	46.5
Other[c]	1	1	4	4	0	10
Unassigned	1	0	54	16	0	71
No information	0	0	13	0	0	13
Total	18	4	78	48	36	184

[a] Gifts to Kambuya's brothers and to Maget in this column probably represent merely a recognition of a proper claim.

[b] Six cows were divided between two brothers; these were scored as 0.5 each.

[c] Includes the ceremonial allocations and prestations connected with the funeral.

ily that had belonged to the former husband of Mangusyo's mother. If that is true, then these animals would be shared between Mangusyo and Maget, for Kambuya had legally been holding them in trust for these boys.

These transactions deserve further analysis. Three general points emerge from them: the frequency of transactions, the ratio of "economic" to "social" exchanges, and the economic rationale underlying the transactions.

It has already been shown that 180 animals were acquired by some kind of transaction (table 2, columns 2 to 6), and that 70 animals were given away and another 136 exchanged out (table 3). In addition to these 386 transactions, other involvements include: 24 cows used in namanya exchanges and returned; 21 animals placed in kamanaktay; 7 ceremonially slaughtered; 3 involved in legal cases; 4 anointed for wives other than those indicated in transfers. Thus Salimu specified 445 economic or social transactions among the 559 animals that lived to maturity and are reported in these genealogies. If there is any error in these data, it would certainly be underenumeration. Furthermore, each of the animals was inevitably involved in at least one further transaction as the result of Kambuya's death, but these transactions are not counted here. Some animals were involved in as many as three separate actions, while 189 had either died or were in the kraal without having had any such involvements. These data clearly show that there are four special actions taken for every five animals in the herd.

Many observers have wondered at the capacity of African herdsmen to retain the details of their animals, or notice that an animal is missing from a herd, without knowing the numbers involved. The matter ceases to cause wonder when we take cognizance of these actions. Indeed, in a very real sense, a man's herd is his autobiography.[3]

[3] In *Sebei Law* (Berkeley and Los Angeles: University of California Press, 1967), I wrote: "With a nice sense of etymological propriety, we may say that the Sebei translate social relationships into pecuniary terms, and conversely, pecuniary ones into social terms" (p. 236). Later I concluded that *"an individual is his property, so that relations between individuals are also relations of property"* (p. 239).

While it is clear that every prestation carries with it some economic implications and every economic exchange carries also some social implication, it does not seem entirely arbitrary to distinguish essentially "economic" exchanges from those that are primarily "social." I would consider the former category all those that were legal exchanges or arrangements: buying, selling, outright exchanges, namanya exchanges, and kamanaktay arrangements. All the remainder might best be scored otherwise, though some like theft and return are certainly ambiguous. These categories perhaps do not differ so much in the nature of the motivation as they do in the fact that they operate under a different sanction system, for economic transactions operate under the sanction of law, of enforceable contract, while the others operate under social pressure only and are not legally enforceable demands.

Accepting these distinctions, we find that there are 145 economic exchanges in the mode of acquisition (table 2, columns 4 to 6), 136 items under "exchange" (table 3), 24 cows that were used in namanya exchanges and returned, and 21 animals in kamanaktay, for a total of 326. Against these are to be set 35 gifts and bride-prices received, 70 gifts and bride-prices given, 7 ceremonial slaughterings, 4 special anointings, and 3 legal cases, for a total of 119. This ratio of nearly three to one expresses what I believe to be an accurate assessment of Sebei attitudes and actions in the realm of herd management.

This ratio does not mean that the social uses of animals are less significant; indeed, it is these uses that establish the unity and continuity of the family, the kota, and the clan. Furthermore, these prestations do represent obligations, and, though cost-accounting methods do not prevail, decisions may nevertheless be made in terms of self-interest. Thus, when Kambuya generously buys off his grandson Chemisto's goodwill, he may more or less consciously be thinking of protection in old age and the continuity of his line of descendants. It is interesting to follow a genealogy of cattle and to discover, for instance, that when an animal was anointed by Kambuya's father for his daughter-in-law, there was established a line of cattle which

ultimately helped to pay for Chemisto's bride and thus to produce the great-great-grandchild of the man who made the original gift, the child whom this woman was carrying at the time of
these hearings, some sixty years later.

Yet the economic exchanges engaged in by Kambuya and
Salimu demonstrate a capitalist's instinct for profit and self-
maintenance. Table 5 shows that in their outright exchanges,
they gave up 18 cows and received 52, in 9 instances having received two heifers for a single bull. Furthermore, the cows that
were exchanged were, in nearly every instance, animals that were
no longer reproductive. It is this kind of concern with maintenance of animals capable of reproducing which made it possible for Kambuya to retain one of the largest herds on the Sebei
plains.

Because of certain inherent difficulties in the analysis, I have
not endeavored to tabulate the namanya exchanges here, but
they appear to run to a ratio of about two heifers received for a
bullock to one heifer given up in exchange. The ratio is also
similar when we examine other namanya exchanges, such as
use of goats, grain, or money; in all instances Kambuya acquired a heifer more frequently than he gave up a heifer.

Kambuya's profit taking is clearly represented in table 6. He
sells more animals than he buys, he buys cows more frequently

TABLE 5
OUTRIGHT EXCHANGES

Kambuya exchanged	Kambuya received			
	Two cows	Cow	Bull	Total
9 bulls	18			18
18 bulls		18		18
12 cows[a]		12		12
6 cows			6	6
2 bulls			2	2
— goats		4	1	5
47 cattle	18	34	9	61

[a] Fifteen of the eighteen cows exchanged, Salimu indicated, were non-productive
(got old, became barren, udders destroyed by hyenas, etc.). Two of the remaining cows were got rid of because they had become *sokoran* ("sinful").

than he buys bulls, and he regularly sells at a higher price than he pays. The result is that he gains more reproductive stock from these transactions but nevertheless manages to obtain a substantial margin of profit, netting opproximately 4,500 shillings on these 59 transactions. It should be noted that there is a very wide fluctuation in price, largely because of the difference in size and quality of animal, though partly reflecting price changes through time; the highest price recorded was 730 shillings, the lowest, 19. I did not discuss with Salimu or any other Sebei the economics of herd management, but from the evidence in these tabulations and other statements, I infer that this profit is the result of the policy already indicated, of acquiring reproductive animals, and also of buying small animals and selling large ones. Salimu frequently noted that money from a sale was used to buy two or three animals. I do not think he enjoyed any market advantage (he sold many animals in the open market or to traders) other than perhaps a greater insight into animal quality.

These data show the importance of an entrepreneurial talent in herd maintenance. They express an attitude toward life itself, for they show that capital accumulation and protection clearly motivated Kambuya and Salimu, and that consumption had to be held in abeyance. It is the obverse side of what was demon-

TABLE 6
SALE AND PURCHASE OF CATTLE[a]

Sale	No.	Sex	Average price	Total	
	17	Cows[b]	183 sh	3,111	
	17	Bulls	227 sh	3,859	
		Total sales			6,970
Purchase					
	22	Cows	100 sh	2,200	
	3	Cows	117 sh	340	
		Total purchases			2,540
					4,430

a Prices were given for thirteen bulls and eleven cows sold; for all bulls and eighteen cows purchased.
b In six instances Salimu indicated that the cow was no longer reproductive.

strated so clearly when Kambuya's pitifully few belongings were
anointed. The data also substantiate Salimu's concern for Andyema's capacity to demonstrate a similar entrepreneurial talent.
The implications for "primitive economics" seem obvious.